The best textbook for teaching an introductory course in religious studies has just gotten better with a new edition. Martin's ability to make critical theory not only understandable, but also useful, to beginning students, is the primary strength of his book. His choice of examples, illustrating the complex theoretical issues he addresses, guarantees student learning will be both significant and – dare I say it – enjoyable.

Charles William Miller, University of North Dakota, USA

A Critical Introduction to the Study of Religion provides key strategies for disentangling the category "religion" and examining religious traditions as complex social phenomena. The text is an effective introduction to explanatory socio-functional approaches, which enable students to ask new sets of questions of their subject. The second edition is a comprehensive model for a new vision of Religious Studies.

Kristian Petersen, University of Nebraska Omaha, USA

A Critical Introduction to the Study of Religion

Second Edition

Craig Martin

Routledge
Taylor & Francis Group
LONDON AND NEW YORK

First published 2017
by Routledge
2 Park Square, Milton Park, Abingdon, Oxon OX14 4RN

and by Routledge
711 Third Avenue, New York, NY 10017

Routledge is an imprint of the Taylor & Francis Group, an informa business.

© 2017 Craig Martin

British Library Cataloguing-in-Publication Data
A catalogue record for this book is available from the British Library.

Library of Congress Cataloging-in-Publication Data
Names: Martin, Craig, 1976– author.
Title: A critical introduction to the study of religion / Craig Martin.
Description: Second edition. | Abingdon, Oxon ; New York, NY : Routledge is an
    imprint of the Taylor & Francis Group, an Informa Business, [2017] | Includes
    bibliographical references and index.
Identifiers: LCCN 2016043235 | ISBN 9781138202245 (hbk) |
    ISBN 9780415419932 (pbk) | ISBN 9781315474410 (ebk)
Subjects: LCSH: Religion—Study and teaching.
Classification: LCC BL41 .M344 2017 | DDC 200.71—dc23
LC record available at https://lccn.loc.gov/2016043235

ISBN: 978-1-138-20224-5 (hbk)
ISBN: 978-0-415-41993-2 (pbk)
ISBN: 978-1-315-47441-0 (ebk)

Typeset in Minion Pro
by Apex CoVantage, LLC

I ask the pardon of those teachers who, in dreadful conditions, attempt to turn the few weapons they can find in the history and learning they "teach" against the ideology, the system and the practices in which they are trapped. They are a kind of hero. But they are rare and how many (the majority) do not even begin to suspect the "work" the system (which is bigger than they are and crushes them) forces them to do.

Louis Althusser, *Lenin and Philosophy and Other Essays* (2001, 106)

This book is dedicated to such heroes, including Erica

Contents

Acknowledgments to the Second Edition

The improvements to the second edition have been facilitated greatly by those who wrote journal reviews, the anonymous reviewers at Routledge, and my colleagues who've generously shared with me their experiences teaching the book. The latter have been particularly invaluable in letting me know what worked well, what did not work well, what was glaringly left out, and what was unnecessarily included. Thanks go to Rebekka King, Pat McCullough, Adam Miller, Dori Parmenter, Kristian Petersen, Erin Roberts, Kevin Schilbrack, and Chris Zeichmann. Apologies to the many colleagues who've given me feedback but whom I've forgotten here.

From St. Thomas Aquinas College—my academic home—I wish to thank those colleagues who, over the last several years, have generously provided me with intellectual stimulation, pedagogical commiseration, or emotional support, including Ellen Chayet, Rachel Golland, Jennifer Hawk, Meghan Mihal, Staci Shultz, Robert Trawick, Ben Wagner, Ryan Wynne, and Barbara Yontz.

I've been lucky enough to be surrounded by generous peers who've offered to read and comment on drafts of various chapters. Thanks to Zoe Anthony, Tara Baldrick-Morrone, Matthew Baldwin, Elliott Bazzano, Daniel Jones, Rebekka King, Adam Miller, Sarah Montello, and Regine Rossi—and apologies again to those whom I've forgotten. As always, the views represented in this book do not necessarily reflect the views of those who helped me improve it.

Thanks go to Tak Toyoshima, creator and illustrator of *Secret Asian Man* comics, for permitting me to reproduce the comic strip in Chapter 2. Thanks to the Minneapolis Institute of Arts for allowing me to use their scan of Andreas Cellarius's "Christian Constellation, First Hemisphere" (plate 22 from *Harmonia Macrocosmica*, included in the institute's Minnich Collection with help from the Ethel Morrison Van Derlip Fund). Thanks also to Malcolm Evans for allowing me to reproduce the comic "Cruel Culture" in Chapter 5.

Last, and most importantly, I would like to thank those hundreds of students who've worked through this book with me over the last four years. I especially want to thank Savannah Finver, Kayla Hunter, and Sarah Montello—three students who've constantly inspired me, pushed me, challenged me, and demanded clarification. I would like to dedicate the material new to the second edition to them, as much of it was inspired as a direct result of the work we've done together and the many engaging conversations we've had.

Acknowledgments to the First Edition

This book has benefitted greatly from the overwhelming generosity of peers and colleagues who were willing to field ideas, read drafts of chapters, or read the entire manuscript.

From St Thomas Aquinas College, I first want to thank my undergraduate students who suffered through the early drafts. Particular mention goes to Emily Hough, Angela Banta, and Dillon Challener for encouraging me to foreground the practical and political consequences of classification in Chapter 3. In addition, for Chapter 8 Valissa Hicks created the visual depiction of the circular relationship of authority and projection; Katie Roepken created the inkblot. Thanks go to Professors C.J. Churchill and Neerja Chaturvedi for organizing the faculty research retreats at which I tried out some of the material in Chapter 5 and received useful feedback. Thanks also go to the participants in the humanities division theory reading group, especially Robert Murray, Barbara Yontz, Nicole de Fee, and Neerja Chaturvedi; the conversations we had on the subject of authenticity helped me work out some of the ideas in Chapter 9. Robert Trawick, my office mate and fellow religion professor, deserves thanks for all of the office conversations and pedagogical commiseration. I want to thank Ellen Chayet for continually encouraging me to foreground questions regarding domination and oppression in the classroom. Last, thanks go to Nicole de Fee and Ryan Wynne for general moral support—they kept me from going crazy as I attempted to balance my research with my teaching.

As I work at a college with only one other faculty member in religious studies, I often depend upon Facebook for intellectual engagement on theoretical and methodological questions related to the study of religion. I want to thank my Facebook friends in general, many of whom engaged me in numerous online conversations while I was working on this book; special mention goes to Russell McCutcheon, Nathan Rein, Tim Murphy, Tim Morgan, Kenny Paul Smith, Bill Arnal, Aldea Mulhern, Chris Zeichmann, Nicholas Dion, and Robert Trawick.

I was fortunate to have many friends willing to read part of the manuscript, including Terry Rey, Marcel Parent, Luke Roelofs, Tim Murphy, and Stephen Benko. Special thanks go to my friends Donovan Schaefer and Jeremy Vecchi, who all but co-wrote Chapter 9; their assistance with that chapter was invaluable. Colleagues who generously read and commented on a manuscript draft in its entirety include Aaron Hughes, Bill Arnal, Jim West, Chris Zeichmann, and Shawn Loner. The number of volunteers willing to read and comment on this book astonished me, and I am greatly in their debt.

As always, I want to note that the views expressed in this book are not necessarily the views of those who helped me improve it.

Thanks go to Tak Toyoshima, creator and illustrator of *Secret Asian Man* comics, who permitted me to reproduce the comic strip in Chapter 2. Some of the material in Chapter 1 previously appeared in "Delimiting religion," *Method and Theory in the Study of Religion* 21/2 (2009). Some of the material in Chapter 8 previously appeared in "How to read an interpretation: Interpretive strategies and the maintenance of authority," *Bible and Critical Theory* 5/1 (2009). Thanks go to the editors for permitting me to use that material here.

Credits for figures within the book are given below the figure caption; those figures without a credit line are either created by me or in the public domain. Figures 3.2–3.4 and 6.1–6.3 are copyrighted using a Creative Commons Copyright 2.0; in each case the individual who owns the copyright has designated the images as available for commercial use with attribution. I have identified the Flickr.com username of the individual who owns the copyright for each in the credit line.

Last, thanks go to Erica, to whom this book is dedicated—you are one of my heroes.

Preface

Christian ministers in the United States once taught that the enslavement of African-Americans was entirely biblical, as blacks were Ham's descendants were cursed to perpetual slavery by Ham's father Noah. The Bhagavad-Gita, a famous text from ancient India, taught that no matter what individuals desired, they must follow the duties of the class they were born into, duties eternally prescribed by the god Krishna; the text reinforced a social hierarchy with four classes, placing priests at the top and servants at the bottom. The Lotus Sutra, a text sacred to many Mahayana Buddhists, includes a story about a princess who magically transformed herself into a man in order to become a Buddha, since women were considered inferior and could not attain a state of Buddhahood in female form.

What these cases have in common is that they are from cultural traditions often called "religions" that present certain forms of social domination—specifically, racism, classism, and sexism—as natural or divine in origin. Despite the fact that religious traditions are often assumed to be the source of benevolent or altruistic moral codes, throughout history these sorts of narratives have been used to reinforce what many of us today would view as unjustified social privilege or oppression.

There are countless introductions to the study of religion, most of which focus on other aspects of religion; however, because I sympathize with those who are victims of oppression, I have chosen to focus this text narrowly on how the cultural elements of religious traditions have been used to legitimate social domination—something which is often ignored in other introductions, or, if addressed, considered briefly or marginally. As an instructor, my primary teaching goals are, first, to demonstrate to students that societies are never set up in ways that serve everyone's interests equally and, second, to give students the skills to identify who benefits and who does not, and how disproportionate social structures are legitimated and maintained. These goals unapologetically drive the organization of the present text.

This introduction is designed to be a text suitable for an undergraduate course, and could be used to anchor an introductory course—whether a so-called "world religions" course or an introductory "theory and method" type of course. In either case it would, of course, require supplementary material. I currently use this text in my introductory course in the following manner: I typically have the students read a chapter, read a primary text or other data, and then ask them to analyze the data using the critical vocabulary in the chapter. For example, my students read the chapter on legitimation (Chapter 7) and watch M. Night Shyamalan's *The Village* (2004), after which we analyze the cultural tools used by the community in the film and consider what legitimating social functions they serve, as well as how the social functions are in some ways more important than their purported "meaning." We follow it up by reading selections from the Bhagavad-Gita and considering how the story could have been used to reflect and reinforce class hierarchy in ancient India.

This book could also be used in a more advanced undergraduate theory and method course in which students are introduced to anthropology of religion, psychology of religion, philosophy of religion, and so on—this text could stand in for critical theory of religion or socio-functional approaches in general.

What follows is not original; rather, it largely draws on the theories of Karl Marx, Émile Durkheim, Max Weber, Antonio Gramsci, Mary Douglas, Peter Berger, Thomas Luckmann, Michel Foucault, Pierre Bourdieu, Judith Butler, Bruce Lincoln, and Russell McCutcheon. This project started, in fact, as a rewrite of the first two chapters of Berger's *The Sacred Canopy* for some students who (understandably) found Berger's vocabulary and diction impenetrable. Almost everything below follows from the spirit of Marx, Durkheim, and Weber, whose theories Berger was attempting to synthesize in *The Sacred Canopy*. In any case, my hope is to make these theorists' ways of seeing how societies and religion work accessible to students or general readers.

I want to emphasize the fact that this book is not designed to introduce students to specific theorists of religion or offer a history of important theories, but rather to give students the skills to analyze cultural traditions from a sociological, critical theory, or cultural studies perspective. Although the works of Marx, Durkheim, and Weber lie behind the material presented, the reader will not find a biography of each thinker or a section introducing the main ideas of each. As an instructor, I am much more interested in having introductory students—who may only take one religion class in their academic careers—be able to understand and use, for instance, Pierre Bourdieu's concept of habitus than to know something about Bourdieu's biography, his basic works, or who he borrowed the concept from.

Readers will notice that there are more examples from Christianity than from other religious traditions in this book. There are two reasons for that. First, my scholarly training has made me much more familiar with Christianity, so I feel more comfortable writing about that tradition than, say, Islam or Buddhism. Second, I teach at a school with a Catholic heritage; most of my students are at least nominally Catholic and have a prior familiarity with the basic cultural content of the Christian tradition. Consequently, Christian examples are the first I reach for in pedagogical contexts. I suspect that many readers will similarly have at least a minimal prior familiarity with Christianity. While I have included examples from a wide variety of other cultural traditions, I introduce those examples without assuming any prior familiarity.

Chapter 1 considers problems with the definition and history of the concept of "religion," and Chapter 2 introduces the critical approach used throughout the book. Chapters 3–6 offer a theory of society, and Chapters 7–9 offer a theory of religion. The last chapter is a case study: I provide a reading of Charles Sheldon's 1896 novel *In His Steps*, demonstrating how the method and theories proposed in this book shed light on a certain form of nineteenth-century Christianity. The matters covered in the chapters on society are assumed by the theory of religion proposed in the later chapters, particularly as I focus primarily on how culture contributes to the reproduction and contestation of social order. However, I have written each chapter so it can be read as a stand-alone essay, and the chapters can be read out of the order I've placed them in.

Chapter Abstracts

Chapter 1—Religion and the Problem of Definition

The concept of "religion" has a long and problematic history. Although we sometimes talk about religions existing prior to the modern era, premodern civilizations did not have a word for religion and did not make distinctions between religious culture and non-religious culture. Our use of the word dates back to early modern Europe arguments for religious tolerance, although it has since been put to use for other—and wildly varying—purposes. Today the word "religion" has so many contradictory uses that it is impossible to specify a definition that fits with the everyday, colloquial use of the term.

Chapter 2—Functionalism and the Hermeneutics of Suspicion

From the perspective of sociology or social theory, those forms of culture we call "religious" appear to serve a number of social functions. In order to draw attention to those functions, we will approach the study of religion using a hermeneutic of suspicion, which invites us to approach the subject matter with scepticism. Rather than take insiders' views on religion at face value, we will ask critical questions about how insiders can use elements of religious culture to accomplish a number of social goals, such as ensuring social cohesion or authorizing moral norms.

Chapter 3—How Society Works: Classification

In order to understand how religion, culture, and society function, we must attend to the classification schemes we use; how do we divide up the stuff of the world, and how are the lines we draw tied up with our political agendas? Whether talking about mushrooms, planets, beer, or gender differences, it is clear that our systems of classification are tied to our interests and desires—and competing groups often use competing classification schemes.

Chapter 4—How Society Works: Essentialism

Once classification schemes are in place, we often attribute essences to the people in the classes we've created. For instance, ancient Indians divided humans into four groups—priests, warriors, commoners, and servants—and claimed that the individuals in each of those classes shared the same core characteristics. However, human classes group together subjects who are almost always very different from one another, and the similarities we see within groups are often fictional. In addition, modern social psychology demonstrates that when placed in groups we quickly produce stereotypes and show in-group bias.

Chapter 5—How Society Works: Structure

Social structures are made up of classifications distinguishing insiders from outsiders, marking hierarchies among insiders, and inviting subjects to fulfil the social roles assigned to their place in the hierarchy. Typically the social structure involves domination: some subjects within the hierarchy have access to power and privilege that are unavailable to subjects below them in the social structure. In addition, dominated subjects often so deeply internalize the social structure that they willingly accept their dominated status.

Chapter 6—How Society Works: Habitus

While we often take the view that anyone who works hard can achieve upward social mobility, sociological research demonstrates that subjects tend to internalize class-based social habits that, insofar as they are viewed as inferior or vulgar by upper classes, prevent subjects from achieving upward mobility. Our bodily habits perpetually mark us as members of a class, leading to collusion within our own group and discrimination from classes whose habits are different. Social stratification can thus be reproduced over time without any intentional efforts.

Chapter 7—How Religion Works: Legitimation

The reproduction of social order often requires legitimations that present the existing conditions as natural or divine in nature. Legitimations can be used to justify or reinforce group boundaries, social hierarchies, and social roles. For instance, American Christians in the nineteenth and twentieth centuries argued that God created white and black races and intended them to be kept separate—such claims were useful for legitimating slavery and segregation. However, legitimations can also be used to challenge the status quo; religious rituals, symbols, and narratives can always be recycled and put to new uses.

Chapter 8—How Religion Works: Authority

Practitioners often appeal to the authority of historical or divine figures in their religious traditions. However, their appeals often involve the projection of their own views onto the figures in question; in this way, the authoritative figures are, for all practical purposes, mirrors of the practitioners themselves. People also subject authoritative texts to selective privileging; we all pick and choose from our inherited culture, privileging what is useful and ignoring what is not. Authority can be challenged or called into question, however, by internal and external critique.

Chapter 9—How Religion Works: Authenticity

Religious practitioners frequently make claims regarding the authenticity of their own tradition and the inauthenticity of others. Since the truth of such claims is not verifiable—authentic essences are not available for empirical investigation—we as scholars cannot adjudicate between them, although we can analyze their social effects. Authenticity claims are always issued from a position of social competition and can be analyzed as rhetorical power plays; in practice, a successful authenticity claim can secure a special authority or privilege for whichever group is received as the authentic one.

Chapter 10—Case Study: What Would Jesus Do?

In Charles Sheldon's late nineteenth century novel *In His Steps*, a group of Christians make a pact, committing themselves for a year to asking "what would Jesus do?" before acting, and following through on whatever answer they come to. This chapter provides an analysis of Sheldon's novel using all of the critical tools described in the previous chapters of this book, focusing on how Sheldon uses Jesus' authority, selectively privileges those parts of the Bible he prefers, naturalizes class difference, and reinforces class-based forms of social domination.

1

Religion and the Problem of Definition

Words and concepts have a history; their meanings, the terms with which they're associated, and the objects or referents they select from the world change over time. A trivial example: the word "thong" once was used to refer to what we today call a "flip flop," but the word now more commonly refers to a particular type of underwear. A more significant example: in ancient Israel, a "marriage" was a social relationship where girls beyond the age of puberty were given by their fathers to other men in exchange for a dowry. When a man raped an unmarried virgin, he was legally required to pay the father a fee and marry the woman, since she was, for all practical purposes, damaged property. A man could have as many wives as he wanted, although wives could only have one husband. Quite literally, the Bible says that men "marry" and women, by contrast, are "taken" or "lorded over." By contrast, in the middle of the twentieth century—at least in the United States—the word "marriage" referred to a mutually voluntary, legally certified relationship between one adult man and one adult woman. Today, at the beginning of the twenty-first century, the word has been changed to refer to voluntary, legally certified, relationships between two adults, of whatever gender or sex. If a community changes the use of a word, the objects (or types of relationships, in this case) to which the word points can be partly or even completely different. In addition, as is clear in the case of "marriage," the changes are contested and highly political. This is especially true of the word "religion," which has changed dramatically over the last several centuries. However, before looking at the complicated history of the word "religion," let's consider a very different politicized word.

Political Definitions: Wetlands

In *Defining Reality: Definitions and the Politics of Meaning* (2003), Edward Schiappa provides an account of how the definition of the word "wetlands" changed in the United States during the early 1990s. At the time, conservationists who wanted to protect wetlands were in competition with developers who wanted to build houses, strip malls, etc. on existing wetlands.

For the conservationists, the keys to defining a "wetland" were threefold. (1) The soil had to be sufficiently saturated with water such that (2) less oxygen could get into the soil, creating conditions in which (3) only certain types of plants adapted to soil with less oxygen—called "hydrophytes"—could thrive. Their definition was not random, and nor was it based on a simple description of patches of land that were sort of wet. On the contrary, the conservationists were concerned first with protecting those species of plants and animals that could only live in these types of wetlands. Second, wetlands—at least on this definition—absorb and hold sediments that we, as humans, don't want in our drinking water, keeping the water table cleaner. Third, this sort of soil can also absorb excess water during heavy rainfall, thus protecting humans to some extent from possible floods. So the conservationists fabricated a definition of "wetland" precisely because they wanted to save certain plants and animals, improve drinking water, and protect us from floods. By contrast, developers had another sort of human interest: they wanted to make money by building on the properties designated and protected as "wetlands."

When George H.W. Bush was running for president of the United States in 1992, "wetlands" were a crucial political issue, and Bush needed to earn the votes of those citizens sympathetic to the conservationists. Consequently, one of his central campaign promises was that under his presidency he would ensure that no wetlands would be lost to development. However, at the same time he also wanted to please the developers so as to continue to get their support—developers can donate more campaign money than conservationists. When Bush finally came into office, he signed into existence legislation that protected "wetlands," but the legislation *completely changed the definition of wetlands* in ways designed to serve the interests of the developers. Specifically, the legislation said that wetlands had to be *very wet*, not just below the surface of the soil, but also at the surface. Bush said, "I've got a radical view of wetlands. I think wetlands ought to be wet" (Schiappa 2003, 87). This benefitted the developers because it greatly reduced the number of "wetlands," as, based on the definition of the conservationists, not all of the "wetlands" were really wet or had water on the surface.

Estimates suggested that probably 30 to 50 million acres of land that had been "wetlands" on the conservationists' definition were reclassified as "not wetlands"—reducing the number of wetlands by a third or by half—so that the developers could build houses and strip malls. A great deal of money was made, and Bush could claim he kept his campaign promise: he *did* in fact approve legislation that protected the "wetlands," even as he redefined the term to suit his purposes. It was a successful bait-and-switch.

The conservationists, of course, were unhappy with these results, insofar as the "really wet" wetlands were so different from the "wetlands" they had singled out that the new legislation no longer served their interests. "Really wet" wetlands couldn't absorb sediments dangerous to human drinking water in the same way, couldn't absorb floodwaters, and didn't sustain the types of endangered species that thrived in the type of "wetlands" that fit their definition. On the new definition, all of the desires of the conservationists were thwarted.

For Schiappa, what is interesting about this case is that both definitions of "wetlands" are tied to human interests, just different sets of interests. What is a wetland? The answer to that question depends on whether one wants a clean water table and to avoid floods, or if one wants to build a suburb. Note: we cannot simply answer that question by going out and looking at one. Whether a particular patch of land is a "wetland" depends not on whether it is wet—just looking at it won't help us. The very same patch of land might look like a wetland for the conservationists but not for Bush and the developers.

Another crucial point for Schiappa is that these definitional decisions are always related to political power, which is why they're so contested. At the end of the day, what is crucial is the legal definition *enforced by the state*. Conservationists can define "wetlands" differently all they want, but their definition has no real-world consequences as long as the state is endorsing and enforcing another definition.

Schiappa concludes that abstract questions like "what is a wetland?"—especially when considered outside of any social or political context—are generally useless. Rather, "the questions to ask are 'Whose interests are being served by this particular definition?' and 'Do we identify with those interests'" (82)? Do we want to make money or save houses from floods?

Political Definitions: Religion

"Religion" is a lot like "wetland": how the term is defined, as well as what's included or excluded in the definition, depends on the interests of those making up the definition. Consider, for instance, two legal cases about whether "yoga" falls under the definition of "religion."

The state of Missouri began taxing yoga studios in 2009, treating them the same as any other business—like gyms—that provides such services. The owners and operators of yoga studios immediately objected to the policy. They insisted that yoga was religious, or spiritual, and as such should be tax exempt, just like churches and other "religious" institutions. "Yoga is a spiritual practice. It's not a purchase. . . . Somehow, we need to get the state to realize that" (Huffstutter 2009). Despite the fact that yoga is a highly profitable, $6 billion industry (Huffstutter 2009), yoga enthusiasts were successful in getting the state of Missouri to change the policy.

By contrast, consider another case from California in 2013. Following the recommendation of yoga enthusiasts, yoga began to be taught in physical education courses in public schools. Soon thereafter, two conservative Christian parents who were uncomfortable with their children being taught yoga filed a lawsuit alleging that, insofar as yoga is "religious," teaching it in public schools violated the separation of church and state. According to the parents' lawyer, "If yoga is a religion and has religious aspects, it doesn't belong in the public schools" (Graham 2013). The lawsuit failed, and the judge ruled—in favor of the yoga instructors—that the yoga was not religious.

So, is yoga religious? If we follow Schiappa's lead, this is an unhelpful question to ask. Instead, let us ask: according to whom and in what social context is yoga religious? What are the interests of the various parties involved? Yoga enthusiasts in Missouri defined yoga as *religious*, because they didn't want to pay taxes to the state. Yoga enthusiasts in California defined yoga as *not religious*, because they wanted to be able to teach it in the public schools. The definition of religion in this case turned on the interests of the parties involved—these definitional games are self-serving. Do we want to make money or get some exercise? Ask other yoga enthusiasts if yoga fits into their definition of "religion," and we're likely to get different answers depending on their individual social and political contexts. What is included and excluded from the definition of religion varies, depending on the politics of the definers. Thus, rather than ask ourselves "What is religion?," it would be better to ask, "Why does this group define religion this way rather than that way, what do they hope to accomplish, and how does the definition serve their interests?" As with wetlands, what do we want to put into our definition, and why? What do we want to protect, or what do we want to sell?

Defining Religion: A Brief Historical Survey

Today people often think of "religions" as special cultural traditions organized around the belief in a god, as well as a set of rituals and communal practices related to that belief. It is often assumed that religion is a matter of individual, personal choice, and a private matter that ought to be kept separate from politics. This contemporary use of the word "religion" has a long history, starting with early modern European politics. There is, in fact, no equivalent word for the modern term "religion" prior to the Protestant Reformation in the sixteenth century. For reasons we'll discuss below, it was not until the Reformation that people began to characterize "religious" institutions as private, separate from politics, and related to spiritual rather than material or bodily concerns.

"Religion" before Modernity

Prior to the Protestant Reformation, the worship of gods was not seen as a special part of life fundamentally segregated from politics or other social spheres.

For instance, in ancient Rome many emperors were worshipped as divine, and people made sacrifices to gods in the hopes that the gods would protect their health, their wealth, or their businesses. Similarly, the Bible presents the kings of ancient Israel as appointed by God; the king's duty was to implement the divine law given to Moses—including, for example, the Ten Commandments. In ancient Greece, ancient Rome, or ancient Israel, a distinction between "religion" and "politics" would have been nonsensical.

If we look at modern English translations of premodern texts, we'll often find that translators do, however, use the word "religion" in their translations. For instance, in the Qur'an—written long before the Protestant Reformation—there is a passage that is typically translated in the following way: "I [Allah] have perfected religion for you" (Surah 5:3). If there is no premodern equivalent for the word "religion," then what ancient Arabic word is being translated here? We could ask the same question about translations of ancient texts from many premodern languages: Hebrew, Greek, Latin, Sanskrit, etc. If there is no premodern word for religion, what are these translators translating? As J.Z. Smith once said in an interview, "It's a well-known conundrum: nobody else has a word remotely like that. If you really want to falsify a translation, find the word religion in any other language" (see https://www.youtube.com/watch?v=iTVeX4Jp418). Translations are often deceptive.

In *Before Religion: A History of a Modern Concept* (2013), Brent Nongbri looks at many of these instances of problematic translation. He finds that the Latin word *religio* is often translated as "religion," but in ancient Rome the word *religio* did *not* mean a private institution, separate from politics, which prepared one for the afterlife. On the contrary, the word meant something like "scruples," "devotion," "reverence," or "rules." Of course, this use overlaps a little bit with some modern uses of "religion," but only slightly. In ancient Rome, one could have *religio* or scruples with respect to any kind of life circumstance—obeying the law could constitute *religio*. *Religiones* were not "religions" but, rather, any set of "rules or prohibitions instituted *either by gods or by humans*" (emphasis added; 28). Similarly, the Arabic word in the Qur'an often translated as "religion" is *dīn*, which simply meant "custom" or "law." Thus, "I have perfected religion for you" is a misleading translation; a translation closer to the Arabic would be "I have perfected the law for you." Nongbri demonstrates the same with many other premodern words that continue to be poorly translated. When we translate premodern terms as "religion," we are actually projecting our own, contemporary ideas back into the past. The scholarly term for this is "anachronism"; an anachronism is something that is out of place in history (for instance, talking about automobiles in ancient Greece would be anachronistic, since automobiles were not invented until much later in human history). Translations that find "religion" in premodern texts are anachronistic, and we must guard against making such errors.

"Religion" in the Early Modern Era

How did "religion" come to be seen as a special kind of institution or culture, fundamentally separate from other forms of culture or politics in general? Prior to the Protestant Reformation, the Catholic church was involved in the political affairs of all Western European states. After the Protestant Reformation—when Protestant churches began to secede from the Catholic church—some European kings sided with the Catholics, and others sided with the Protestants. Those kings who had allied with the Catholic church attempted to suppress the growing Protestant movement, as they saw Protestantism as a threat to the unity of their state. Many people were killed, and several wars ensued.

The Protestants responded to the violence and attempts at suppression by claiming that their institutions should be tolerated, as they were not, in fact, a threat to political unity (although the fact that they were literally warring with the Catholics made this a bit of a disingenuous argument). Martin Luther—the initiator of the Protestant Reformation—argued that states and churches had completely separate jurisdictions. The duty of a king was to oversee bodies and the welfare of the nation; the duty of ministers was to oversee the preparation of souls for the afterlife. In an important treatise on the essential differences between religious institutions and state institutions, Luther wrote that the state is supposed to oversee "laws that extend no further than the body, goods and outward, earthly matters" (Luther 1991, 23). Since the jurisdiction of churches did not overlap or interfere with the jurisdiction of the state on Luther's account, the state should tolerate minority religious groups whose affairs were indifferent to "earthly matters" (see Martin 2010 for a summary and critique of these arguments).

This was a very radical view at the time: the Catholics certainly understood the duty of the church as concerning *both* this world and the next. However, the Protestants were eventually successful in earning the right to be tolerated, largely because, at some point, ongoing war between Catholics and Protestants became a losing situation for all parties. Tolerance of hated enemies became preferable to perpetual fighting. In this instance, defining religion as a cultural sphere separate from politics and law first served the interests of the Protestants, protecting them from Catholic oppression, and eventually served the interests of everyone who wanted to avoid the wars over these competing political allegiances.

The philosopher John Locke wrote what is probably the most famous defense of religious tolerance. The basis of his argument was, as with Luther, jurisdictional:

> The care of the souls cannot belong to the civil magistrate, because his power consists only in outward force; but true and saving religion consists in the inward persuasion of the mind . . . And such is

the nature of the understanding, that it cannot be compelled to the belief of anything by outward force. Confiscation of estate, imprisonment, torment, nothing of that nature can have any such efficacy as to make men change the inward judgment that they have framed of things.

(Locke 2003, 219)

The latter claim is, of course, clearly false: governments persuade people to "believe" things all the time through mandatory state education, propaganda campaigns, outlawing competing views, etc. Nevertheless, making the distinction between persuasion and force led him to the following conclusion:

The church itself is a thing absolutely separate and distinct from the commonwealth. The boundaries on both sides are fixed and immovable. He jumbles heaven and earth together, the things most remote and opposite, who mixes these societies, which are, in their original, end, business, and everything, perfectly distinct, and infinitely different from each other.

(226)

This too was false; Locke was making an argument in favor of tolerance *precisely because* states were mixed up in the business of the churches. However, it was a useful lie: insofar as the claim was received as persuasive, the assertion that states and churches don't have anything to do with one another—even though they obviously did—was a way to get states to *stop* interfering with churches. (Notably, Locke allowed for several exceptions to his rule; he thought that some "religions," like Islam, were such a threat to the commonwealth that the state should obviously outlaw and repress them (see Martin 2010)).

What is crucial here is that—much like "wetlands"—this jurisdictional definition was a new invention; before this time no such "religion-as-a-private-matter" was thought to exist. Just like George H.W. Bush or our enterprising yoga instructors, Martin Luther and others invented a new definition in order to serve their unique political interests.

Notably, however, even though tolerance was won with the argument that the jurisdiction of churches did not overlap with the jurisdiction of the nation, it is clear that churches—both Catholic and Protestant—continued to involve themselves in social and political matters. The idea that "religions" were private matters was a useful fiction to end wars, but by no means did it change the churches' behavior or end their involvement in political matters. This is unchanged still today: institutions we presently call "religions" continue to be involved in social and political matters, and vice versa. Indeed, the stereotypes that "religion makes people moral" or "religion can help make the world a better place" presume that the jurisdiction of "religion" concerns social welfare and thus overlaps with the jurisdiction of the nation-state.

"Religion," Colonialism, and Cultural Chauvinism

The only "religions" of particular concern in the definitional disputes of the sixteenth century were Catholicism and Protestantism. However, in the seventeenth century Christian Europeans begin to consider other cultural traditions as potentially deserving the status of "religions." At the time, their concern was primarily to separate out the definition of "true religion" from "false religion," and thus books on "religions" tended to focus on distinguishing the merits of "true religion"—that is, Christianity—from the errors of "false religions," such as Judaism or Islam, as well as what they called "idolatry," "paganism," or "heathenism." In the eighteenth, nineteenth and early twentieth centuries, Europeans (and later, North Americans) developed an evolutionary schema, according to which they defined religions and cultures as entities that evolved over time from worse to better. Thus they separated the "backwards" religions like those of "primitive savages" from the "advanced" religions like Christianity and Judaism; these accounts put "Christianity" at the peak, as the most advanced—and therefore the best—religion among all the others. In his devastating critique of theories of "primitive religion," E.E. Evans-Pritchard writes,

> [i]n these theories it was assumed, taken for granted, that we [Europeans] were at one end of the scale of human progress and that so-called savages were at the other end, and that, because primitive men were on a rather low technological level, their thought and custom must in all respects be the antithesis of ours. We are rational, primitive peoples prelogical, living in a world of dreams and make-believe, of mystery and awe. . . .
>
> Primitive man was thus represented as childish, crude, prodigal, and comparable to animals and imbeciles.
>
> (Evans-Pritchard 1965, 105)

Evans-Pritchard concludes that

> [a]ll this fitted very well with colonialist and other interests, and some were prepared to admit that some of the discredit must go to the American ethnologists who wanted an excuse for slavery, and some also to those who desired to find a missing link between men and monkeys.
>
> (106)

In summary, presenting "primitives" as evolutionarily backward was useful for justifying colonialism and slavery. *Their definitions and caricatures of "religion" were blatantly acts of cultural chauvinism.* These theorists found "in primitive religion a weapon which could, they thought, be used with deadly effect" (15).

Although his work did not directly support colonialism, Christian theologian Rudolf Otto defined "religion" as a sensing or feeling of "the Holy." On the surface that doesn't sound particularly chauvinistic, but when we look into the details, we find that his definition was designed to present Christianity—and, more specifically, Protestant Christianity—as the most "rational" religion and "unsurpassable" (Otto 1958, 82). For Otto, Christians sensed or felt "the Holy" and put that feeling into rational terms better than any other religion. By contrast, Otto argued that Judaism and Islam were slightly less rational, and, in the case of Islam, more "fanatical" (91). Otto viewed the "barbaric" (130) religions of "primitive savages" as so far behind in the progress of evolution and so "rudimentary" (117) that they shouldn't be considered "religions" so much as "pre-religions" (124). For Otto, the definition of the word "religion" was useful not for an objective account of how "religions" are different from other cultural traditions; rather, it was a tool for ranking cultures and putting his favorite at the top. Otto too was reinventing the definition of words to serve his interests, thereby presenting his culture as superior to all other cultures.

Scholars have long noted the connections between these types of definitions of "religion" and European colonialism. Starting in the fifteenth century, European nations developed and expanded their empires by sending ships all over the world to conquer territory, seizing foreign land as their own, and appropriating natural resources for sale or trade. The ideology of the "white man's burden" was used to justify colonization; that is, the so-called "more evolved" races had a moral duty to help the more "primitive" races catch up in the march of progress. Similarly, the view that there are advanced and primitive religions taught that it was acceptable to conquer and subjugate "backwards" religious groups in order to help them "evolve." It is therefore no surprise that one of the early definers of "religion," Samuel Purchas, defended the East India Company's administration of the British colonial endeavors in India—the British invasion of India was seen as being for the greater good, insofar as it modernized trade and brought Christian missionaries to the region (see Fitzgerald 2007). Of course there is always a great deal of "collateral damage" in colonization; countless natives across the globe were killed as European nations expanded their empires. Quite literally, as Evans-Pritchard put it, definitions can be deadly weapons of war. These early definitions of "religion" and the ranking of cultures they entailed were chauvinist and imperialist in nature, justifications for colonizing whatever areas of the globe the Europeans saw as profitable.

The Christian Ideal

Most scholars of religion have moved away from this explicitly ethnocentric, Christian perspective. Many scholarly definitions leave out the ranking aspects of the earlier definitions, and instead define "religion" more neutrally as including the religion of Christianity and other forms of culture that are structurally similar—usually Judaism, Islam, Buddhism, and Hinduism, among others. However, some scholars argue that one problem of this more neutral approach is that we're still left setting up "Christianity" as an ideal against which all other religions are compared. Even if scholars no longer accept that Christianity is somehow intrinsically superior to other religions, we may still be setting it up as a universal standard. On this type of definition, religions:

1 are started by a founder—like Jesus;
2 have central beliefs and doctrines that practitioners must believe in—like the Christians' Nicene Creed;
3 have sacred texts in which those core beliefs are recorded—like the Bible;
4 have rituals designed to reinforce remembrance of those doctrines—like the Eucharist; and
5 have communities of worshippers organized around the sacred texts, doctrines, and rituals—like the Christian church.

This definition of religion encourages comparisons between the Bible and the Qur'an as sacred texts, or comparisons between Jesus and Muhammad as founders, or between the Eucharist and Muslim rituals such as praying five times a day or traveling to Mecca. In a way this approach is less biased than the earlier attempts at definition, insofar as Christianity is considered *alongside* other religions, rather than above them.

Unfortunately, this approach still sets up Christianity as the *ideal type*, which has resulted in a kind of Christian privilege, especially when it comes to the history of legal cases related to "religious freedom"—particularly in the United States. For a long time, Native American practices weren't protected by laws governing religious freedom because the Native Americans didn't have sacred texts or churches like the Christians did. Indeed, at some points in the history of the United States, Native American practices were outright prohibited by law, in part because American Christians considered them demonic. As Suzanne Owen writes in *The Appropriation of Native American Spirituality* (2008), "[i]n 1883, despite the First Amendment of the United States constitution that guarantees religious freedom, Henry Teller, Secretary of the Interior, developed laws prohibiting Native American ceremonial activity. Those who were caught disobeying were imprisoned" (30–31). To secure some of the freedoms that Christians enjoyed, Native Americans eventually had to present their culture as somehow fitting the mold of Christianity. Black Elk was one figure who made great efforts in this cultural battle by creating narratives that became the basis of a Native American "spirituality." In order for the Lakota tribe to be seen as having "a 'true' religion not unlike Christianity . . . Black Elk . . . employed a Catholic framework to explain Lakota ceremonial traditions," inventing both a "founder" of the religion and a set of seven "sacraments" (43). To earn the rights that Christians already enjoyed, Black Elk and others had to manipulate and transform their cultural traditions until they looked like a "religion" that Christians could recognize as familiar.

Similarly, religious freedom laws protected Christian "conscientious objectors," giving them the right not to kill in war, while for a long time "conscientious objectors" who weren't part of a "religious" tradition that looked like Christianity weren't protected. In one interesting court case, analyzed by Winnifred Fallers Sullivan in *The Impossibility of Religious Freedom*, (2005) some Jews and Catholics in Florida lost a "religious freedom" lawsuit—the lawsuit concerned whether they could decorate cemetery graves with "religious" shrines—because the Protestant judge didn't see the litigants' "religion" as sufficiently "religious" to warrant legal protection; to him, their religion didn't look enough like his religion to count. This is what happens when Protestant Christian views of their own tradition are set up as the norm or the ideal model for all other forms of culture potentially deserving of legal protection.

Irrational "Religion"

One major shift in the way scholars talk about "religion" took place in the nineteenth and twentieth centuries, when scholars increasingly began to define "religion" as essentially irrational in some way, as opposed to other forms of knowledge that were considered rational or scientific by contrast. Rather than seeing religions along a continuum from better to worse—or from civilized to barbaric or savage—these scholars presented "science" as civilized and defined all "religion" as backward, unscientific, or intrinsically misguided in some way. This approach holds on to the evolutionary schema like Otto's discussed above, except that it puts "science" or "secular" forms of knowledge at the peak of evolution rather than "Christianity." The problem with this approach is that there's no clear way to demarcate "scientific" reasoning from so-called "religious" reasoning. Social scientific research shows us that all groups—whether labeled "religious" or "nonreligious"—appeal to authoritative figures or texts, have unquestioned background assumptions, show in-group bias for their own group's views, etc. (see Chapter 5 for more on this). From the perspective of social science, all human groups behave in similar ways, and thus the presentation of "nonreligious" groups as more reasonable than "religious" groups looks a lot like the self-serving narratives written by those scholars who presented Christianity as the highest evolved religion.

Consider those who defined "Islam" as essentially irrational after the 9/11 attacks on New York in 2001. Al Qaeda's attack killed almost 3,000 civilians and was publicly viewed as irrational and immoral. By contrast, the subsequent invasion of Afghanistan by the United States resulted in the deaths of 92,000 people, more than 26,000 of whom were civilians (see costsofwar.org, hosted by Brown University, for more information about the death tolls of recent global conflicts). Despite the fact that *this resulted in almost 9 times the number of civilian deaths* as Al Qaeda's attack, almost no one views the invasion of Afghanistan as "irrational." As William Cavanaugh notes in his book on the myth that religions are intrinsically and irrationally violent, "revulsion toward killing and dying in the name of one's religion is one of the principle means by which we become convinced that killing and dying in the name of the nation-state is laudable and proper" (Cavanaugh 2009, 4–5). Defining religion as irrational is a convenient way to justify killing enemies we can successfully label as irrationally "religious." Once again, we have a situation where the contested terms are defined in ways that serve the interests of the definers.

Finally, it is worth pointing out that one of the legacies of the tradition of distinguishing and ranking advanced religion and primitive religion is that people make a distinction and ranking between individual religion and organized religion, or—which seems to be the same thing—between spirituality and religion. The stereotype is that while organized religion is oppressive and constraining of individuality, spirituality is more liberating in that it allows for individual creativity. What counts as "religion" and "spirituality" is, as before, tied to the interests of those using the terms. In practice, "organized religion" seems to refer to any "religious tradition" a group dislikes, and "spirituality" is any "religious tradition" a group likes (see Martin 2014, especially the chapter titled "Our 'Religion' of the Status Quo"). Ironically, there are organized communities of "spiritual" people who oppose "organized religion," and those communities have their own rules, social norms, and demands for conformity—just like all human groups. The claim that their group's ideology is "spirituality" rather than "organized religion" is in many ways little different from the chauvinistic rankings of the imperialists who saw fit to conquer indigenous communities who had only a "primitive religion"—the only difference is that the insulting caricatures of "primitive religion" are recycled and revised, and then used to malign "organized religion."

***

In summary, these are just some of the problems with the history of the word "religion":

- Although we talk about "religions" existing prior to the modern era, this is problematic because premodern civilizations did not have a word for "religion," nor did they see what we might call "religion" as distinct or separate from other forms of culture or society.
- Protestant reformers appealed for tolerance on the basis of the fact that "church" and "state" had completely different jurisdictions, thereby obscuring the fact that those institutions we call "religions" are always actively involved in social and political projects (and vice versa).

- Many accounts of the nature of "religion" were designed to justify the cultural superiority of Christian Europe and to justify imperialism and colonialism.
- Even when different "religions" are seen as equal rather than better or worse, Christianity often gets used as the ideal model for what "religion" looks like, thus resulting in a legal bias in favor of Christians when it comes to religious freedom court cases.
- Although scientific studies show that all human groups require conformity, show irrational bias, and discriminate against other groups, "religions" are often assumed to be more irrational or more violent—despite the fact that we have no evidence for that assumption.
- Some groups today claim to be "spiritual" and contrast themselves with "organized religions," but in doing so repeat the rhetorical gestures of imperialist Europeans who separated "Christianity" from "primitive religion" in order to claim superiority for their own group and justify colonial endeavors.

All of these uses of the term "religion" and "spirituality" are normative, meaning that the definitions of the terms are tied to a set of subjective and often controversial evaluative norms or values. This is problematic from an academic perspective because the definitions of academic terms are not supposed to center around the subjective, normative assumption that one's own group is superior to others' groups. Academic standards prohibit scholars from merely cheerleading for their own favorite institutions, even when their cheers are disguised beneath clever definitional work. "Religion" is a term with perhaps too much normative baggage, as almost all uses from the early modern period to the present are tied up with assertions of cultural superiority. Can the word be saved?

Toward a Better Definition?

Would it be possible to come up with a definition of religion that avoids the biases that existed in previous uses of the term, or a definition that isn't simply self-serving for the group using it? Some scholars have attempted just this—to come up with a definition of religion without normative baggage, or one that would be neutral or unbiased. The problem, however, is that we cannot formulate a non-normative definition—that is, a definition that isn't tied to problematic or subjective social norms—that fits with the everyday colloquial use of the word. Usually when we try to formulate a definition, we look at all the different things that word is applied to and try to see what they have in common with each other—what's the lowest common denominator among all of these things? For instance, we could look at lions and tigers and try to figure out what they each have in common with their own species that simultaneously

Table 1.1 Forms of culture potentially called religious

Judaism	Indigenous cultures	Feng shui
Christianity	Practice of yoga	Visiting a medium
Islam	Personal meditation	Marxism or existentialism
Hinduism	Reading self-help books	The Metallica fan club
Buddhism	Reading astrology reports	American nationalism

distinguishes them from the other species: those big cats we call tigers all have stripes, and those big cats we call lions have manes (at least when it comes to the males in the species). "Stripes" would go into our definition of tigers—since they all have that in common—and "manes" would go into our definition of lions. There would be more to it than this, but this would be a start.

However, this method of formulating a definition will not work when we come to all those things we commonly refer to as "religion," because *there are no features that are uniquely common to all the traditions we typically call religions.* People have tried to make an official definition that fits our colloquial everyday use, but they inevitably fail. Consider the things in Table 1.1 that one might find in the world, and which the word religion might or might not group together.

Which of these things would be picked up by the word religion? I think most people would generally agree that the colloquial use of the term would probably group together all of the things in the first column (with a small question mark next to Buddhism for all of those people who say it is a philosophy and not a religion). From the second column, the term might include indigenous cultures or the practice of yoga (another couple of small question marks), but probably not the other things. Colloquial uses of the term religion rarely, if ever, include anything in the third column.

Now look at the following definitions of religion; we can see that none of them will pick up the same thing that the colloquial use of the term picks up.

- *Religion as a "belief system."* This definition includes both more and less than the colloquial use. It will probably pick up Marxism or existentialism, for example. In addition, the Metallica fan club may well be organized around the belief that Metallica is the best band there ever was. However, some Jewish and Buddhist practitioners specifically emphasize that one's practice (ritual or meditative) is all that is important to them, and that one's beliefs are irrelevant for membership in their community. This definition would probably not pick up those particular forms of Judaism and Buddhism.
- *Religion as something that specifically concerns "supernatural" matters.* This definition will also group together more and less than the colloquial use. Insofar as some forms of Christianity and Buddhism are atheist, this

sort of definition would not include those forms, although the colloquial use probably would. Also, this term might pick up astrology, feng shui, or visiting a medium, and some uses of Ouija boards, although the colloquial use probably would not.

- *Religion as "matters of faith."* This sort of definition often trades on the association of "religion" with "faith" and the association of "science" with "reason." However, if we understand "faith" to be "faith in things that cannot be proven," then one will find "faith" in elements of *all* of the things on the list. It cannot be "proven" that Metallica is the best band ever, nor can the nationalist faith in America be "rationally" justified. At the same time, if we understand "reason" to concern "things that can be proven," then one will also find "reason" in elements of *all* of the things on the list. It seems "reasonable" to claim that a man named Gautama preached about *dukkha* a few centuries BCE, to claim that a man named Jesus lived, preached, and developed some sort of following in the first century, to claim that Metallica is a heavy metal rock band, or to claim that the 4th of July celebrates the day on which the Declaration of Independence was signed. These things are part of Buddhism, Christianity, the Metallica fan club, and American nationalism, but they are not simply matters of faith; they are facts. There are *both* matters of "faith" and matters of "reason" in every cultural tradition; the faith/reason binary will not neatly segregate those traditions colloquially called religions from other traditions.

- *Religion as concerning "the meaning of life."* Concerns about the so-called "meaning of life" are rather recent and bourgeois. Ancient Jews and first-century Christians, for instance, didn't talk about the "meaning of life," and most poor people spend their lives searching more for the satisfaction of minimal needs than the "meaning of life." This vocabulary is really one of recent coinage, and is used most often by those who have the leisure time to search for this sort of "meaning." This definition would not pick up much of anything prior to the twentieth century. However, we can take part of this idea, and transform it slightly; perhaps concerns about the "meaning of life" belong under the category of "concerns about one's place in the universe." This more general category will pick up all of the things the colloquial use of the term religion does, and several more. One can find concerns about one's place in the universe in some forms of yoga, self-help books, Marxism and existentialism, and some forms of American nationalism (those forms that focused on manifest destiny, for instance).

- *Religion as concerning "spirituality" or "spiritual well-being."* What this will pick up will depend on what one means by "spiritual," a vague term that is easily exploited on account of its vagueness. Nevertheless, if we let "spiritual" be used broadly, this definition of religion will probably pick up all of the things the colloquial use does, as well as yoga, meditation, self-help books, and perhaps feng shui.

- *Religion as "communal institutions oriented around a set of beliefs, ritual practices, and ethical or social norms."* This definition—which is close to some scholarly uses of the word—will probably pick up all of the things the colloquial use does, but it will probably also pick up some forms of yoga (maybe not those forms that are simply exercise, but probably those that are communally practiced), Marxism, the Metallica fan club, and American nationalism. In fact, this definition is very broad, and would probably pick up a whole host of things not colloquially understood to be religious: karate centers, Oprah's book club, businesses that have an important corporate culture, the local university's department of religious studies, etc.

One might come a little closer to the colloquial use by combining the last definition with some qualification about the importance of supernatural elements. However, such a definition would still pick up American nationalism, which often has a theistic inflection, and would fail to pick up atheist forms of some traditions colloquially called religions. *None of these definitions match the colloquial use exactly.*

The problem here is simple: the reason why we can't formulate a definition that fits the colloquial use is because *the colloquial use groups together dissimilar things.* This is, of course, in part because of the long history of the term, where its application shifted over time depending on the interests of those using the term. Since the word was used in many competing ways, of course the term has come to refer to a lot of dissimilar things. All of those things we colloquially call "religions" simply do not share a set of core properties.

A radical consequence of recognizing this fact is that we will not be able to make any generalizations about those cultural traditions we call religions. It is easy to make generalizations about something that is used with precision: all "fish" live in water and breathe with gills. But a term like "sea creature" is broader than "fish," and groups together a wider variety of things, many of them dissimilar. We could say that "all fish breathe with gills," but we couldn't say "all sea creatures breathe with gills," because whales and dolphins do not. The word "religion" is much more like "sea creatures" than "fish"—a lot of different things are grouped together under the word religion—and that prevents us from making any substantial generalizations. Anyone who begins a sentence with the phrase "all religions . . ." is certainly saying something false. It is therefore incorrect to say that all religions are about private matters, belief, faith, the supernatural, spirituality, mystical experience, or anything else. Because the colloquial use of the word "religion" groups together so many dissimilar things, these generalizations are simply not true.

In addition, if the word "religion" groups together dissimilar things, there will not be anything that fundamentally distinguishes those things called religions from other sorts of cultural traditions. Consider the "sea creatures" example. We might try to make an essential distinction— "sea creatures are fundamentally different from land animals because the former breathe with gills and the latter breathe with lungs"—but it will not work, since the characteristics of both groups overlap: some sea creatures do, in fact, breathe with lungs, like some of the land animals. The same problem is true with "religions"—they cannot be essentially distinguished from other cultural traditions.

For instance, what is it that fundamentally distinguishes "religion" from "nationalism"? One might say that "nationalism" is concerned with *politics* but "religion" is not, but that would be false: many of those traditions we call religious are extremely political. American evangelical Christians, for instance, are very politically active. One might say that nationalism concerns a *national territory*, but religions do not, but that would be false: some of those traditions we call religious are in fact linked to a territory or piece of land. Hindu nationalism is an important contemporary movement in India, and one that sees Hinduism as intrinsically linked to "Mother India" as a specific territory. One might say that nationalism doesn't have any *supernatural elements*, but religions do, but that too would be false: many forms of nationalism have supernatural elements. For instance, Hindu nationalism has a number of supernatural elements, as does American nationalism—as evidenced by the slogan "In God We Trust" on US money, and the inclusion of "one nation, under God" in the US pledge of allegiance. And, even if we eliminated all of these references to God from American nationalism, we would still have mysterious, almost supernatural ideas like "unalienable rights" which, according to the American constitution, were given to us by God. In the end, it turns out that there aren't really any fundamental differences between those things we colloquially call nationalisms and those things we colloquially call religions. There is no substantial reason to call the 4th of July a nationalist celebration as opposed to a religious one—the only reason why we call the 4th of July nationalist rather than religious is force of habit.

Before concluding, I would like to clarify what I am not arguing. I am not saying that religion can't be defined. Just like a "wetland," "religion" can be defined in lots of different ways, depending on whose interests we want to serve. However, what I am saying is *we can't come up with a definition that fits all of the everyday uses of the term.* Of course conservationists can define "wetland" in a particular way; what they cannot do is define "wetland" in a way that fits the colloquial use, their usage, and the usage of George H.W. Bush at the same time—simply because the word is used in competing ways across different contexts. Similarly, we can define "religion" in a lot of different ways, but none of our definitions will simultaneously fit the colloquial use and the use of the word by folks like Martin Luther, *and* Rudolf Otto, *and* scientists who think religion is irrational—they're using the word in competing or potentially even opposite ways, so there isn't a lowest-common-denominator to be found.

Conclusion

The history of the word "religion" is tied up with normative interests, Reformation-era politics, Christian ethnocentrism, European imperialism, and more. In each of the historical cases considered, "religion" was defined in a way specifically to serve the interests of some groups at the expense of others. In addition, even if we attempt to set aside the problematic history of the definition of "religion," our common, everyday use of the word "religion" is relatively sloppy, arbitrary, and unsophisticated. I'm sure that psychologists refer to some of their patients as "crazy" on occasion, but you wouldn't find an entry for "crazy" in a psychology textbook, simply because it's an unsophisticated term. Similarly, there is nothing particularly wrong with utilizing the word "religion" in everyday conversation; however, as scholars we must be aware of the normative baggage associated with the term, resist making generalizations, and avoid positing any fundamental distinctions between "religion" and other types of cultural traditions. "Religion" might be no more useful in an academic setting than "crazy" is in a psychology class.

In addition, it would presumably be more neutral for us, as scholars, to resist taking sides with some definitions over others. Rather than say "yoga is religious" or "yoga is not religious"—that is, rather than taking sides with those who want to dodge taxes or those who think it makes for great exercise—perhaps we should simply point out how the game of definition works. In his analysis, Schiappa did not say "this is what a wetland really is"; on the contrary, he merely noted how this definition serves these interests, and that definition serves other interests. Similarly, perhaps we—in our role as scholars—should avoid taking sides in contested political battles and instead confine ourselves to pointing out how the different definitions of "religion" serve different social or political interests in different contexts. Much like sportscasters who don't take sides in their commentary, we as scholars could strive for less bias by limiting ourselves to analyzing how others play the game.

What follows in this book does not presume that any particular form of culture is fundamentally "religious" or "not religious." Since all forms of culture tend to function in similar ways, making a distinction between "religious" and "not religious" does not appear to be particularly fruitful. Thus we will look at forms of culture commonly considered "religious," but we will also draw analogies or make comparisons to forms of culture often considered "not religious." Although this book is intended as an introduction to the critical study of religion, it could just as well have been called *A Critical Introduction to the Study of Culture*. What we say about so-called "religious" culture will be transferable to culture in general.

2

Functionalism and the Hermeneutics of Suspicion

How should we approach the study of religion? Because we are going to treat religion as no different from culture more broadly, we can borrow approaches from anthropology, sociology, cultural studies, and other academic disciplines that offer sophisticated ways of thinking about the relationship between culture and social power. More specifically, we will look at what scholars call "functionalism" and "the hermeneutics of suspicion." However, before turning to those approaches, it is important to consider the approaches we're explicitly going to avoid.

Problematic Approaches to Avoid

One of the most common ways people study religion is based on the assumption that their own religious tradition is the correct one; we can call it the "my religion is true" approach. For instance, many conservative Christians are taught that Christian beliefs are true, and that other religious beliefs are false at best and demonic at worst. On this view, studying religion might amount to looking into how Christianity is true, how other religions are false, and how to convert people away from false religions. Indeed, some Christian colleges offer courses on "world religions" that do just that, offering students a survey of the differences between "true religion" and the "false religions."

Most scholars in religious studies think this approach is problematically biased. Since the early modern period, academic study has made *questioning everything* a central goal. Of course, we can never question everything all at once; we all have some unquestioned assumptions. However, most scholars think those unquestioned assumptions should eventually be sought out and rigorously interrogated. Unfortunately, the "my religion is true" approach tends to set aside some assumptions as so sacred as to be unquestionable. For this reason, most scholars reject this approach as unacceptable for academic study.

A second common way people tend to think about religion is as a "belief system." On this view, religious practitioners subscribe to a system of beliefs, and the beliefs they hold inform or shape their behavior. "Belief" in religious doctrine is assumed to be a causal force that directs people's behavior. Why do most Muslims avoid pork? Because they believe that pork is unclean, following Allah's words in the Qur'an. This general theory of religion, however, simply does not work.

There are several problems with the theory that religions are essentially belief systems that direct practitioners' behavior. First, as noted in Chapter 1, not all cultural traditions colloquially called religions focus on "beliefs," as this theory implies. Despite the fact that most people refer to "Buddhism" as a "religion," some Zen Buddhist practitioners even go so far as to say that doctrines or beliefs are *completely irrelevant* to their tradition. Rather than emphasizing doctrine, these Zen Buddhists focus instead on the practice of meditation, which they say will transform you no matter what beliefs or doctrines you hold. Obviously, some cultural traditions do focus on what scholars call "orthodoxy," which means "right belief" or "correct doctrine." However, other traditions focus on what scholars call "orthopraxy," which means "right practice." Many of those cultural traditions we call "religious" focus on orthopraxy and ignore orthodoxy altogether.

Second, even those who say beliefs are important—those who emphasize orthodoxy—rarely if ever have a *system* of beliefs. Social and psychological research shows that people tend to hold a collection of contradictory beliefs that cannot be put together into a completely coherent system. Every cultural tradition has tensions or contradictions within it—especially because cultures evolve and change over time. No culture is a systematic, coherent whole.

Third, people often behave in ways that explicitly contradict their stated beliefs. Many people who believe they are not racist nevertheless behave in extremely racist ways. Similarly, many Buddhists who believe in the teaching that we should practice compassion are not compassionate, and many Christians who believe in "loving your neighbor" do not, in fact, love their neighbors.

A fourth problem with the idea that religions are belief systems is the fact that few practitioners fully subscribe to the apparently "official" beliefs or doctrines of their religious tradition. For instance, most American Catholics support the use of birth control despite the fact that official Catholic doctrine says it is immoral. Similarly, although pork and alcohol are prohibited in the Qur'an, many Muslims around the world eat pork and drink alcohol. No one accepts *everything* in the cultural tradition they inherit. Indeed, the scope of any sizeable historical tradition is so broad that it is unlikely any particular individual could even know all of the teachings, doctrines, and practices that have been emphasized in the history of the tradition. Modern

Hindus claim their religion is thousands of years old; who among us could keep track of three or four thousand years of doctrine? Thus the assumption that people believe everything that's in their so-called "belief system" is untenable.

Fifth, and most importantly, research shows that people's behavior is often based on something *other than* their stated beliefs. Motivations for human behavior are extremely complex, and we often act without ever consciously thinking about our stated beliefs or religious doctrines. For example, social scientific research shows that our behavior is often more influenced by the perceptions of our immediate peers than our conscious beliefs—we frequently but unconsciously act in ways designed to mimic or impress those we like. It is quite possible that individual Muslims who avoid pork do so not because of any doctrines found in the Qur'an but rather because that's what all of their immediate peers do. Similarly, Catholics who refuse to use birth control might do so not because Catholic doctrine forbids it but because that's the social norm in their local community—which could help explain why Catholics in *other* communities might have no problem with using birth control. When asked "why did you do that," practitioners may of course give reasons that appeal to their religious doctrines; if we asked Muslims about their avoidance of pork, they're more likely to point to the Qur'an to explain their behavior than to say "we do it because our friends do." However, their behavior could be motivated by either of those two things. The automatic assumption that we consciously determine our course of action after consulting our beliefs is deeply problematic.

In summary, we have seen that:

1 some traditions emphasize orthopraxy over orthodoxy;
2 even in those religious or cultural traditions that emphasize belief or doctrine, rarely are the beliefs ever systematically connected to one another;
3 people's behavior may openly conflict with their stated beliefs;
4 people in cultural traditions rarely accept all of the "official" beliefs or doctrines they inherit from their tradition; and
5 social scientific research shows that human behavior is often motivated by social conditions—of which we're typically unaware—rather than consciously stated beliefs.

This idea that religion is a belief system that straightforwardly directs practitioners' behavior quickly collapses under investigation. Stated beliefs or doctrines are clearly *part of* those many cultural institutions we call religions, but those beliefs are often contradictory, ignored, outright rejected, and so on—in which case the overly simple claim that "religion is a belief system" is nonsense.

This book will therefore reject the "my religion is true" approach and the "belief system" approach; instead, we will approach the study of religion using what is called "functionalism" and the "hermeneutics of suspicion."

Functionalism and the Hermeneutics of Suspicion

"Functionalism" is an approach to culture that looks for how a particular element of culture *functions* in a society; functionalists ask, how is this element of culture used, and what is it being used for? The doctrine of the "divine right of kings" is a useful example. The doctrine was created in the early modern period when European kings were battling with the Catholic church on a variety of social and political matters. According to the doctrine, God appointed kings to their position, and thus their rule was divine in origin and in some way uncontestable. In retrospect, it is clear what function this doctrine was created to serve: it was invented by those who wanted to defend the authority of kings over and against the authority of the Catholic popes—if kings were divinely appointed by God, they could perhaps freely ignore some of the popes' demands. *The social function of the doctrine was to protect the authority of royalty and to challenge the authority of the popes.* "Functionalism" is the academic approach that looks precisely at how elements of culture work or function in particular social contexts.

Although most people are not familiar with the term "hermeneutic," its definition is simple: the word "hermeneutic" is a technical term that means "method of interpretation." A "hermeneutic of suspicion" is a *method of interpretation* that is *suspicious* of whatever is being studied. A hermeneutic of suspicion requires us, when faced with religious claims or religious practices, to approach those claims with scepticism. This is, in fact, what we do most of the time. Everyone is a sceptic about some things; if we found ourselves faced with a murderer who says "God told me to do it," we would probably begin by doubting that claim and looking for other explanations or understandings of what is going on. We are liable to suggest, "perhaps he is schizophrenic," or "maybe he is using 'God' as an excuse for what he has done." By adopting a hermeneutic of suspicion, we train ourselves to approach the study of culture like homicide detectives approaching possible murder suspects—with a very critical eye. Those who employ a hermeneutic of suspicion become culture detectives, taking nothing at face value, and looking for hidden motivations, unstated assumptions, or unseen effects in how elements of culture are formed and used.

One brilliant example of how elements of culture could serve unseen social functions is presented in E.E. Evans-Pritchard's book, *Witchcraft, Oracles, and Magic among the Azande* (1976). Evans-Pritchard, an anthropologist, did research on the Azande—an African tribe in the Sudan—in the 1920s, focusing on their practices of witchcraft and their use of witch doctors. The Azande believed that witches were born with a magical substance inside their body that permitted them to perform witchcraft. However, there was no way for individuals to know whether or not they were born with it—most people in the tribe assumed that the majority of witches were ignorant of their own abilities. However, even if an individual witch was unaware of his abilities, he could still bewitch others unconsciously. A witch could, unknowingly, become angry with another person and magically cause illness or death. Whenever anyone became ill or died, the general assumption within the community was that it had been caused by a witch who bore ill will. Evans-Pritchard notes that *all* unfortunate events were attributed to witchcraft. The actual circumstances of the particular misfortune were unimportant. Whether a man died from an illness or from his house collapsing was irrelevant—the tribe would assume that the cause behind the illness or the falling house was witchcraft. He recounts one example:

> [s]hortly after my arrival in Zandeland . . . a hut had been burned to the ground. . . . Its owner was overcome with grief as it had contained the beer he was preparing for a mortuary feast. He told us that he had gone the previous night to examine the beer. He had lit a handful of straw and raised it above his head so that light would be cast on the pots, and in so doing he had ignited the thatch. He, and my companions also, were convinced that the disaster was caused by witchcraft.
>
> (20)

Although they did not know which particular witch had done it, they all took for granted that witchcraft was the cause of the misfortune.

When an illness occurred that the villagers attributed to witchcraft, the family of the sick person would worry that they had angered a witch. To protect themselves and the sick individual, the family would go to a witch doctor (which is not the same as a witch), who could perform a magical ritual in order to determine which particular witch was causing the illness. One such ritual involved feeding a mild poison to a chicken and asking its spirit questions like, "if so-and-so is the witch, kill the chicken; if so-and-so is not the witch, let the chicken live." Whether the chicken lived or died would tell the answer, and the witch doctor had to ask multiple times, reverse the phrasing of the questions, and try different names. He had to get the same answer at least twice for it to be confirmed—several chickens might be required to get to a firm answer, making this an expensive ritual. When a witch was decisively identified by the spirit in the ritual, the sick person's family would make arrangements for a messenger to speak to the witch.

> Almost invariably the [accused] witch replies courteously that he is unconscious of injuring anyone, that if it is true that he has injured the man in question he is very sorry. . . . He says . . . that if he is a

witch he is unaware of his state and that he is not causing the sick man injury with intent. He says that he addresses the witchcraft [substance] in his belly, beseeching it to become cool (inactive).

(42)

In cases where the illness persisted—or if the illness resulted in death—the family would likely hire a witch doctor to curse the witch to death. Whenever the witch identified by the chicken ritual eventually died—whether immediately or years later—his death would be attributed to the curse. Because those who had been identified as witches feared being cursed, they were of course motivated to be as courteous as possible to whoever was bringing the complaint.

Evans-Pritchard analyzes these ritualized social interactions as an outsider; he did not believe in witchcraft or magic. "Witches, as the Azande conceive them, clearly cannot exist" (18). However, he notes that these practices served the social function of "eliminating friction" within the community (43). Because everyone fears that everyone else may be a witch, or even fears that they themselves may be witches subject to witch doctor curses, they are constantly on guard against offending their neighbors.

> It is in the interest of both parties that they should not become estranged through the incident. They have to live together as neighbors afterwards and to co-operate in the life of the community. It is also to their mutual advantage to avoid all appearance of anger or resentment. . . . The whole point of the procedure is to put the witch in a good temper by being polite to him. The witch on his part ought to feel grateful to the people who have warned him so politely of the danger in which he stands.
>
> (43)

Evans-Pritchard later concludes, "Belief in witchcraft is a valuable corrective to uncharitable impulses, because a show of . . . meanness or hostility may bring serious consequences. . . . Since Azande do not know who are and who are not witches, they assume that all their neighbors may be witches, and are therefore careful not to offend any of them without good cause" (54–55).

Evans-Pritchard's work is, first, an example of a hermeneutic of suspicion: he doesn't accept the existence of witchcraft or curses, and thus looks for alternate explanations of what might be going on in the community with all the talk about witches and witchcraft. Second, he provides a functionalist explanation of what's going on: he argues that even though witchcraft isn't real, the *belief in* witchcraft and practice of witch doctoring serves the social function of encouraging everyone in the community to be polite to one another. Even if witchcraft isn't real, belief in witchcraft might nevertheless serve an extremely useful social function within the community.

It is important to note that Evans-Pritchard's view of Azande culture is an outsider's view rather than an insider's. Scholars make a distinction between the view practitioners have of themselves (the insider's or "emic" view) and the view scholars have of them (the outsider's or "etic" view). If we asked members of the Azande community why these ritual interactions are performed, they would likely say: "we have to protect ourselves from witchcraft." If we asked Evans-Pritchard, he would say they function to eliminate tension or friction between individuals or families in the community. The understanding of the function of the culture would thus be completely different on the insider's and outsider's approaches. Evans-Pritchard's theory is also called "reduction-ist" because he "reduces" these cultural interactions to a social function; for him, the function of witchcraft can best be explained using the language of anthropology.

Bruce Lincoln, a functionalist who utilizes a hermeneutic of suspicion, argues that:

> [t]he same destabilizing and irreverent questions one might ask of any speech act ought to be posed of religious discourse. The first of these is "Who speaks here?", i.e., what person, group, or institution is respon-sible for a text, whatever its putative or apparent author. Beyond that, "To what audience? In what immediate and broader context? Through what system of mediations? With what interests?" And further, "Of what would the speaker(s) persuade the audience? What are the consequences if this project of persuasion should happen to succeed? Who wins what, and how much? Who, conversely, loses?"
>
> (Lincoln 1996, 226)

In focusing on these questions, he points out, we will "insist on discussing the temporal, contextual, situated, interested, human, and material dimensions of those discourses, practices, and institutions that characteristically repre-sent themselves as eternal, transcendent, spiritual, and divine" (226). That is, whereas insiders will often describe their beliefs and their actions in terms of magical powers, gods and goddesses, supernatural events, or eternal and transcendent values, if we use functionalism and a hermeneutic of suspicion we will explain their beliefs and actions in terms of historical contexts and material consequences. This form of functionalism translates (or "reduces") everything into social terms.

Using this approach does not mean that we are personally sceptics about all things religious—it just means that we will approach religious traditions *as if* we were sceptics *for the purpose of our study*. This means that when we come across insiders' claims about gods or goddesses, miracles, supernatu-ral phenomena, or eternal truths, we will approach those claims with suspi-cion, set them aside, and look for alternative descriptions or explanations of what's going on. This element of the hermeneutics of suspicion is called "methodological atheism."

Methodological atheism is often misunderstood: people sometimes assume that approaching religious traditions or practitioners with suspicion or scepticism is unfairly critical. However, this is not necessarily the case. Many scholars in the academic study of religion are devout practitioners, but nevertheless approach their *academic studies* with this method. As one scholar puts it, "no matter what religion or irreligion we personally pursue, and no matter what religious tradition we study, we are *as scholars* outsiders to the thing we are trying to grasp" (emphasis added; Jaffee 1999, 281). Adopting this approach for their academic studies is not necessarily at odds with their religious faith or practice. There are many scholars who are—for all practical purposes—atheists at work, but devout practitioners at home. In addition—and as we'll discuss below—there are very good reasons for approaching the academic study of religion from this sceptical perspective.

In summary, this approach to the study of religion will first consider some cultural element—a myth, set of symbols, ritual, etc. Second, we will approach the material with suspicion and methodological atheism—we will assume for the sake of our study that any supernatural claims are false and will question what might motivate a group of practitioners to make such claims if they are not true. Finally, we will look for a functionalist explanation for the data under consideration—if this myth might not be true, for instance, might it nevertheless serve some sort of social function for the community that tells it?

Further Defending this Approach

There are several reasons we can offer in support of functionalism and the hermeneutics of suspicion. The first reason for this approach is that, as we have already suggested, it turns out that almost everyone *already uses this method.* Even if one believes in the Christian god or the Muslim god, one probably does not believe in Ahura Mazda, or Asherah, or Chemosh. Everyone is an atheist *about someone else's gods.* Christians generally do not believe in Hindu gods; consequently, they tend to approach claims about what Hindu gods have done or said with a great deal of suspicion. Similarly, Jews and Muslims generally do not believe that Jesus was divine; consequently, they tend to approach Christian claims of Jesus' divinity with a great deal of suspicion. Everyone tends to be critical toward *other* religious traditions, but uncritical toward their own. Rather than be unevenly critical by excepting our own personal tradition from criticism while criticizing everyone else's, as scholars we should be *equally suspicious* across the board.

A second reason for this approach—and this is probably the most important one—is that if we adopt a functionalist approach and a hermeneutic of

Figure 2.1 *Secret Asian Man* comic strip (© 2009 Tak Toyoshima, reproduced with permission)

suspicion, we will notice a number of interesting things we might not otherwise see. Consider the comic strip in Figure 2.1. Let's try to answer the question, "What's going on here?" If we are *not* suspicious, and we take the characters at their word, what's going on—from an insider's perspective—is that God apparently does not want this boy to eat candy. However, if we approach the question using a hermeneutic of suspicion, we will notice things we might not otherwise attend to. Perhaps what is going on—if we assume that gods don't exist—is that the father is appealing to the authority of divine beings to persuade his son not to eat candy. In fact, we might go on to notice that this is practically a universal phenomenon: "the gods want you to do this" often carries more authority—when it is persuasive—than "I want you to do this." If we assume a suspicious attitude toward claims about gods, we will more easily notice that saying "God wants you to do this" might function to *add authority to one's claims.*

Max Gluckman, another expert on indigenous African communities, provides us with a real example rather than a fictional one. He writes about how trading practices among Barotse tribes are believed to develop supernatural properties; according to the insider's perspective,

> where a Barotse barters regularly with another they become "friends" and then perhaps "blood brothers"—quasi-kinsmen. Similarly, when a Barotse doctor treats a patient for a serious illness their relationship expands so that after the cure they are still "mystically" bound together by supra-sensible bonds, and, for example, if the patient does not pay him, the doctor's medicines will renew the illness.
>
> (Gluckman 1965, 78)

According to the Barotse, if an individual does not pay the doctor then the medicine given for the illness will magically make the illness return. However, from an outsider's perspective we can utilize a hermeneutic of suspicion and look for a functionalist explanation: if we assume that this claim is, in fact, *not true*, why might people in this community make such a claim? This one is easy to answer: if people believe this they will be more likely to pay their doctor's bills for fear of getting sicker. This is a myth that *serves the function of ensuring that doctors will be paid.*

Consider an example more relevant in Europe or North America: the Catholic church officially insists that when priests pray over the bread and the wine—which is central to the ritual act of communion or the Eucharist—the bread literally turns into Jesus' body and the wine literally turns into Jesus' blood. In addition, the church insists that *only* certified priests can do this—the magical saving power that is offered through the ritual will not work if administered by a priest who is not certified by the Catholic church. Maybe this insider's claim is true and maybe it is not, but as scholars we can approach this using methodological atheism and look for a functionalist explanation. If we assume it is not true, what might be going on here? The answer is not obvious, but we can speculate that this belief and the associated practice is one that *serves the function of reinforcing the authority of the Catholic Church itself.* Catholics are told by the Church that they cannot go to other churches; the practice of communion in the other churches is *not real*—and therefore lacks any real power—because it is not administered by a Catholic priest. This claim—where it is persuasive—functions to protect the authority of the Church and make sure that practitioners do not leave the Catholic Church and go to other churches.

A third reason in support of functionalism and a hermeneutic of suspicion is related to the previous one: even if our suspicion is unwarranted—that is, if it turns out that the supernatural claims under consideration *are true*—our functionalist explanation can still be true. To put it in other words, in many cases an insider's view and an outsider's functionalist explanation could both be true at the same time. I gave three examples above, and with each and every one of them, even if the supernatural explanations offered were true, our functionalist explanation of "what's going on" remains true as well:

- Even if it is true that God doesn't want this boy to eat candy, *it is still true* that the father's appeal to the gods *functions to lend a special authority* to the claim that wouldn't be there if the father said "I don't want you to eat the candy."
- Even if it is true that the Barotse doctor's medicines will make the patient sick if she does not pay, *it is still true* that this belief *functions to ensure that the doctor will be paid.*
- Even if it is true that communion only works when it is administered by a priest certified by the Catholic Church, *it is still true* that this belief *functions to reinforce the central authority of the Catholic Church.*

A related issue is the fact that whenever scholars deal with religious traditions, they are almost always faced with competing and contradictory claims. As we will see in a later chapter, Christians have utilized the figure of Jesus to support a wide range of contradictory social and political positions. In fact, for just about any modern political position one could dream up (pro-capitalism, pro-communism, pro-life, pro-choice, progressive sexual norms, conservative sexual norms) we could find a book where Jesus has been said to support that position. However, it is not possible that Jesus could support all of those positions at once: some or most of these depictions of Jesus' social or political views *have to be false*. Of course, this poses no problem if we are using a hermeneutic of suspicion: it is easy to see, using this approach, that putting one's own values in Jesus' mouth gives them a special authority that they would not otherwise have. Since Jesus could not personally have supported all the values attributed to him, statistically speaking the sceptical functionalist explanation of what is going on—"these people are projecting their own values onto Jesus in order to make their views more authoritative"—is likely to be the right explanation *most of the time*.

A fourth reason we should use a hermeneutic of suspicion is that sometimes religious claims are demonstrably false. Religious practitioners often make claims that we can fact-check, and we sometimes find out that they have gotten the facts wrong. Christians once insisted that their god created the Earth and placed it at the center of the universe, and some still insist that the earth is only about 6,000 years old. But these beliefs are demonstrably false—the Earth is not at the center of the universe and it is much older than 6,000 years. Some Christians claim to believe that the Bible is "literally true" in its entirety, but that is nonsense. Just ask them if they believe that it is "literally true" that Jesus is "the bread of life." Of course they don't think that—Jesus wasn't a baked good. Despite the popular claim that religion is always a matter of "faith"— and therefore beyond proof or disproof—religious practitioners often make claims that are demonstrably false, contradictory, or just plain nonsense, and these things both invite and deserve critical inquiry. All religious practitioners are human, and all humans make mistakes, make up stories, contradict themselves, and so on. When they do so, there is no reason to give them a free pass on their error just because the error was related to their "religion." As Lincoln rightly suggests, "Reverence is a religious, and not a scholarly virtue. When good manners and good conscience cannot be reconciled, the demands of the latter ought to prevail" (1996, 226).

Finally, we should utilize a hermeneutic of suspicion because every other academic discipline is suspicious of religious claims, and *we shouldn't give "religion" a special privilege we wouldn't give any other object of study.* Consider scientists: Galileo didn't turn away from a critical analysis of the solar system just because the Catholic church told him that the Earth was at the center of the universe. On the contrary, he was sceptical of this claim—and his scepticism led him to important investigations that rightly challenged what the church believed (of course, eventually the Catholic church came

29

around to his point of view). Consider medicine: people once believed that when we sneeze we are expelling demons from our bodies. Thankfully medical doctors didn't take this for granted and investigated the ways in which allergies or illnesses cause sneezing—if they hadn't challenged this we would not have allergy medicine. Consider historians: the history professors who work down the hall from me read stories all the time where historical events are attributed to the actions of gods, but that does not stop them from looking for other descriptions or explanations for these events. Academic disciplines are supposed to look for the truth, even when the truth challenges deeply held religious beliefs. Academics are not supposed to put up roadblocks that stop critical inquiry just because some religious group disagrees with their findings. Anthropologist Mary Douglas puts it perfectly: "It does not help our understanding of religion to protect it from profane scrutiny by drawing a deferential border around it. Religion should not be exempted at all" (1986, 24).

So we have five reasons we might want to use functionalism and a hermeneutic of suspicion:

1 Most people already use this method, except in an uneven way—they are uncritical toward their own tradition and critical toward others; by contrast, we should apply criticism evenly.
2 If we use this approach we are apt to notice things we might not otherwise notice, such as the fact that stories about gods often function to add authority to one's social agenda.
3 Even if an insider's view turns out to be true, an outsider's, functionalist explanation could also be true simultaneously.
4 Despite the popular but false idea that what we typically call religion is completely a matter of faith, we can sometimes prove that religious claims are false or contradictory.
5 There are no good reasons to give "religion" special privileges; "religion" should not be exempted from criticism, even if criticism sometimes conflicts with people's religious beliefs.

The fact that religious claims conflict with one another forces us, as scholars, to be suspicious. Contradictory views cannot all be true at once, and thus we have to be critical when investigating competing claims—just as a homicide detective must be suspicious when approaching suspects with competing claims. A hermeneutic of suspicion works the same way: if these claims about gods and goddesses cannot all be true, how might religious practitioners benefit by talking about gods and goddesses? By attending to these sorts of questions we will notice all sorts of things we wouldn't otherwise see. In sum, we are not using a hermeneutic of suspicion because no religious claims are true; we are employing this method because it is *useful*.

To summarize: the functionalism and hermeneutic of suspicion used in this book

- starts by considering what insiders say and do,
- remains suspicious or doubtful of all supernatural claims (methodological atheism),
- seeks to understand "what's going on" by reducing or translating religious claims or practices into social terms and social functions (reductionism and functionalism), while
- focusing on whose interests are served, in order to
- discover things of interest that we might not otherwise notice.

Before moving on it is worth noting that functionalism and a hermeneutic of suspicion can be turned against those who use it. I encourage readers to be sceptical of the claims I make in this book. What might I seek to accomplish? Do I challenge or reinforce the status quo? Whose interests are advanced or undermined by the claims made?

Studying Religion versus Being Religious

Many insiders resist outsiders' critical study of their own religious tradition. No one likes their views and actions to be picked apart, as if under autopsy. Some object to the academic study of religion altogether. A critic of the academic study of religion once suggested that studying religion will not help people become religious; the critic used an interesting metaphor, comparing the study of religion to the study of birds: "no amount of theory can help an ornithologist to fly" (see Smith 2004, 208). Another scholar responded by saying, "Precisely! An ornithologist is not a bird *but one who studies birds*" (Smith 2004, 208; emphasis added).

Similarly, the point of religious studies is not to be religious but to study religion. On this view, one need not be religious to study religion, any more than one needs to be a bird to study birds, to be a plant to study plants, to be a Nazi to study Nazism, or to be sexist to study sexism. The last analogy is particularly instructive: there are lots of feminist scholars of religion who study how religious traditions are sexist, and in doing so their goal is obviously not to be religious, but to criticize religions. As scholars we are outsiders for the purposes of our study, not insiders. As we go along, we will take it for granted that as scholars of religion our job is to study religions, understand how they work, and so on, *not* to advance religious agendas or convert people to a particular religious tradition.

However, by no means does it follow that this approach will be entirely "neutral" between competing views. We noted above that many religious claims are demonstrably false. For instance, modern astronomy flatly contradicts the medieval Catholic church's claim that the Earth is at the center of the universe. Our hermeneutic of suspicion will, in some cases, work against some religious claims or interests. I agree with Russell McCutcheon when he suggests that scholars should be "in the business of provoking unreflective participants in social systems into becoming reflective scholars of social systems" (McCutcheon 2001, 170). My goal is not to make readers more or less religious—my goal instead is to help them see how societies are constructed and maintained, especially when those societies contain oppression or domination. It would be disingenuous to deny that this latter goal is, in many cases, at odds with the interests of, for instance, elites in patriarchal religious groups. Those feminists who study patriarchal religions are obviously not in the business of serving the interests of the patriarchs they study.

In conclusion, religious piety is, in principle, separable from religious studies, and this book will be concerned with the latter rather than the former. Our agenda is organized around questions of how religion and culture are tied to power relations, not around promoting any particular cultural tradition. We will be outsiders, rather than insiders, for the purposes of our study.

3

How Society Works: Classification

"A rose by any other name"?

William Shakespeare once wrote, "a rose by any other name would smell as sweet." The idea, of course, is that a thing is what it is, independently of the label placed on the thing. On this view, the process of labeling or naming is a secondary process, and one that does not change the nature of the thing named.

First → Second
Thing → Name/Label

If we found what we commonly call a rose in our flower garden and renamed it a "feces flower," that would not give the flower a foul smell. Changing the name does not change the thing itself.

Shakespeare's idea fits with common sense, but—as we will see—it is completely wrong much of the time. The most obvious counterexample to Shakespeare's claim is with respect to things like "money." Something is money only on the condition that a community recognizes it as money. If we cease to recognize a thing as money, it ceases to be money. Francs, which used to be money in France, are no longer recognized as money—the French have moved on to use euros. As such, francs are no longer money. Money by any other name *will not* be the same thing.

The reason for this is that some things are what they are not because of their material properties but because of a set of human social relations. In these cases, the relation between the thing and the human practice makes it what it is. Human categories often work similarly. One can be a "friend" not because of one's material make-up, but because of one's relationship to other humans. I am a "husband" because I have a partner who I married; if she died I would cease to be a husband and become a "widower." There is nothing about my physical make-up that makes me a husband or a widower—it is the *social relationship* between me and someone else. We are always in social contexts that determine who we are in ways that are relational: I was not a "professor" until my college hired me and made me one. You are not a "student" unless you are a student *of* someone or something.

Mary Douglas once similarly argued that there is nothing about the intrinsic material qualities of something that makes it "dirt." What makes something "dirt" is not its material constitution, but where it stands in relationship to humans. The drop of "soup" on my spoon is soup; the drop of soup on the floor is "dirt." The crumbs of bread on my plate are "crumbs"; the crumbs on the floor are "dirt." The hair on my head is just "hair"; the hair on the floor is "dirt." A common phrase gets at this point in a different way: "One person's trash is another's treasure." What makes something trash or treasure is not its intrinsic qualities, but its relationship to humans, human communities, or human interests.

Despite Shakespeare's insistence, sometimes what a thing is depends on the label given. What a "thing" is may *follow* rather than precede the name given to it. A copper disc *is* money *only when* it is given the name "penny." In such cases, the label comes first, and what the thing is comes second. In these cases we have to reverse the model Shakespeare gave us above:

Second ← First
Thing ← Name/Label

Although a chapter on how language works might seem out of place in a book on religion and society, this subject matter is fundamental for two reasons. First, many important theorists—such as Émile Durkheim, Mary Douglas, Pierre Bourdieu, and J.Z. Smith—have argued that the way we classify or divide up the world is fundamental to understanding how religious and cultural traditions function to reinforce social order. Second, most of us inherit the sort of common-sense view of language and the world assumed by Shakespeare, but because of the sorts of reasons we will consider below, this view started to be rejected by philosophers in the eighteenth century and became widely rejected by all critical scholars in the twentieth century (whether in philosophy, religious studies, history, sociology, etc.). Getting past the common-sense view of language is the first step to sophisticated, critical scholarship, and all of the remaining chapters of this book assume the view of language presented in this chapter.

Words Create Worlds

The basic idea of social constructionism is that we, as humans, make the world what it is for us. The world is not just there for us to find and discover—rather, we make the world what it is through our use of language. Philosopher Hilary

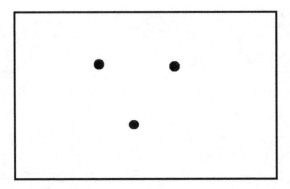

Figure 3.1 How many things are in the box?

Putnam provides a great example of how this works (see Putnam 2004, 38ff). How many things are in the box in Figure 3.1? An obvious response, of course, is *three*. However, as Putnam goes on to point out, this answer only makes sense if we are counting in a particular way. We could count other "things" in the box. How many *possible pairs* of circles are there? *Three.* How many *possible groups of three* circles are there? *One.* How many "things" are there if we add circles and groups of circles? *Seven.* How many square inches of white space are there? How many molecules of black ink are there? We could go on and on, of course, but the problem is clear: how many "things" there are in the box depends on how we are counting.

If a doctor looks at a human body using an MRI machine and an X-ray machine, she will see completely different things (Figures 3.2 and 3.3). What tools we use to "see" make up what we see. For social constructionists, the same thing is true of everything in the world—the *concepts* we use to "see" the world make up what we see. A political scientist could come into my class-room and, using a particular set of concepts, perhaps find 45 percent Republicans, 45 percent Democrats, and 10 percent unaffiliated. A religion scholar could come into my classroom and, using a different set of concepts, perhaps find 80 percent Christians, 10 percent Jewish, and 10 percent unaffiliated. A chemist could come into my classroom and may find certain percentages of oxygen, nitrogen, etc., in the air. What the world looks like to them—what they see—depends on what concepts they use to look at the world.

Some readers are no doubt unconvinced: "there are only three things in the box—a 'group' isn't a thing." But this clearly will not work. All concepts *group together* stuff in the world. The "head" in the picture on the next page is a *grouping* of a skull, a brain, blood vessels, facial muscles, nasal cavities, etc. The "brain" itself is a *grouping* of brain matter, nerves, blood vessels, etc. Even the "circles" in the box are *groupings* of ink molecules in a particular formation. The only things in the universe that might not be groupings would be subatomic particles, and no one has ever seen those—they are products of scientific hypotheses.

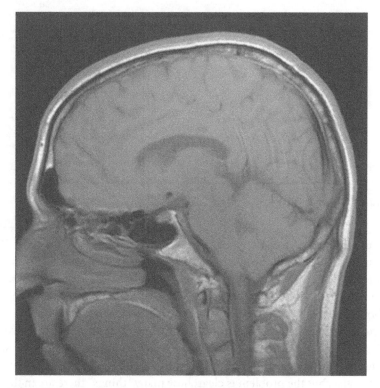

Figure 3.2 MRI scan (Creative Commons Copyright (cc) erat)

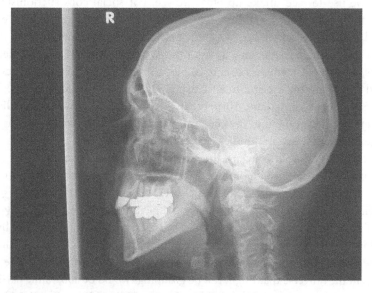

Figure 3.3 X-ray image (Creative Commons Copyright (cc) erix!)

Figure 3.4 Cookie dough (Creative Commons Copyright (cc) SarahInDisguise)

"Things" are not just there as things in the world—our concepts "group" stuff and *only then* is that stuff there for us as "things."

To my knowledge, the best metaphor is to think of the stuff of the world like a roll of cookie dough (see Figure 3.4). What cookies are contained therein? Of course that depends on what cookie cutters we select. For all practical purposes, we can consider concepts as cookie cutters: with them we bring into relief the stuff of the world for us. If we use different concepts, we get different results. Also, consider Andreas Cellarius' constellations, created for his 1660 volume *Harmonia Macrocosmica* (see Figure 3.5). The constellations we pull out from among the various stars in the sky depend on what interests us. The Greeks and Romans pulled out figures such as Orion, Cancer, and Cassiopeia, figures drawn from Greco-Roman mythology. Cellarius, a Christian who rejected Greek and Roman polytheism, pulled out Christian saints, Noah's ark, and the Ark of the Covenant, creating all new constellations. These are not the same constellations with different names—they are altogether different groupings based on different interests.

The categories we use are always linked to our human interests. Rodney Needham puts it well:

> in order to think about the world, and also to act upon it, we need to divide phenomena into classes. We have to group things together according to what we think are significant resemblances as, for example, when we discriminate a class of objects as edible mushrooms.

And we need to distinguish a contrasted class by significant difference, as when we circumscribe a further class of objects as poisonous
mushrooms.

(Needham 1979, 17)

Just as with the "wetlands" discussed in Chapter 1, what is important is that it
is *we* who divided mushrooms that way. Mushrooms do not appear to us in the
world in those two categories: *we* are the ones dividing them into categories,
and for *our* purposes. In addition, if our interests change our categories may
change as well. When I was young I was allergic to all nuts *except* peanuts and
almonds. Consequently, my family made a distinction between that category
of nuts ("the safe ones") and all the other ones ("the bad ones"). There was
nothing natural about that distinction—it resulted merely from my family's
concerns. Families without such allergies would have no use for this classification. However, when I grew up those allergies went away; I no longer make
this distinction as it's no longer useful. My changing body led to changing
classifications.

Figure 3.5 "Christian Constellation, First Hemisphere" (plate 22 from *Harmonia Macrocosmica*,
1660; scan reproduced with permission of the Minneapolis Institute of Arts)

There are seven key principles to social constructionism, and we already have the first two. First principle: *words are tools that humans use to delimit from the stuff of the world what is of interest to them*. Second principle: *the tools we use produce the world for us; if we used a different set of tools, we would have a different world*, just the same as if we used a different set of cookie cutters, we would have different cookies.

The third principle of social construction is that *the uses of words are variable*. For instance, much like the "wetlands" discussed in Chapter 1, the way people use the word leprosy is today different from the way it was used two millennia ago; back then, the word was used to pick out a number of kinds of skin diseases. Consequently, when we read about Jesus healing "lepers" in the New Testament, the author may not be talking about the same thing we mean when we think of lepers—perhaps those "lepers" just had what we call psoriasis.

The fourth principle is that *variable uses are all we have—there are no intrinsically right or wrong uses of words, just different uses*. If what is counted as a leper depends on the specific use of the word in a particular context, and if there are no right or wrong uses, it would be nonsensical to ask what a leper "really is." Asking what a leper "really is" would be tantamount to asking how the word leper is used outside of any particular social context, or asking what the word means when no one is using it. From a social constructionist perspective, rather than ask what a leper really is, what is important is figuring out exactly how we and others use or have used the word in specific contexts.

Consider how these four principles bear on our understanding of the use of the word "planet." In 2006, a team of astronomers at the International Astronomical Union voted to change the definition of the term "planet," such that Pluto no longer fitted the definition, and would no longer officially be considered a planet. The purpose behind this definitional change was the simplification of the taxonomy of astronomical objects: astronomers have found objects in the solar system bigger than Pluto—it was apparently easier for them to narrow the definition of a "planet," such that it excluded Pluto, rather than to call all of these newly found objects "planets" as well. Among the scientific communities that view this union as authoritative, Pluto is now considered a "dwarf planet," rather than a "planet."

Now, if we had a time machine, and one of these astronomers from 2006 went back in time to 2005, it is possible that she might get into an argument with a 2005 astronomer about Pluto's status. Our friend from 2006 could claim that Pluto is not a planet, and our astronomer from 2005 might well claim that that is absurd. There may be no disagreement about what Pluto looks like, what Pluto is made of, its mass, its orbit, its gravity, etc. One would hope that the differences between them would be resolved were they to find that each is using a different definition of "planet," and a different taxonomy of astronomical objects. Presumably, their argument would end with the sudden realization: "Oh, you're using the term 'planet' differently than I am." These two astronomers need not establish what a planet "really is." Indeed, what could that even mean? To understand each other, our astronomers only need to establish clearly how each is using the term.

We might, of course, disagree about which definitions are ultimately more useful, but this is a pragmatic matter: which definition is more useful for such and such context, given such and such purposes? Edward Schiappa puts it this way:

> Instead of posing questions in the time-honored manner of "What is X?" ([such as] "What is a planet?," "What is a terrorist?," "What are sexual relations?"), I suggest that we reformulate the matter as "How *ought* we use the word X?" given our particular reasons for defining X.
>
> (Schiappa 2003, xi)

The discussion that would follow the last question would be much more clear and navigable than the one that would follow the question about whether Pluto is "really" a planet.

People sometimes conclude from the fourth principle that social constructionists are saying that anything can mean anything and therefore nothing can be false, but that is not true at all. If we have agreed to use the old definition of "planet," then Pluto *is* a planet. If we have agreed to use the new definition of "planet," then Pluto *is not* a planet. Social constructionism does not suggest that "anything goes"; it suggests that when determining whether a claim is true we will have to carefully attend to the definitions our community is using, and the truth or falsity of the claim will only extend as far as our community (or other communities using the same concepts in the same way). For this reason, the fifth principle of social constructionism is that *although the uses of words change, this does not mean that anything is true—whether a claim is true depends on the agreed upon use of the words for a particular community.*

When we change the concepts we use, we bring into relief different things from the world—changing a concept is like using another cookie cutter to slice up dough. However, it would be silly to think that changing the concepts we use always changes the world as it is. Pluto is indifferent to the concepts we use to bring it into relief—we can call it a planet, a dwarf planet, an asteroid, or a hemorrhoid, and that will have no effect on its mass, gravity, orbit, atmosphere, etc. Those properties of Pluto do not change when we change its name. However, the same thing is not at all true of humans. Our properties *do* change if we categorize ourselves differently.

This is the sixth principle of social constructionism: *what we are as humans is a result or product of the concepts and practices in our societies.* I am all of the following:

- a doctor (of philosophy, not medicine),
- a guitar player,
- a cat owner,
- a car driver,
- an internet user,
- a reader,
- a voter,
- a citizen, and
- a professor.

All of those things that I am only make sense because I live in a particular type of society—I could not be any of these if I grew up as a caveman. From a social constructionist perspective, we, as humans, are a *product* of society. I cannot be a king in my society, although I could be a president. Similarly, a man in fifteenth-century Europe couldn't be a president, although he could be a king. Kings and presidents are what they are *only because* there is a social system set up to recognize those social roles. No society, no kings. No society, no professors. No society, no college students. We cannot emphasize this enough: we are what we are because society makes us that way—*humans are products of societies.*

This point deserves emphasis because we tend to forget it. Usually, we take it for granted that we just are what we are; we assume that our identities are natural features of the world. But the social constructionist insists: there's nothing natural about it—*our identities are social.* Calling Pluto a dwarf planet does not change Pluto, but calling someone a president instead of a king *would change* him. Because humans can respond to what they're called, there's a circular relationship between what we are called and what we are. We organize ourselves in response to what we call ourselves:

> The responsiveness to new labels suggests extraordinary readiness to fall into new slots and to let selfhood be redefined. This is not like the naming that . . . creates a particular version of the world by picking out certain sorts of things, for instance, naming stars, foregrounding some and letting others disappear from sight. *It is a much more dynamic process by which new names are uttered and forthwith new creatures corresponding to them emerge.*
>
> (Douglas 1986, 100; emphasis added)

Louis Althusser calls this "hailing": we are "hailed" by others and, in responding to hails, become what we called (Althusser 2008, 44ff). Ian Hacking calls it "making up people": "human beings . . . come into being hand in hand with our invention of the ways to name them" (Hacking 2002, 113). Whatever we call it, philosophers, anthropologists, sociologists, and social theorists across disciplines agree that what humans are is not established prior to the advent of the classifications and labels we use to sort humans into different categories.

This is even true of human groups organized around such seemingly natural traits as race, sex, hair color, etc. There was once a famous experiment where a 3rd grade teacher divided her class between brown-eyed and blue-eyed students:

> On the first day, the blue-eyed children were told they were smarter, nicer, neater, and better than those with brown eyes. Throughout the day, [Jane] Elliott [the teacher] praised them and allowed them privileges such as a taking a longer recess and being first in the lunch line. In contrast, the brown-eyed children had to wear collars around their necks and their behavior and performance were criticized and ridiculed by Elliott. On the second day, the roles were reversed and the blue-eyed children were made to feel inferior while the brown eyes were designated the dominant group.
>
> What happened over the course of the unique two-day exercise astonished both students and teacher. On both days, children who were designated as inferior took on the look and behavior of genuinely inferior students, performing poorly on tests and other work. In contrast, the "superior" students— students who had been sweet and tolerant before the exercise—became mean-spirited and seemed to like discriminating against the "inferior" group.
>
> (Frontline 2003)

Of course the teacher did not make her students have blue eyes or brown eyes, but the teacher did teach the students to organize themselves around these categories. There is nothing natural about privileging those particular categories: we could organize human groups around height, weight, hair color, hair length, skin color, clothing, and so on. There is no intrinsic reason for us to privilege one set of categories over another, except for particular purposes (perhaps we want to divide people by height when we are taking a group picture, so the tall ones do not cover up the short ones). Judith Lorber notes,

> in Western societies, we see two discrete sexes and two distinguishable genders because our society is built on two classes of people, women and men. Practically every form you fill out asks whether you are male or female, even though your psychology or biology may be irrelevant for what the form is used for.
>
> (Lorber 1994, 38)

It might make sense to emphasize the difference between male and female for the purposes of sexual reproduction—sexual difference matters at a sperm bank—but we segregate according to sex even when what we are doing has nothing to do with reproduction. I know of no one who has tried to conceive a child while in a public restroom, but for some reason our society separates bathrooms for men and women. Why divide restrooms by sex rather than by size, age, ability (that is, divide them for able-bodied or handicapped individuals), or group type (that is, divide for adult individuals or adults with children)? The last two ways of sorting would be much more practical, which is perhaps why we are seeing restrooms set aside for families—once a rare thing—more and more often.

As Pierre Bourdieu notes in his discussion of rite of passage rituals for males (such as ritual circumcisions that take place at the onset of puberty),

> [this ritual] says: this man is a man—implying that he is a real man, which is not always immediately obvious. It tends to make the smallest, weakest, in short, the most effeminate man, separated by a difference in nature and essence from the most masculine woman, the tallest, strongest woman, etc. To instate, in this case, is to consecrate, that is, to sanction and sanctify a particular state of things, an established order, in exactly the way that a constitution does in the legal and political sense of the term. An *investiture* (of a knight, Deputy, President of the Republic, etc.) consists of sanctioning and sanctifying a difference (pre-existent or not) by making it *known* and *recognized*; it consists of making it exist as a social difference, known and recognized as such by the agent invested and everyone else.
>
> (Bourdieu 1999, 119)

Social rituals (and social practices in general) invest the most insignificant natural differences with an incredible social significance. Blue eyes or brown eyes, white skin or dark skin, and so on: these are not socially significant in and of themselves; they become significant when they are socially constructed as such. Shared ways of thinking "assign disparate items to classes and load them with moral and political content" (Douglas 1986, 63). And social consequences almost always follow from assigning an individual to a class or category.

We tend to think of language as *mapping* the world around us. The world is just there, and we draw a map tracing its outlines. This was basically Shakespeare's view when he said "a rose by any other name would smell as sweet." However, for social constructionism, this is terribly false and misleading, especially when it comes to social facts. Our concepts did not originally map the social world—they were *blueprints* for the social world. In the United States, there is a president, a supreme court, a congress, and so on. However, the concepts "president," "judge," and so on did not originally map a pre-existing system, they *created* the system. No constitutional democracy was possible before humans came up with the concepts of "constitution" and "demos." Americans could not have their political system without their particular set of political concepts, which served as blueprints of the social world they live in.

Here we are circling back to where we began: the penny in my pocket is money only because I live in a society where people believe, as a part of a mutual agreement, that it is a legitimate form of currency. Because we believe this, it actually *is* a legitimate form of currency. Even though it is a social fact rather than a natural fact that euros rather than francs are legitimate currency at this time in France, there is nothing unreal or untrue about this. The common sense idea that something is true or false independently of human beliefs or human conventions does not work here; whether something is true or false necessarily results in part from a particular relationship between the stuff of the world and human beliefs and conventions. A hair on my head is a hair, but when it falls on the floor it becomes dirt. Of course nothing about the hair is materially changing, but its status *for us* changes. What makes it go from being just hair to being dirt is its *relationship to a human community*.

So we have the seventh principle of social constructionism: *social facts, although social, are nevertheless real facts—if only for the community that recognizes them as such.* The last part of the principle is an important qualification— my dollar bill *really is* legitimate currency, but only for those communities that recognize it as such. My dollar bill may cease to be legitimate currency if I leave America and travel to a country that will not accept US currency.

This last principle complicates things because people within communities almost never completely agree about their system of classification. Philosopher Chiara Bottici notes:

> In the case of social entities such as nations, classes, and states, we are not dealing simply with abstract notions, but with socially constructed beings: it is because there are narrating bodies [i.e., communities of individuals that tell stories about them] that behave *as if* such beings existed, that they do *actually* exist.
>
> (Bottici 2007, 241)

However, there are almost always *multiple* stories or narratives about nations and states, and it is not always possible to combine them into a common narrative or common identity. As a result, "the plurality of stories may turn into the recognition that *there is no common story* to be told" (Bottici 2007, 242; emphasis added).

Today, the United States is no longer a colony of Great Britain. However, was it independent on July 4th, 1776, the day the Declaration of Independence was signed? It *was* independent of Great Britain in the minds of the Americans who signed, but it certainly *was not* independent in the minds of King George III and most British citizens. The recognition of America's "independence" was at first recognized by some but not others, and only several years later did it come to be recognized by all. And often there is *never* a universal recognition of a social fact, in which case it seems that it never entirely becomes a "fact." Although, to my knowledge, everyone today recognizes America's independence from Great Britain, there are different stories to be told about places in the world like Palestine or Kashmir, over which people continue to fight. "[T]here is never the guarantee that all these stories can be reconciled into a single plot" (Bottici 2007, 245).

An Important Example: Sexual Difference

In modern Western culture, one can be one of only two sexes: male or female. We usually take this to be a straightforward, natural, biological fact, but things are not that simple. Considering how social constructionists think about the seemingly simple distinction between male and female will shed light on how valuable (and how radical) social constructionism really is.

   1 *Words are tools that humans use to delimit from the stuff of the world what is of interest to them*

Whether or not one is "male" or "female" is of considerable interest to most people in our society, particularly because—for better or for worse—we tend to treat people differently based on how we identify their sex. When we meet new people, their sex is often one of the first things we notice.

   2 *The tools we use produce the world for us; if we used a different set of tools, we would have a different world*

The male/female distinction has been the dominant one throughout human history, but it is not the only one. Some cultures have *three* sexes, rather than two (and a feminist biologist once suggested that it would be useful to recognize five sexes in our own culture—male, female, and three types of hermaphrodites in between; see Fausto-Sterling 1993). Our society would be very different if we divided people up into three sexes. Sexual preferences would multiply: there wouldn't be just heterosexual, homosexual, and bisexual—we would have to create a range of new categories, such as trisexual. Dating rituals and sexed social codes (such as the current practice of the male proposing to the female) would get a lot more complicated.

   3 *The uses of words are variable; the way in which people have used the words "male" and "female" has changed over time*

One great example is found in Anne Fausto-Sterling's book, *Sexing the Body*. There she points out that for the Olympics there is a sexual division for each event—men are not allowed to compete with women. But how do they decide whether someone is a man or a woman? In the past, they would line women up before a panel of judges and require them to pull down their pants—those individuals with penises could not compete as females. However, the people who run the Olympics changed their system several years ago, presumably because they thought forcing women to strip was too invasive. Later, they began to do DNA tests: those individuals with XY genes competed as men and those individuals with XX genes competed as women (see Fausto-Sterling 2000, 1–3).

So, what's the difference? *Not everyone with XX genes has "female" genitalia, and vice versa.* Studies estimate that 1½ to 2 percent of the human population has genitalia that do not match up to their DNA the way most people think they would (51–3). In a college class of 30 to 50 students, it is more likely than not that there is an "intersexed" person in the class. There are about 1,200 to 1,400 students at my college; that means there are probably 20 or 25 intersexed students on campus. Several years ago, there was a "woman" ("she" had "female" genitalia) who, surprisingly, discovered after her DNA test that "she" had "male" XY genes. As a result, "she" was disqualified from competing as a woman (1–3). The use of words is variable: on the old system, the Olympic Committee would have categorized this individual as a "woman," but on the present system the Olympic Committee categorized this individual as a "man." Whether one is identified as a male or female depends on what way we decide to sort out the differences between male and female. On one system of classification an individual might be female, but on another she might be male. And if we had three sexes instead of just two, one might be neither.

As Ian Hacking rightly notes, our uses of classifications and categories are constantly shifting:

> New slots [are] created in which to fit and enumerate people. Even national and provincial censuses amazingly show that the categories into which people fall change every ten years. Social change creates new categories of people, but the counting is no mere report of developments. It elaborately . . . creates new ways for people to be.
>
> (Hacking 2002, 100)

4 Variable uses of words are all we have—there are no intrinsically right or wrong uses of words, just different uses

There seems to be no reason to say that one way of defining sex is the right way.

5 *Although the uses of words change, this does not mean that everything is true—whether a claim is true depends on the agreed-upon use of the words for a particular community*

Just because the way sex is determined is variable does not mean that anything can be anything. If our operative definition of "male" is "has a penis," then an individual with a penis will be male *for this given definition*, even if he has "female" XX genes. However, if our operative definition of male is "has XY genes," then she will be female *for that definition*, a female who just happens to have a penis. What is true will depend on what classification system we have in place.

6 *What we are as humans is a result of the concepts and practices in our societies*

This is true when it comes to sex in at least three ways. First, if I were born in a society that had three sexes, I might not be male, so my male identity is, in part, a product of the concepts my society uses.

Second, identities carry rights and privileges in societies. It is pretty clear that whether one is identified as male or female has a great deal to do with the rights and duties assigned to one in our society. The woman/man who wanted to compete as a woman, but couldn't because she/he had "male" DNA, was stripped of some rights and duties and assigned an alternative set once her DNA was determined. These rights and privileges become a part of our identity. Who we *are*, socially speaking, is a product of the rights and responsibilities assigned to us by our communities.

Third, as Judith Lorber notes,

> there is ample evidence that once gender is assigned, boy and girl children are handled and reacted to quite differently.
>
> Take the phenomenon of boys' boisterousness or girls' physical awkwardness in Western societies. When little boys run around noisily, we say "Boys will be boys". . . . But are boys, universally, the world over, in every social group, a vociferous, active presence? Or just where they are encouraged to use their bodies freely, to cover space, take risks, and play outdoors at all kinds of games and sports? Conversely, what do we mean when we say, "She throws like a girl"? . . . In fact, she throws like a person who has already been taught to restrict her movements, to protect her body, to use it femininely.
>
> (Lorber 1994, 39–40)

Just as parents tend to encourage boys to behave in certain ways, so girls are discouraged (and vice versa). During our childhood, most of us heard our parents say—innumerable times—"boys don't do that" or "girls don't do that." Because of this, scholars have begun talking about sex and gender as analogous to muscle memory: we are habituated to behave in certain sexually different ways until they become natural to us, although there is nothing natural about these behaviors to begin with. As a result, who we are or who we become, as far as our sexual and gendered identities are concerned, is a product of the practices in our societies.

7 Social facts, although social, are nevertheless real facts—if only for the community that recognizes them as such

Things in the world are what they are because we identify them as such. Although this woman/man's genitalia didn't change when he began to be called a man by the Olympic Committee, it nevertheless remains a fact that on the Olympic Committee's criterion, she/he was a "man." That it was a social fact does not make it any less of a fact, although its truth *extends only as far* as those communities that share the committee's definition of male and female. For communities with a different criterion (such as the *old* Olympic Committee), she/he would, as a matter of fact, have been a "woman."

***

The social construction of something like a "college" is fairly easy to understand: without a community that recognized these roles, we couldn't have a president, a dean, professors, students, etc. By contrast, understanding the social construction of something like sex or race is much trickier. One's sex or race seems natural, rather than social—but this is only because we forget (or never noticed) that people have divided up the sexes and the races in different ways at different times. As a result, we misrecognize social categories by taking them as merely or simply natural categories. As Bourdieu rightly notes, the practice of sorting people into apparently natural categories "is an act of social magic that can create difference . . . by exploiting as it were pre-existing differences. . . . The distinctions that are the most efficacious socially are those which give the appearance of being based on objective differences" (Bourdieu 1999, 120). Consider the teacher mentioned above who divided her students into blue-eyed and brown-eyed groups: this is exactly what Bourdieu is talking about. There is something seemingly "natural" about the distinction—clearly there are some students with blue eyes and some with brown eyes. This "natural" difference lent a certain credibility to the social grouping of students, although the social effects of that particular grouping were far from warranted by nature. Social rituals (and social practices in general) invest the most insignificant natural differences with an incredible social significance. And, once constructed, social categories tend to take on a life of their own. When they do this, and when their constructed nature is made to appear as if it were natural—for example, religious traditions often suggest sex binaries were divinely ordained—this is called "naturalization," a concept we will discuss further in the next chapter.

Beer and Roses

In conclusion, let us briefly revisit Shakespeare's rose. When it came to Pluto, we noted that changing its name from "planet" to "dwarf planet" would not affect its orbit or its mass. Would the smell of a rose be equally resistant to a change of name? Would a rose, in fact, smell as sweet if we called it a "feces flower"? Interestingly, more than a little research has been done on how labels and expectations appear to alter our experiences of the world. In *Predictably Irrational: The Hidden Forces that Shape Our Decisions* (2010), Dan Ariely reports on studies his academic team performed on the taste of beer. In one experiment, they made two batches of beer: one batch was simply unaltered Budweiser, and the other was Budweiser with balsamic vinegar added to it—which they called "MIT Brew" since they performed the experiment on the Massachusetts Institute of Technology campus (see Ariely 2010, 201ff). Bar patrons were offered a free beer of their choice, but were required to sample both beers prior to choosing which they wanted. The results? Those who were *not told* what the "secret ingredient" was predominantly preferred the MIT Brew after sampling both; by contrast, those who *were told* before sampling what the secret ingredient was predominantly asked for the Budweiser afterward.

> [W]ithout foreknowledge about the vinegar, most of them chose the vinegary MIT Brew. But when they knew in advance that the MIT Brew had been laced with balsamic vinegar, their reaction was completely different. At the first taste of the adulterated suds, they wrinkled their noses and requested the standard beer. The moral, as you might expect, is that if you tell people up front that something might be distasteful, the odds are good that they will end up agreeing with you.
>
> (203)

In this case, it appears that changing the label altered the way the beer tasted to the participants in the experiment. While I know of no similar experiment on roses, it's quite possible that people would wrinkle their noses at "feces flowers" and develop similarly negative associations with its smell. Perhaps we tend to like the smell of roses because they're romanticized in our culture and associated with love and beauty. Perhaps "escargot" tastes better than "snails," and "caviar" tastes better than "fish eggs." Perhaps one person's trash is another person's treasure, and—in addition—one person's delicacy is another person's disgust. In any case, there are many reasons to call into question Shakespeare's common sense view of the relation between language and reality.

To summarize, we have argued—contrary to Shakespeare—that the labels we use to divide up and organize the stuff of the world have a constitutive role in creating the world we inhabit. In addition, unlike inanimate objects, humans *respond to* the concepts we use to organize ourselves into different groups; the identities we internalize literally make us who we are and alter our experiences of the world. Last, the uses of these concepts and identities are sometimes in conflict; when competing groups use different conceptual schemes, they may literally see, taste, smell, and inhabit different worlds.

4

How Society Works: Essentialism

Animism and Essentialism

According to some of the theories of "primitive savages" and "primitive religion" discussed briefly in Chapter 1, religion originated when ancient peoples attempted to understand and explain mysterious forces whose causes were beyond their "primitive" understanding. What causes thunder? It must be animated by a thunder god. What causes rain? It must be animated by a rain god. According to this theory of religion—called "animism" by early anthropologists—these "primitives" imagined and projected invisible agents behind natural phenomena when guessing as to their causes. According to E.B. Tylor, one of the first anthropologists to make this claim, these spirits they projected onto natural phenomena were of course completely illusory, but "savages" were nevertheless attempting to be rational. "Tylor wished to show that primitive religion was rational, that it arose from observations [of the natural world], however inadequate, and from logical deductions about them, however faulty; that it constituted a crude natural philosophy" (Evans-Pritchard 1965, 26). That is, they were like toddlers trying hard to explain natural phenomena—and thus they deserved some credit for their efforts—but they were still for the most part ignorant toddlers. For E.E. Evans-Pritchard—a later anthropologist—theories of animism presented natives as if they were "childish and in obvious need of fatherly administration . . . [as well as] superstitious . . . [and] incapable of either critical or sustained thought" (8). Evans-Pritchard rightly rejected Tylor's theory as an unfair caricature, especially insofar as Tylor had never "been near a primitive people" (6) and instead based his theory almost entirely on speculation.

While "animism" as a general theory of religion has largely fallen out of favor, there is nevertheless probably a bit of truth to it. Contemporary theorists and cognitive scientists have demonstrated that most mammals have some tendency toward animism—in the sense of a tendency to project agency where there is none: "cats see fluttering leaves as prey, horses see blowing bags as threats, and dogs hear sirens as howls" (Guthrie 1993, 39). When we hear noises in our houses at night, we wonder if there are prowlers, burglars, or ghosts—unless we have pets, in which case we tend to assume it's just the cat running around. We seem to automatically assume that there is an agent of some sort causing the noise, rather than dismissing it as the house settling. Presumably this tendency offers us an evolutionary advantage: animals that hear noises, perceive a predator behind them, and run away are more likely to survive longer than those who aren't predisposed to detect predators at all— even if they end up with a few false positives, such as when the wind is just rustling the bushes. "[I]f you don't startle at dangerous motions, you'll soon be somebody else's supper" (Dennett 2007, 109).

While few of us today are persuaded that there is a rain god behind rain or a thunder god behind thunder, I would argue in a way that we are all still animists—in the sense that we project causal agency where none exists—every time we assume that there is some "essence" to individuals in a social group, an essence that organizes and determines their behavior. "Essentialism," however, is perhaps a better word for this than "animism."

One of the most obvious examples of essentialism in recent human history is race essentialism. Prior to the nineteenth century—and for most of Western history—Christians assumed that all races had their origin in Adam and Eve. This view was called "monogeneticism," meaning that all races had a single origin or genesis. However, in the nineteenth century scientists attempted to discern distinct essences that could be used to separate the white race from other races. Often the essences were read off physical characteristics. In his history of scientific racism, *The Mismeasure of Man* (1981), Stephen Jay Gould quotes the work of a scientist named Louis Agassiz:

> It was in Philadelphia that I first found myself in prolonged contact with negroes. . . . I can scarcely express to you the painful impression that I received, especially since the feelings that they inspired in me is contrary to all our ideas about . . . the unique origin of our species. . . . I experienced pity at the sight of this degraded and degenerate race. . . . It is impossible for me to repress the feeling that *they are not of the same blood as us*. In seeing their black faces with their thick lips and grimacing teeth, the wool on their head, their bent knees, their elongated hands . . . I could not take my eyes off their face in order to tell them to stay far away.
> (Emphasis added; quoted in Gould 1981, 44–45).

Agassiz was forced to conclude that Adam and Eve were the parents of the white race, but that other races had separate origins; in addition, he went on to rank the races, placing whites at the top. The view that different races had separate origins came to be called "polygeneticism," and it was used to jus-tify differential treatment of whites—who were seen as superior—and other races—who were seen as inferior.

Scientific accounts of essential racial differences of course changed over time; as Gould notes in his historical survey, later scientists attempted to dis-cern the unique essences of races in the size and shape of the skull, then in the size and shape of the brain, and in the twentieth century shifted to trying to find essences in intelligence, IQ, or DNA. The hope in all of these inves-tigations was to discern the singular essence that determined the behavior of minority races, an essence that made them fundamentally different from whites. Much like the so-called animists who were thought to find an invisible rain god behind the rain clouds, if whites could find a unique essence of some sort inside black bodies, they could justify slavery, segregation, or discrimi-nation as naturally following from the essential differences between the races. Gould concludes that all of these attempts to discern racial essences had cru-cial weaknesses, that the attempts to find such essences were driven by social and political motivations, and that "science" is perhaps not as "objective" as we would like to think it is.

While publicly overt or explicit racism is far less popular in the twenty-first century than in the nineteenth, gender essentialism persists without showing any signs of abating. "Men are from Mars and women are from Venus," as the saying goes—a sentiment that is still fairly widespread. Much like scientific racism, scientific sexism has attempted to discern unique essences in men and women's bodies. As Anne Fausto-Sterling recounts in *Sexing the Body* (2000) and Rebecca M. Jordan-Young in *Brain Storm: The Flaws in the Science of Sex Differences* (2010), scientists over the last two centuries have attempted to read gendered essences off of brain size, external genitalia, internal organs such as the uterus and fallopian tubes or seminal vesicles and vas deferens, testes or ovaries, testosterone or estrogen, DNA, etc. Again, as with race, the hope was to find an essence that differently determines the behavior of men and women. If we could find such essences, we could justify differential treatment of men and women. Why shouldn't we permit women to vote or run for political office? Because their brains are inferior to men's. Why must women remain in the home to raise children? Because their hormones make them more nurtur-ing. Some contemporary conservative Christian propagandists quite explicitly use sex essentialism to justify differential treatment of men and women. James Dobson, for instance, writes that "nothing can be done to change the assign-ment of sex God made at the instant of conception. That determination is car-ried in each cell, and it will read 'male' or 'female' from the earliest moments of life to the point of death" (quoted in Bartkowski 2001, 45). On the basis of this difference, Dobson insists that women must be subordinate to men, and that a woman's place is in the home, raising children and cleaning the house (see Bartkowski 2001, especially chapters 4 and 5).

However, much like Gould, Fausto-Sterling and Jordan-Young find that the scientific attempts to discern fundamental essences to men and women suffer from crucial weaknesses. Both are scientists, and both insist that "genes matter, hormones matter, and brains matter" (Jordan-Young 2010, 20), but that the evidence for the existence of competing, dual essences is nevertheless "surprisingly disjointed, even contradictory" (3) and that the essentialist conclusions many would like to draw from the evidence—such as Dobson's view that all women have abilities that make them fundamentally better-suited than men at tending a home or raising children—are overreaching.

In addition to gender essentialism and race essentialism, we also often see religious essentialism: the idea that everyone in a particular religious group shares in some essence that determines their behavior from the inside out. Many people today think that there is some sort of violent essence to Islam that makes all Muslims act violently. These people—many of whom are Christian— will point to violent passages in the Qur'an that recommend taking up arms against idolaters. The presumption seems to be that because it is in the Qur'an, it must be part of the Muslim essence, and every Muslim must therefore want to kill idolaters. One obvious problem with this is, of course, that there are many more injunctions to kill idolaters in the Christian scriptures. There are commands to kill idolaters, commands to attack cities and kill everything that breathes, and Jesus himself is reported as saying "I came not to bring peace, but a sword." It turns out that Muslims, Jews, and Christians ignore a great deal of what is contained in their authoritative texts (a matter to which we'll return in Chapter 8). Despite this fact, we frequently see critics of religion making claims such as the following: "The DNA of early Judaism, Christianity and Islam code for a lot of violence" (Hagerty 2010). However, this presumption that these religions have DNA is just as essentialist as scientific racism and scientific sexism.

The Process of Essentializing

In Chapter 3 we saw that people collect various phenomena and place them together under categories, concepts, or labels, sometimes even when those phenomena have no common denominator or shared characteristics. Essentialism depends on that prior act of collection or classification, and works something like this: a label is attached to a group of phenomena—that is, we group together things we call "rain clouds," or "negroes," or "women"—and then we project an essence as lying somewhere behind the label, an essence that determines the behavior of all members of the group. On the basis of the essence, additional characteristics are attributed to whomever carries that label, and various social roles are often prescribed.

Consider a superficial example: the application of the label "blonde." If someone is blonde, perhaps we can project an essence on that person—there must be something intrinsically or essentially *dumb* about that person. From that we can attribute additional characteristics, and then assign a social role: because blonde people are not smart, they will make mistakes on the job, and as such we should avoid giving them any real responsibility at work. The first step is to assign a label, project an essence behind the label, and the other steps follow from there:

Projected
hidden   ← Label →   Additional   →   Social role
essence   characteristics

Dumbness ← Blonde →   Will make   →   Do not give
                      mistakes   responsibility

This is, of course, a very silly example—to my knowledge no one takes seriously the idea that blondes are intrinsically dumb and need to be treated as such (although some people seem to take seriously the idea that blondes are essentially more attractive, sexier, or that "blondes have more fun" as the saying goes). However, race and gender essentialism were and are very real. Even today the category of "woman" often involves the attribution of characteristics such as "weak," along with the behavioral recommendation that "women should be protected by their men"—despite the fact that there are a lot of women in the world who are stronger than a lot of men, and we do not recommend that weak men need to be protected by stronger men, or that strong women should protect weak, elderly men.

All of this is, of course, a more precise way of talking about what we normally refer to as stereotypes. When we stereotype or essentialize, we treat an individual not as an individual but rather as a member of a group. If we label someone as a part of a group, we often project the characteristics presumed to belong to the group on the individual in question, whether or not that particular individual has those general characteristics. The fact that the individual is a member of the group is all we need to know about them, and we usually do not let matters of fact get in the way of our stereotypes. It is for this reason that weak men might be expected to protect strong women. I'm certain my wife is stronger and more physically capable than my 85-year-old grandfather, but if we were in a sinking ship I'm sure my grandfather would recommend sending the "women and children" to the lifeboats first—as if the women on the boat were as weak as children and in need of his protection. The stereotypes we use may have nothing to do with the reality in front of us.

Those cultural traditions we refer to as "religious" are often centrally concerned with creating and assigning categories of persons and projecting

essences. For instance, in the Bhagavad Gita—an ancient Hindu text—the god
Krishna tells Arjuna the following:

> The actions of priests,
> warriors, commoners, and servants
> are apportioned by qualities
> born of their intrinsic being.
>
> Tranquility, control, penance,
> purity, patience and honesty,
> knowledge, judgment, and piety
> are intrinsic to the action of a priest.
>
> Heroism, fiery energy, resolve,
> skill, refusal to retreat in battle,
> charity, and majesty in conduct
> are intrinsic to the action of a warrior.
>
> Farming, herding cattle, and commerce
> are intrinsic to the action of a commoner;
> action that is essentially service
> is intrinsic to the servant.
>
> Each one achieves success
> by focusing on his own action;
> hear how one finds success
> by focusing on his own action.
>
> (Miller 1986, 141)

Here, Krishna is saying that those born in each of the four classes have an
essence (which he calls their "intrinsic being"), from which it follows that we
can attribute additional characteristics and a social role:

Warrior's			Heroic,		Social role
"intrinsic	←	Warrior	→	energetic,	→	of soldier
being"				etc.	

For anyone born into the warrior class we can project a warrior's essence.
Because of the warrior essence, we can attribute additional characteristics, and
ones that will make those in this class suitable for the social role of a soldier or
fighter. This projected essence is merely projected, of course—there have been
people born in the warrior class who do not, in fact, possess all the qualities
attributed to them (as a result, they were probably not particularly well-suited
to the social role and tasks assigned to them). No matter their actual abilities,
weak warriors would still be included in the warrior class and potentially more

capable farmers or servants would be excluded. In the end, this sort of attribution of an invisible essence works in the same way as the forms of racism and sexism discussed above.

As anthropologist Rodney Needham rightly suggests,

> An individual, in being associated with one of these divisions, participated in all the other members of that symbolic class; his character and his destiny are determined by it. The members of a division in this classification were ... thought of as constituting a unity.
>
> (Needham 1979, 11)

For Needham, one's destiny is determined by one's class *not* in the sense of having an actual, real essence that determines one's behavior, but rather in the sense that *the community determines one's destiny* on the basis of the identity they assign: rights and duties are assigned on the basis of one's category or class (Needham 1979, 21). Once this sort of animism or essentialism is engaged, there is little one can do to escape from it.

Perhaps there would be nothing wrong with using categories in this way if all things in a category really were identical.

> In the traditional definition of a class in western philosophy, its members share at least one common feature; it is by virtue of this point of resemblance that the individuals belong to the class. At its logical extreme this definition is taken to mean that the principle of substitution will apply: i.e., that whatever we know of one object in a class we know of other objects, to the extent that they are alike. For a great many practical purposes, this common-feature definition of a class is appropriate and useful. Once we classify a thing as a knife we may assume that it can be put to use in certain ways that a fork could not. What we know about one carburetor we know, by and large, about any other carburetor; they may not be identical, or interchangeable, but we can at least get a conceptual grasp on them and understand where they fit.
>
> (Needham 1979, 63)

All "sharp knives" are good for cutting simply because they are in the group of things that are "sharp." The assignment of a use on the basis of the category makes sense in this sort of case. The problem, of course, is that the same is not at all true of groups of humans. Not all women are weak, and not all weak people are women. Not all warriors are heroic, and not all heroic people are warriors.

> In other cases—probably in the majority—the ethnographic evidence provides no reason to think that the members of a symbolic class are

connected by features that are common to all. . . . It might be that the only common feature uniting the members of such an extensive symbolic class was that they belong together, to that class.

(Needham 1979, 63–4)

The members of a class may be so different that the only common trait might be that they are members of the same class. For instance, perhaps the only thing common to all "whites" is that they are called "whites," and perhaps the only thing common to all "women" is that they are collectively called "women."

The Science of Group Bias

There is a great deal of sociological and social psychological research demonstrating that our social labels or group identities determine our sympathies—that is, those to whom we are sympathetic and friendly—as well as our antipathies—those toward whom we experience opposition, dislike, animosity, or hostility. Group identities are almost magical in the power they have over us. Consider three people: a seventeenth-century Christian Pilgrim in Plymouth, Massachusetts, a twenty-first-century evangelical Christian college student in New York, and a twenty-first-century Muslim student at the same college. The twenty-first-century Christian will have very little in common with the Pilgrim: they live in different centuries, subscribe to different political views, work with different technology, experience completely different educational levels, have different tastes in music, have different career goals, etc. By contrast, the Christian student may have much in common with the Muslim student: they may wear similar clothing, speak the same language, take the same classes, share the same college major, attend the same College Republicans meetings, enjoy the same music, and work at the same store in the mall. And yet—despite all these similarities—the Christian student may see the Pilgrim as "one of us" and the Muslim student as "one of them." Group identities can unite people across time and space who have little or nothing in common and can separate people who have just about everything in common.

The hierarchical self- and other-classifications we've internalized can sharply accentuate our social perception. Consider skin color: judged in terms of wavelengths of light, the colors of skin available to us appear in a *continuous* range from light to dark. By contrast, we tend to use *discontinuous* categories: from white, to brown, to black, etc. (depending on our social context—not all contexts use the same racial categories). When classifying races, rather than classify according to a continuous scale—on which there could be thousands and thousands of varying shades—we use only a handful of categories.

These categories, in turn, shape our perception of the various shades. As Henri Tajfel demonstrates in *Human Groups and Social Categories: Studies in Social Psychology* (1981), subjects who show racial prejudice exaggerate the differences of shades. Those classed as "white" will be perceived as lighter than they are, and those perceived as "black" will be perceived as darker than they are: "when skin color, or height, or some facial traits of social 'value' are concerned, there will be a marked sharpening of differences in the degree of these characteristics perceived as belonging to individuals who are assigned to different categories" (Tajfel 1981, 70). In these cases, individual differences in the shade of skin color are discarded for the general category in which the individual is placed, although—as Tajfel notes—this happens more often with "ambiguous cases toward the middle of the range, such as those of relatively light-skinned negroes and dark-skinned whites" (82). Social psychologists have studied these effects in the way we categorize and report skin color, in the way we categorize and report ethnicity, intelligence, and economic class, and even in the way we categorize the length of lines drawn on pieces of paper. In each case, they have found that our systems of classification predispose us to impose sharp differences where no such differences exist.

Perceived differences are further sharpened when tied to matters that are of great social significance to us.

> If a man is prejudiced, he has an emotional investment in preserving the differentiations between his own group and the 'others.' . . . [T]he preservation of [inaccurate] judgments is self-rewarding, and this is particularly so when prejudiced judgments are made in a social context strongly supportive of hostile attitudes toward a particular group.
>
> (134)

Our judgments are often self-serving: we want to think well of ourselves, and constantly calling our own judgments into question would be painful.

This raises the puzzling question as to how we as humans can successfully function on an everyday basis if we systematically over- and under-estimate differences. For instance, individuals who over-estimate the distance of an oncoming car when crossing the road are more likely to get run over, and individuals who under-estimate jumping distances when rock-climbing are more likely to fall off a mountain. What is perhaps different when it comes to social groups is our social distance from those to whom we strongly oppose ourselves—when "they" belong to a competing group, live on the far side of town, or perhaps even across the globe, we're likely to be ignorant of what "they" are like. As such, few opportunities for a "reality check" arise (134). In addition, some research demonstrates that, as children, we form attitudes toward other groups prior to acquiring knowledge of them—that is, we develop attitudes before we discern facts (211). For example, one study demonstrated that a group of British children exposed to a number of WWII stereotypes about Germany at a young age liked Germans much less than their immediate peers, despite actually having less factual knowledge about them; it turns out that "knowledge is not an essential prerequisite for the development of emotional reactions" (220). Our prejudices may be largely based on our ignorances and, unfortunately, prejudice discourages us from correcting that ignorance: why would we want to learn more about groups toward which we feel antipathy? There are rarely social incentives to correct our stereotypes.

For Tajfel, stereotypes result in systematic, over-simplified caricatures of the individuals that make up other groups. All of the following occurs:

- we ignore complexity and think in terms of simple differences (139);
- we over-estimate the similarities of people within other groups, seeing "them" as an undifferentiated whole and ignoring their individual differences (243),
- we explain the action of individuals in terms of a presumed essence of their group as a whole (139);
- we tend to ignore evidence that contradicts our stereotype of other groups (152); and
- we depict group essences as "inherent and immutable," that is, as unchanging over time (139).

On the other hand, our own group identity biases our self-perceptions: we see our in-group as just as unified and coherent as we see the out-group, and ignore or minimize evidence to the contrary. The fact that "we" as a group are not as similar to each other as we think we are is difficult for us to see. Or, to put it another way, we may tend to essentialize our in-groups as much as we essentialize out-groups.

One of the effects of in-group bias is that we are more likely to notice when others make these cognitive errors, and less likely to notice them when we are the ones making the errors. "We" like to think of "them" as racist or sexist— we think "we" are rational and reasonable by contrast. However, these social effects appear to be universal: *we all suffer from these biases*. Much like the early theorists of "animism," we like to think that it is the others who are fools; it is not us but the "savages" who project invisible, animating spirits. However, these theorists *essentialized* those whom they called "savages"; that is, they projected an invisible essence onto the group that they presumed determined the behavior of all members—in which case, these early theorists were arguably doing practically the same thing that they accused the "primitives" of doing. There is perhaps nothing more "animist" than assuming that "they" are essentially "animist" and "we" are essentially not.

It is for this reason that it is perhaps not particularly useful to distinguish between "religious" communities and "non-religious" ones. In many contexts—such as in the writings of those who criticize religion—this distinction invites us to assume that groups labeled as "religious" are essentially less rational than others; on their view, "religious" people are perhaps essentially stupid, like "blondes." However, as we have seen, the sociological and social psychological research demonstrates that we are all in the same cognitive situation when it comes to biases that affect our self-perception and our perception of others (and—as we will see in Chapter 7—the forms of legitimation used by so-called "religious" groups function identically to the forms of legitimation used by groups that are not considered "religious"). Consequently, rather than seeking to discern—or project—essential differences that separate "whites" from "blacks," "women" from "men," "savages" from "moderns," or "religious" from "not religious," we will seek to avoid essentializing any of these groups, of whatever sort.

Against Essentialism

Part of the problem with essentialism is that no one has ever seen an essence. The racist scientists sought to read essences off of external characteristics like skull size or performance on IQ tests, but those characteristics were presumed to be visible markers of an invisible essence, not the essence itself. If you cut up and autopsied a man's body, you would not be able to put your finger on a "male" essence. Try as you might, you cannot see a woman's essence under a microscope. You might be able to see DNA under a microscope, but it is clear from our discussion above that scientific studies have not been able to demonstrate that essential distinctions between men and women can be pinned on our genetic codes. Similarly, consider something like a nation: can you see an essence in the nation as a whole? Even if you gathered all Americans together and took their picture, would "freedom" or "democracy" appear in the resulting photograph? No: these invisible essences *are projected by those attributing an essence to a group.*

However, even when we do find some similar characteristics—even if not an "essence"—shared by members of a group, there are at least two reasons to doubt that there is an invisible essence underlying the shared label. We have already noted the first: categories or labels often group together dissimilar things. My cat's fur is black and my car's seats are black, but I doubt they are both black as a result of an identical, shared cause or essence—the former is probably tied to DNA while the latter is likely the result of chemical dyes. We should not project essences behind shared labels (like "black") because the things that fall behind the labels may be similar in some respects but are likely dissimilar in others.

Second, the things that fall under a classification or category always change or evolve. As the famous saying goes, "you can never step in the same river twice." If one steps in the Mississippi river, steps out, and then steps back in, the river is—quite literally—now something different than it was the first time. Rivers are made out of water that is constantly moving, shifting, and changing. The same is true of everything in the world. It is obvious with things like "rivers" or "tornadoes," but less obvious with things like "Craig Martin." However, "Craig Martin" is constantly changing too. Not only does one's body constantly change—cells are being created and dying, digestion is taking place, oxygen is moving in and carbon dioxide moving out—but one's mind is constantly changing as well, especially as one gains new experiences, discards old ideas for new, and so on. To return to an example used above: the range of stuff that falls under the category "woman" shifts as people change their use of the word, but the body of any particular "woman" is also constantly changing. As soon as we try to essentialize a "woman," perhaps by attributing to her the "ability to carry and bear a child," she may go through menopause and, in fact, no longer be able to carry or bear children. (This is, of course, leaving aside that many of those persons classed under the category of "woman" are never capable of bearing children in the first place, or the fact that many "women" make a conscious choice to be child free.)

In addition, even apparently "solid" things like those that fall under the classification "tables" change: underlying the appearance of solidity are molecules and atoms constantly swirling, moving, and shifting. The wood that the table is made out of is slowly decaying. It might not decay in our lifetimes, but it will not be here in a million years. Every bit of "solid" matter is shifting and moving like a river, even if it is not noticeable to a human eye. To return to another previous example: the range of stuff that falls under the category of "planet" changes as the use of the word changes, but even a particular thing falling under a specific use of that term is itself changing. Whether or not we call Pluto a "planet," the material out of which Pluto is made is shifting and changing (the changing nature of "planets" is even more obvious with gas giants such as Jupiter, which are basically clouds of swirling hydrogen and helium). Projecting an unmoving, stable essence behind our categories results in making us forget the shifting, changing nature of the stuff grouped together by those categories. As we have noted, the assumption that those things that fall under our categories are immutable or unchanging—especially when we are talking about other groups—seems to be a feature of cognitive error bias.

Conclusion

We regularly project stable, unchanging essences where there are none to find, despite all these obvious problems with essentialism. Projecting a causal essence behind a group or a class is much like projecting a causal animating spirit behind rain: the rain god *causes* rain to pour, and the female essence of women *causes* women to behave the way they do. Despite all of our so-called "scientific progress," we moderns frequently commit the same cognitive errors that we attribute to so-called "primitive animists," insofar as our causal accounts of group behavior tend to outrun the available data. From the perspective of methodological atheism, we should instead be very sceptical of claims about invisible essences that secretly lie behind group phenomena, for when we peek behind group labels we usually find only diversity and change.

5

How Society Works: Structure

Socialization, Social Roles, and Social Order

Societies are largely constituted by systems of classification and related social roles and behavioral practices. All large societies are made up of categories that distinguish between who is included and who is excluded—with relative degrees of affinity and estrangement—and, in addition, categories that distinguish different social classes or social positions *within* the group. Sometimes these classes are implicit and informal; for instance, friendship circles tend not to have rigid insider/outsider boundaries. Sometimes these things are explicit and very formal; an associate professor of religious studies at a college has a strict set of privileges, duties, etc., unique to that position—as opposed to other positions such as "assistant professor," "dean," or "provost"—and written down in an official contract protected by law.

For the most part, we inherit rather than create these social systems. For instance, we are born into a world in which certain social expectations are placed on men and women. In America, most of us are taught that when a man wants to marry a woman he needs to buy a diamond ring and propose to her. There is nothing natural about this—diamond rings have not always existed, and there have been societies in which a woman (or her family) makes the proposal, sometimes even with a dowry. We as individuals did not create the diamond ring practice; rather, a long time ago others created it by altering existing engagement practices. Some businesses found they could make a lot of profit by encouraging and thereby perpetuating the practice; eventually it became a tradition that most Americans follow. By the time I was born, it was long since a tradition that was almost inviolable: I did not buy a diamond ring when I proposed to my partner, and both I and my fiancée got in trouble with our families; some families might even have prohibited the marriage.

These sorts of practices are created by human beings, but then are repeated over and over, so much so that they take on a life of their own and begin to appear to be necessary. Sociologist Peter Berger writes about such social practices as if they were "tools" created by human beings. When these systems are created, they attain the same sort of reality that a tool does:

> Once produced, the tool has a being of its own that cannot be readily changed by those who employ it. Indeed, the tool (say, an agricultural implement) may even enforce the logic of its being upon its users, sometimes in a way that may not be particularly agreeable to them. For instance, a plow, though obviously a human product, is an external object . . . in the sense that its users may fall over it and hurt themselves as a result, just as they may by falling over a rock or a stump or any other natural object. . . . The same objectivity, however, characterizes non-material elements of culture as well.
>
> (Berger 1967, 9)

Berger is suggesting that a society might invent a cultural product like a plow, which, once created, has a reality of its own that is to some extent outside the control of any particular individual humans. The same thing is true of nonmaterial things in culture, just like the engagement ring practice. We could not physically cut ourselves on that practice in the way that we could trip and fall over a plow—thereby scraping our knees—but because others have adopted the practice we could face significant social consequences were we to violate it. The first person to wear pants probably did so out of sheer preference or pragmatism; however, wearing pants has crystallized into an inviolable social practice. For most of us, if we went to work without pants we would lose our jobs. As social practices become deeply habituated, to a large extent—although never entirely—they extend beyond our control.

The same goes for many religious traditions. Some Jewish communities forbid tattoos and require men to wear yarmulkes. Amish women are required to wear dresses and bonnets. Where such social codes are strictly enforced, violation of the code can result in serious censure. According to Berger, "Man concocts institutions, which come to confront him as powerfully controlling and even menacing constellations" (1967, 9). It would be a mistake for us to assume that these sorts of social strictures apply only in exotic or alien communities, and that there are no equivalents in, for instance, mainstream US culture. On the contrary, I have known many people who have been censured by their family for wearing tattoos or facial piercings, and some who have been threatened with termination from their jobs for violating dress codes (it is worth noting that social standards on piercings and tattoos are beginning to change, with some workplaces relaxing their bans—no social standards are eternal).

Once these social practices are set in motion, become habitual, and are systematically socialized into future generations, they tend to reproduce themselves automatically. Sociologist Émile Durkheim points out, it is patently obvious that all education consists of a continual effort to impose upon the child ways of seeing, thinking and acting which he himself would not have arrived at spontaneously. From his earliest years we oblige him to eat, drink and sleep at regular hours, and to observe cleanliness, calm and obedience; later we force him to learn how to be mindful of others, to respect customs and conventions, and to work, etc. If this constraint in time ceases to be felt it is because it gradually gives rise to habits, to inner tendencies which render it superfluous; but they supplant the constraint only because they are derived from it.

(Durkheim 1982, 53–4)

Durkheim makes a counter-intuitive claim that is almost definitely true: as children we experience the control parents have over our lives as constraining, but we eventually become so habituated to these practices that they are no longer felt as constraints. Through habituation these practices can move from being forced on us to being actively desired by us. There is no doubt that many Muslim women enjoy wearing a hijab. The reverse is probably true as well: most Muslim men are probably perfectly happy being *denied* the freedom to wear a hijab.

Through socialization we internalize not only these sorts of practices, but also the social positions and social roles assigned to us. These positions and roles are fundamentally inter-related to the practices—one's role in the practice of engagement rituals will depend upon whether one has been assigned (and internalized) the identity of "male" or "female." According to Berger, "The roles of, for instance, husband, father or uncle are objectively defined and available as models for individual conduct" (1967, 14). Berger notes that an individual can "put on" these roles like he or she is putting on clothes. However, he goes on to suggest that these roles are typically internalized at a much deeper level. Along with the social roles assigned to us we receive a related identity that makes us what we are: "the individual is not only expected to perform [a role] as husband, father, or uncle, but to *be* a husband, a father, or an uncle" (Berger, 1967, 14). As noted in Chapter 3, we are not naturally "male" or "female": because the significance of genitalia, gonads, or DNA varies depending on the classification scheme in place, we are *made* male or female in part by the classifications and social conventions we've inherited. But, again, these identities are often so deeply internalized that most individuals do not feel that they are "playing" at being a male or a female; rather, most feel that they simply *are* a man or a woman. As Durkheim rightly insists, when we internalize these identities, they go from being "outside" us to being "inside":

collective force is not wholly external to us; it does not entirely move us from the outside. Indeed, since society can exist only in individual minds and through them, it must penetrate and become organized inside us; it becomes an integral part of our being.

(Durkheim 2001, 157)

In addition, as sociologist Anthony Giddens notes, what is particularly important about social identities are the *rights and responsibilities* assigned to them. For Giddens, a social position is

> a social identity that carries with it a certain range (however diffusely specified) of prerogatives and obligations that an actor who is accorded that identity ... may activate or carry out: these prerogatives and obligations constitute the role-prescriptions associated with that position.

(Giddens 1984, 84)

That is, what rights one can claim and what responsibilities one is assigned are related to the identity one's society ascribes. These rights and responsibilities do not strictly determine how a particular individual will behave, but they undeniably limit the range of socially acceptable behaviors open to her.

As we saw in Chapter 4, the assignment of an identity is often presumed to be based on an essence. We pretend to discover an essence and attach a label to it; the truth, of course, is that we attach a label to a group and then project an essence (and, as social constructionists note, our labels often group together dissimilar things that lack any sort of common characteristics). We usually attempt to justify the rights and responsibilities we assign on the basis of that essence. We project the essence of "dumbness" behind the label "blonde," and assign rights and responsibilities accordingly:

Dumbness ← Blonde → Will make mistakes → Do not give responsibility

Again, this is a silly example, but we see the same thing done throughout history with very real categories, such as "man" and "woman," or "white" and "black." It is an almost universal feature of those cultural traditions we call religions that they assign essences and categories to groups of people. For instance, ancient Hindus divided people into four classes: priests, warriors, farmers, and servants. Significant rights and responsibilities—as well as prohibitions— were assigned to these identities on the basis of a projected essence. Similarly, ancient Israelite texts divide Israel into twelve tribes and assign specific rights and responsibilities to some of them—for instance, the male Cohanim of the Levite tribe had the duty of serving as priests. The Catholic Church makes a fundamental division between men and women—only the former are permitted to be priests and only the latter are permitted to be nuns, and the rights and responsibilities assigned to these groups are substantially different in important ways.

Many of the identities and roles we internalize are not like our career identities. Most professors could, at some point in the future, decide they did not want to be professors anymore and quit their jobs—thereby altering their professional identity. But other identities, like race, sex, gender, and family identity, are assigned at birth and are unlikely to be changed. These identities will be almost impossible to shake, although they too are just social constructions. In premodern societies "white" was not a category; if one was born in the first century, one could not have been "white," no matter one's skin color. "Whiteness" was created during the period of European colonization, in part as a way for Europeans to collectively distinguish themselves from the people they were conquering and enslaving. In the US, the so-called "one drop rule" was invented and implemented in order to determine whether an individual was "black." If the individual had even "one drop" of blood from African descent—that is, any African ancestry whatsoever—she would be considered "black" rather than "white," even if her skin was literally white. As Mark Twain describes in his tragic satire, *Pudd'nhead Wilson*, more than a few white-skinned babies were born to black women who had been raped by white slave owners, resulting in "black" slaves whose skin was just as white as their owners'. One such character in the novel was named Roxy:

> To all intents and purposes Roxy was as white as anybody, but the one-sixteenth of her which was black outvoted the other fifteen parts and made her a negro. She was a slave, and salable as such. Her child was thirty-one parts white, and he, too, was a slave, and by a fiction of law and custom a negro.
>
> (Twain 1981, 9)

As Twain notes, it was the "fiction of law" and not nature that made people "white" or "black" when it came to social identities, social roles, and legal rights in the American South.

The "one drop rule" remained a part of American jurisprudence well into the twentieth century; after slavery was abolished it was used to prohibit "whites" from marrying "blacks" during the time of segregation. When the "one drop rule" was eventually given up, some white-skinned "blacks" could be re-classified as "white" (interestingly, during the time of Apartheid in South Africa, people who legally changed their racial classification were called "chameleons"). In addition, insofar as rules regarding race varied from country to country during the twentieth century, the same person could have been considered "black" in one country but "white" in another. However, since race, sex, and familial classifications are *usually* rigidly fixed and assumed to be completely natural, we tend not to notice their constructed nature and—as a result—fully internalize them without question. Through the socialization process an individual internalizes the roles assigned to him in this context and apprehends his own identity in terms of these roles. Thus, he not only plays the role of uncle, but he *is* an uncle. *Nor, if socialization has been fairly successful, does he wish to be anything else.*

(Berger 1967, 17; emphasis added)

Or, as Pierre Bourdieu puts it,

The work of inculcation through which the . . . imposition of the arbitrary limit [between one social identity and another] is achieved can seek to naturalize the decisive breaks that constitute an arbitrary cultural limit—those expressed in fundamental oppositions like masculine/feminine, etc.—in the form of a *sense of limits*, which inclines some people to maintain their rank and distance and others to know their place and be happy with what they are, to be what they have to be, thus depriving them of the very sense of deprivation.

(Bourdieu 1999, 123)

That is, if one is classified as "male" and has successfully internalized one's society's construction of "male" identity, one will *want to be* male, and one will *want* things associated with maleness. In contemporary North America, this means one will want blue rather than pink clothes, will want to wear pants rather than skirts, or will want to keep short rather than long fingernails. Of course, there is nothing natural about any of these things—pink was a popular color for boys in past centuries—but once one has internalized one's male identity and the coordinated male practices in my society, one will want these because they are what males are supposed to want. In addition, as Bourdieu notes, one will learn to be happy with the fact that one is prohibited from wearing skirts—one will be deprived of the sense that one is being deprived of the ability to wear skirts. As noted above, once a subject identified as both "Muslim" and "male" has internalized these identities, it is unlikely that he will have any desire to wear a hijab.

Social positions are often coordinated, and the social system only works in part because individuals who have internalized the system act in concert with one another—although it is clear that the system, in fact, never works entirely smoothly because people never fully internalize the dominant order of things. Members of each social position play their part in the whole, just as on the football field quarterbacks, running backs, linemen, etc. play their part in the whole, or just as in a symphony violinists, cellists, and bassists work in concert. Society only works "if the individuals who compose it are assembled and act in common" (Durkheim 2001, 313). American evangelical Christians, for instance, sometimes have a very strict coordination of separate but complimentary gendered parenting roles. They insist that because of the way their god created human beings, men have the ability to teach children certain

necessary skills every child needs to learn, but which women cannot teach—
and vice versa. Consequently, they sometimes vehemently oppose gay parenting on the grounds that two men (or two women) cannot teach their children
both sets of skills the children need to know. (Evangelicals also tend to oppose
single parenting for the same reason, but interestingly without the vehemence
they reserve for gays and lesbians.)

When we so deeply internalize a particular social system, we tend to take it
completely for granted. We rarely, if ever, question the ways in which we have
been classified. Social theorist Bruce Lincoln puts it this way:

> [u]nderstanding the system of ideology that operates in one's own
> society is made difficult by two factors: (i) one's consciousness is itself
> a product of that system, and (ii) the system's very success renders
> its operations invisible, since one is so consistently immersed in and
> bombarded by its products that one comes to mistake them (and the
> apparatus through which they are produced and disseminated) for
> nothing other than "nature."
>
> (Lincoln 1996, 226)

This tendency not to question the social order we have inherited and internalized is, of course, good for social stability:

> [i]t is much better (better, that is, in terms of social stability) if [an
> individual] looks upon [the identities assigned to her] as part and
> parcel of the "nature of things." If that can be achieved, the individual
> who strays seriously from the socially defined programs can be con-
> sidered not only a fool or a knave, but a madman.
>
> (Berger 1967, 24)

People who do not follow the expectations of the identity assigned to them are
sometimes seen as extremely disruptive of the social order, and they often are.
It is for this reason, for instance, that interracial families were seen as a threat
to social order during America's era of segregation, or that intersexuals (that is,
people who in some way do not fit into modern medical definitions of either
"male" or "female") are seen as a threat to a social order oriented around a
strictly binary sexual division of labor. Intersexuals are, of course, not seen as
equally threatening in communities—and there are many (see Nanda 2000)—
that are less strict or even flexible about sexual difference.

In general, however, roles are created, reinforced, and then strictly coordinated, and when they are, people are expected to march in unison to the beat
of the drum. If one person steps out of line, she may knock other people out of
line and create general disorder—as many of us have seen when one person in
a marching band trips and falls, creating a domino effect. Religious traditions
are often extremely strict when it comes to organizing and policing gender

roles so that they remain stable. It is not very often that we find an Amish woman building a house or an Amish man cooking dinner, nor do we see Catholic women serving as priests or Catholic men serving as nuns.

It is worth noting however—and we'll have more to say about this below— that not all people view social order as necessarily a good thing, and there are often competing visions of what counts as "order." One significant problem with social coordination is that the system is often set up to exploit some people for the benefit of others—such as in societies where there are "slave owners" and "slaves"—in which case stepping out of line might later be seen as justified in retrospect even when it throws society into disorder. Social order in the American South prior to the Civil War was considerably dis- rupted when slaves ran away from their owners, but in these sorts of cases some individuals—such as those who organized the Underground Railroad— saw social disorder as preferable to social order. Whether disruptions of the social order are seen as good or bad may in fact depend on the hindsight of future generations and who writes the history books.

Elements of Societies

In general, it is useful to think of social groups as having—at the very least— the following key elements:

- insider/outsider boundaries (with varying degrees of rigidity or fluidity),
- social hierarchies and social positions,
- assigned behaviors, including
    - social roles for particular positions,
    - moral codes,
    - behavioral codes,
    - etc.

First, for every community there are *boundaries* designating an inside and an outside. Everyone is a member of his or her own family, but is necessar- ily genealogically excluded from most other families. Some insider/outsider boundaries are mutually exclusive: in the United States one cannot, technically speaking, be a member of the Democratic Party and the Republican Party at the same time. Many religious communities see their religious identities as mutually exclusive; that is, most people believe that one cannot be, for instance, both a Christian and a Jew at the same time. This is not always the case; there are many people who consider themselves *both* Jewish *and* Christian. (And, in fact, many of those we call the first Christians—such as Jesus' disciples—were Jews who probably saw the Jesus movement as just another branch or sect within Judaism.) Most insider/outsider boundaries are obviously not mutually exclusive. One can be a member of a number of classes all at once: "female,"

"Catholic," "nun," "sister," "daughter," and so on—there is nothing mutually exclusive about these identities or group memberships.

As noted above, there are almost always privileges and duties associated with community membership. There will be a wide variety of social expectations, prohibitions, and privileges placed on one identified as "female," "Catholic," "nun," and so on—not the least of which is that one will be absolutely prohibited from administering certain Catholic rituals, such as the Eucharist, as that is reserved strictly for those who wear the identities "male" and "priest." In addition, there will often be material or bodily signifiers used to signal group membership, such as robes, hoods, collars, etc.

Every community has *social hierarchies*. Usually there are unique privileges and duties associated with each level of the social hierarchy. The Catholic Church has an obvious social hierarchy: there is a pope at the top, and that position is followed by a variety of bishops, priests, nuns, laypersons, etc. There is a very specific division of labor, where each level in the hierarchy is assigned a specific set of tasks. However, not all religious traditions have a formalized hierarchy. There is no Muslim or Jewish equivalent of the Catholic pope, for instance; the hierarchies in Judaism and Islam tend to be less centralized and more variable from community to community.

It should be noted that people are almost always a part of *multiple* communities or contexts at the same time. A college professor of religion could be a minister at a local church. If the college's president is a member of that church, the professor would stand above the president in the church's hierarchy but below the president in the college community. Similarly, some scholars have noted that in highly patriarchal religious communities the men may hold positions of privilege in the overall community, but as women are given charge over domestic tasks, they may have authority over men in their kitchens.

Finally, every community has certain behavioral demands or expectations for individuals in the community. College professors are obliged to dress in a manner appropriate for someone of their rank in the social hierarchy: professors need not wear suits (as the deans or vice presidents do), but at many colleges they are highly discouraged from wearing, for example, jeans and T-shirts like students. As noted above, if individuals have been successfully socialized—that is, if they have successfully internalized the social system—they will desire to comply with these behavior demands, rather than find them as restrictions. The same often goes for religious practitioners that are required to wear yarmulkes, bonnets, hijabs, and so on.

One important caveat: because societies are subdivided and because subjects wear multiple identities, some subjects are caught between competing social expectations. For instance, while some Muslim women might be socialized to desire to wear a hijab within their Muslim community, they may live in a larger society that objects to the practice. When subjects are situated on the boundaries of groups with competing expectations, they may have to adjust as they move from group to group. This is something that we all do to some extent; most of us speak differently when we are dining with friends compared to when we are dining with our parents. Navigating competing expectations is much more difficult, however, when one of our social circles finds offensive the behaviors that are central to another of our circles.

Naturalization, Domination, and Social Reproduction

Societies and social orders are not intrinsically stable. Subjects in a social structure have competing desires and interests, and what is good for some is bad for others. What prevents people from leaving or revolting? Social reproduction—that is, the reproduction of the social structure over time—is facilitated by what scholars call "naturalization."

Naturalization takes place when things that are social are perceived *as if* they are natural—their social nature is obscured, covered over, or made invisible. Sociologists Peter Berger and Thomas Luckmann write, "Social order is not part of the 'nature of things,' and it cannot be derived from the 'laws of nature.' Social order exists *only* as a product of human activity" (Berger and Luckmann 1967, 52). However, we often act *as if* social relations are natural, as if they were "facts of nature, results of cosmic laws, or manifestations of divine will" (89). As anthropologist Mary Douglas notes, obviously practical social conventions are usually not naturalized but rather are typically recognized as social or cultural—we drive on the right side of the road in North America because it is a useful or convenient social code, and the fact that it is merely a convention and that other nations do it differently is generally obvious. However, most social practices or social institutions are not like this:

> most established institutions, if challenged, are able to rest their claims to legitimacy on their fit with the nature of the universe. A convention is institutionalized when, in reply to the question, "Why do you do it like this?" . . . the final answer refers to the way the planets are fixed in the sky or the way that plants or humans or animals naturally behave.
> (Douglas 1986, 46–7)

When one simply assumes that one is, by nature, "white" or "black," the fact that racial categories are social constructions is forgotten. The socially constructed aspect of that identity has been covered over or covered up—that is, "mystified"—or presented as natural when it is not—that is, "naturalized."

One time I wore traditionally female make-up to work as a social experiment (specifically, I painted my nails pink and wore lipstick). One can imagine the responses I got: "that's just wrong!"; "but you're a guy!"; and so on. When people said these things to me they were mystifying or naturalizing certain gendered practices. There's nothing natural about our society's make-up practices—there is nothing about nail polish that makes it inherently better suited for women than for men. However, when people respond to a male wearing nail polish by saying "but you're a guy!", they are talking about that particular social norm *as if it were natural*, or as if it were built into the way the universe works. Naturalization is one of the most powerful tools for social control available. When one breaks a social code that has been naturalized, it seems as if one has broken one of the rules of the universe—it seems like defying gravity or messing with the space–time continuum.

In addition, when people say "but you're a guy!", it seems like they are making a *descriptive* statement: it is just a matter of fact that I am a "guy." However, much more than this is going on: there are obligations affiliated with the position of a "guy" that are being *prescribed*. If I wear fingernail polish and someone says "but you're a guy," they are implicitly saying, "*and guys shouldn't do that*." That is, the "matter of fact" turns out to contain a value judgment and an order to comply with a social norm. It is for this reason that Bourdieu says, "[e]very time we use a classificatory concept . . . we are making both a description *and a prescription*, which is not perceived as such because it is (more or less) universally accepted and goes without saying" (Bourdieu 1998, 66; emphasis added). When our prescriptions—what we think "should" be the case—are buried beneath our apparent descriptions—what we claim "is" the case—they are mystified, covered up, kept hidden, and therefore less likely to be overtly challenged. "Boys don't do that" or "girls don't do that" are among the most powerful means of social control, insofar as they disguise social norms or values as mere matters of fact.

Berger suggests that when human identities, practices, social structures, etc. are naturalized, they are given a "fictitious necessity." That is, it seems like they are necessary when, in fact, they are not. I could have been born in a society that has three sexes, instead of two—there is nothing necessary about a two-sex or two-gender system. However, when people say "but you're a guy!", they are naturalizing the two-sex system and making it seem *as if* it were necessary. We are constantly surrounded by fictitious necessities: it seems necessary that "guys" should buy engagement rings. Because we take these social practices as if they were natural and necessary (as natural and necessary as gravity, for instance), we tend to keep the practices in place. It is for this reason that Bourdieu insists that individuals "tend to reproduce this [social] order without either knowing they are doing so or wanting to do so" (Bourdieu 1998, 26). We may not *want* to keep a set of arbitrary social practices going, but because we assume they are necessary we maintain the practice without thinking about it. Indeed, for Bourdieu we all contribute to social order without intending to, simply by habitually repeating and reinforcing as natural the practices we've inherited without question.

It might seem as if all such naturalized social norms are merely oppressive or constraining on individuals—as if society was simply about the control of individuals. However, such a perspective seriously misunderstands the positive aspects of societies. According to Giddens, social structure "is not to be equated with constraint but is always *both constraining and enabling*" (Giddens 1984, 25; emphasis added). For example, the identity of a "professor" does, of course, *constrain* professors in some ways—there are many things that it is considered improper, unwise, or even illegal for professors to do—but that identity is also *enabling*. At the very least, it enables many professors to do what they love (i.e., to teach) and to earn an income at the same time. So while professors might grumble at times about their constraints—for instance, some professors chafe against the dress codes—we can nevertheless recognize that those constraints are simultaneously coordinated with a number of positive possibilities or opportunities that would not otherwise be possible. The system constrains me even as it makes my career and lifestyle possible.

Similarly, Catholic priests are required to take a vow of celibacy—this clearly restricts them in some way, but simultaneously frees up their life so they can accomplish more in their role within the church. For some Hindu traditions, complete devotion to the path to liberation requires "householders" to renounce their family life. Toward this end, Gandhi—in consultation with this wife—famously renounced sex at one point, since "procreation and the consequent care of children were inconsistent with public service" (Gandhi 1993, 206). He describes abstinence as difficult at first, but goes on to say it became a "matter of ever-increasing joy" (209). Thus it began as a constraint but gave way to something that was experienced as pleasurable in itself, in addition to the fact that the choice permitted him to devote more effort to his social and political agendas.

When we assume that constraints are merely negative we miss the positive role of social constraints in making us what we are. When we miss this, we might assume that the best way to social liberation would be to remove all restraints or limitations. If social constraints are merely oppressive, perhaps we could maximize freedom and liberty by eradicating them. However, the individuals arguably *least constrained* by human social norms are those feral children whose earliest childhood is experienced without human contact, such as the two Indian children—Kamala and Amala—who were famously raised by wolves as infants but later found and adopted by Christian missionaries in the early twentieth century.

As Douglas Keith Candland documents in *Feral Children and Clever Animals: Reflections on Human Nature* (1993), what many cases of feral children share is that the children can develop very different bodily or cognitive abilities than children raised by human parents. Kamala and Amala, for instance, could only eat food on the floor—sometimes eating with the family's domesticated dogs—were able to digest raw meat, were able to run quickly on all fours, but could not walk upright. Like other feral children, they would sometimes eat dead animal carcasses they came across. Some feral children show heightened ability to see at night. Most of them are unable to learn much, if any language, and even those who memorize or recognize a few words rarely appear to understand their significance or usefulness. Feral children are famously uninterested in human society or human clothing, typically ignore toys that appeal to other children, and many do little more than eat, sleep, run around, and stare at the walls of whatever room they are placed in. Kamala would typically urinate or defecate wherever she was at, and would only use a restroom when watched by her parents—"[i]f they were not in sight, she would urinate at will" (67). One famous boy—named "Victor" by a scientist who worked with the boy for many years at the beginning of the nineteenth century—was described by a contemporary as:

> a degraded human being, human only in shape; a dirty, scarred, inarticulate creature who trotted and grunted like the beasts of the fields, ate with apparent pleasure the most filthy refuse, was apparently incapable of attention to even elementary perceptions . . . and spent his time apathetically rocking himself backwards and forwards like the animals at the zoo. A "man-animal," whose only concern was to eat, sleep, and escape the unwelcome attentions of sightseers.
>
> (quoted in Candland 1993, 18)

This report no doubt reflects a problematic rhetorical bias, but even with the negative, pejorative terms removed it is unlikely that many of us would find this boy's situation enviable. Arguably, these feral children are about as free from human social constraints as possible, but would we describe them as "free" or "liberated"? On the contrary, I suspect most of us would interpret their lack of human socialization as resulting in them being greatly restricted, perhaps even enslaved to their biology, basic instincts, or animal desires. Complete liberation from social constraints would result in us being very constrained. It is crucial that we not ignore the positive role of social constraints in endowing us with needs, desires, enjoyments, and capabilities that most non-human animals never experience.

On the other hand, however, it is clear that although in many ways positive, social constraints and social structures are frequently set up in ways that exploitatively serve the interests of some individuals or groups more than others. For instance, even after the abolition of slavery in the United States, strict, legal racial segregation persisted for about a century (and there is good evidence that it still persists in other forms today). The practice of segregation was so taken for granted that it was a fictitious necessity. If a black person went into a "white" restaurant, people might have responded by saying "but you're black!", just as people responded to my nail polish by saying "but you're a guy!" Such a statement is not merely a description, but carries with it a set of social *prescriptions* as well, and ones that reinforced the oppression of racial minorities. "But you're black" meant "get out." The complete internalization and naturalization of social positions and social practices can be good for a stable social order, but it can also reproduce oppression or domination.

Crucially, dominated groups sometimes *willingly participate in their own domination*: there were women in nineteenth-century America who actively campaigned *against* their own right to vote (see the newspaper advertisement in Figure 5.1). They had so thoroughly internalized their subordinate social

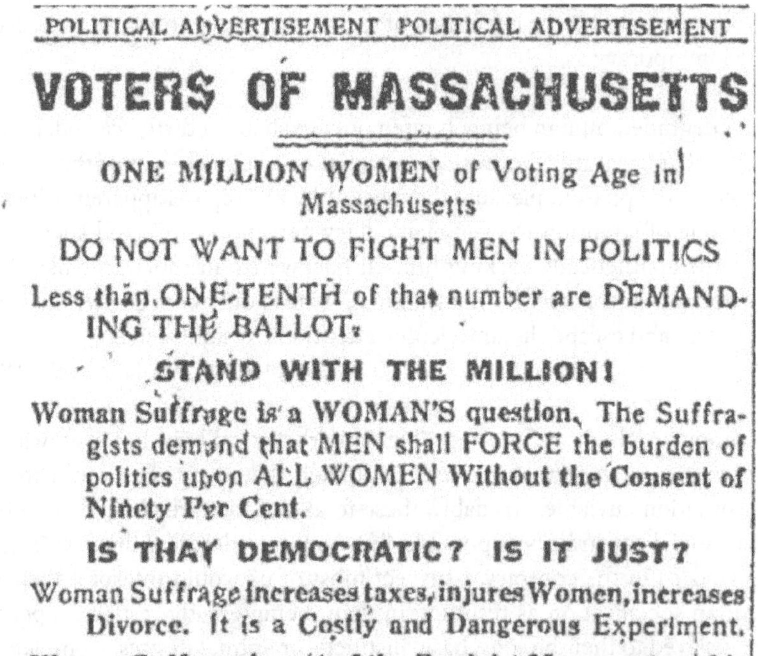

POLITICAL ADVERTISEMENT POLITICAL ADVERTISEMENT

VOTERS OF MASSACHUSETTS

ONE MILLION WOMEN of Voting Age in Massachusetts

DO NOT WANT TO FIGHT MEN IN POLITICS

Less than ONE-TENTH of that number are DEMANDING THE BALLOT.

STAND WITH THE MILLION!

Woman Suffrage is a WOMAN'S question. The Suffragists demand that MEN shall FORCE the burden of politics upon ALL WOMEN Without the Consent of Ninety Per Cent.

IS THAT DEMOCRATIC? IS IT JUST?

Woman Suffrage increases taxes, injures Women, increases Divorce. It is a Costly and Dangerous Experiment.

Woman Suffrage is part of the Feminist Movement, and is wanted by every Socialist, every I. W. W., and every Mormon.

DO NOT JOIN HANDS WITH THESE ENEMIES OF THE HOME AND OF CHRISTIAN CIVILIZATION.

The men of New Jersey voted to Protect their Women from Politics, to Maintain the Family as the Unit of the State.

WE APPEAL TO YOU TO FOLLOW THEIR EXAMPLE. VOTE "NO" ON WOMAN SUFFRAGE next Tuesday in

Justice to Your State and to

ONE MILLION WOMEN

WOMEN'S ANTI-SUFFRAGE ASSOCIATION OF MASSACHUSETTS,
685 Boylston Street, Boston
Mrs. John Balch, President.   Mrs Charles P Strong, Secretary.

Figure 5.1 Women against women's right to vote

role that they accepted it as natural, right, and necessary. In a sense, this was good for a stable social order—women were "kept in line," so to speak—but these women were unintentionally reproducing a social order in which they were assigned a subordinated or dominated status. We can call this "internalized domination."

In *Emerging from the Chrysalis* (1981), Lincoln draws from anthropological accounts of societies in cultures across the world—including the Navajo in North America, the Tiyyar in India, and the Tiv in Africa—and demonstrates how rituals that initiate girls into womanhood often function to assign an identity to women that enables them to experience the privileges associated with adulthood but simultaneously assigns them a status subordinate to adult men. The title refers to the central metaphor of the book: like a caterpillar that wraps itself in a cocoon or chrysalis and later emerges as a beautiful butterfly, so young girls enter rites of passage and later emerge as women. This is a perfect example of naturalization: Lincoln presents social processes (initiation rituals) as if they were natural processes (caterpillars turning into butterflies), thereby mystifying their social origin.

For Lincoln, much of what is significant is that the girls who participate in the ritual attain a divine cosmological significance for themselves. For the Tiyyar, these rituals are necessary for the young women to be eligible for marriage and bearing children; participation in the ritual "is sufficient to alter her life permanently, and as a result of it the girl becomes a woman, assumes new duties, is given a new honorific title . . . and is considered eligible for marriage" (Lincoln 1991b, 7). For the Navajo, the ritual involves singing songs about a respected goddess named "Changing Woman," who is associated with fertility; singing the songs is understood to confer a symbolic identification of the young woman with the goddess. Lincoln notes,

> Social and religious factors are not separate, but inextricably tied. Respect for Changing Woman and respect for women in general are one and the same, for each woman *is* Changing Woman, and becomes so through performance of the . . . rite
>
> (Lincoln 1991b, 33)

The Tiv ritual involves not only a symbolic transformation brought about through song, but bodily transformation brought about through ritual scarification. Young women who undertake the Tiv ritual have concentric circles drawn around their navel with a razor, as well as lines drawn from the navel to the throat. The scars are "said to promote fertility," and the ritual's effect

> is transformative: it is the means whereby a girl becomes a woman. . . . The scars themselves are simultaneously the means of her

79

transformation and the visible mark that this transformation has been completed, making each girl a woman and a sacred object for all to see.

(Lincoln 1991b, 48–49)

By means of such rituals, girls were transformed into women and thereby earned all the rights and privileges associated with the new status.

When the first edition of his book appeared, the text focused on the positive nature of these rituals:

> What rituals can do is to transform necessary activities from unremitting drudgery into something rich and satisfying, and filled with meaning. Ritual thus makes hunting or planting into sacred activities by defining them as repetitions of divine primordial gestures or acts necessary to preserve the cosmic order. In this way, ritual makes it possible for people to derive profound emotional and intellectual satisfaction from otherwise pedestrian affairs, because it points to something cosmic, transcendent, or sacred concealed within the tedium of mundane existence.
>
> (Lincoln 1991b, 107)

Because of such rituals, these young women are not just planting crops in the hot sun—they become goddesses making the earth fertile for the purpose of bringing life to the cosmos. The former might be boring, but the latter confers emotional satisfaction. For Lincoln, these rituals should be understood as fundamentally enabling meaning and happiness for those who undergo them.

However, ten years later Lincoln issued a second, revised edition of *Emerging from the Chrysalis*, in which he emphasized the more oppressive side of these rituals. He wrote a new afterword, pointing out that he had somewhat changed his mind since the book first appeared. He did not deny that rituals such as these can enable meaningful lives for women, but he noted that there is a darker side to the rituals that he had previously ignored. In part, these rituals naturalize and assign social roles these women might not otherwise have chosen:

> Successful initiation . . . thus produces Navajo women who will put their abundant labor at the disposal of others: husbands, children, friends, relations. It produces women who serve food, keep house, tend children, till the land, herd the animals, and what is more, who learn to derive satisfaction and pride from all this.
>
> (Lincoln 1991b, 113)

Lincoln suspects that this serves the interests of these women's husbands and children more than it serves the interests of the women themselves: such rituals lead "subjects to desire (or think they desire) for themselves precisely what society desires of them" (112). For Lincoln, it is as if these rituals make women into slaves for their societies, but slaves who have so deeply internalized their naturalized social role that they actively desire the "positions, statuses, and modes of being that society desires for and demands of them: persons it can use for its own purposes" (112). Thus in the second edition of his book, the rituals of the Navajo, Tiyyar, and the Tiv are depicted as more constraining than enabling, more exploitative than beautiful. Rather than seeing them only as beautiful rituals that enable a meaningful life, Lincoln has come to see them also as tools to help women internalize their own domination.

Lincoln focuses on the domination of women, but at the same time he's also describing what makes social reproduction in general possible. Why don't these women leave society? Why don't they revolt against men? First, insofar as the relations of domination are fully naturalized by the myths and rituals they live by, another way of life likely doesn't seem possible or even imaginable. Second, these women do benefit in some way by gaining a number of social privileges that come with their new status as an "adult." Dominated subjects often comply with the system that dominates them because they can benefit themselves—relatively speaking—by "playing by the rules." For instance, modern Western societies place a disproportionate number of demands on women's bodies compared to men's. As Tina Fey humorously puts it in *Bossypants*, women are expected to have "Caucasian blue eyes, full Spanish lips, a classic button nose, hairless Asian skin with a California tan, a Jamaican dance hall ass, long Swedish legs, small Japanese feet, the abs of a lesbian gym owner, the hips of a nine-year-old boy, the arms of Michelle Obama, and doll tits" (Fey 2011, 23).

> Now if you're not "hot," you are expected to work on it until you are. . . . If you don't have a good body, you'd better starve the body you have down to a neutral shape, then bolt on some breast implants, replace your teeth, dye your skin orange, inject your lips, sew on some hair, and call yourself Playmate of the Year.
>
> (24)

How are these disproportionate expectations maintained or reproduced over time? Why don't modern women revolt against the system that treats them unfairly in relation to men? Arguably, modern women internalize these relationships of domination because by playing by the rules—even unfair rules—they can benefit themselves in the short term, and, in any case, it's unlikely that they could successfully overturn the whole system of expectations.

Some scholars call this sort of "playing by the rules" the "patriarchal bargain." Yes, in this system women are in many ways subordinated or disadvantaged in relation to men, but by accepting and playing the patriarchal game they can improve their station relative to other women. Sociologist Lisa Wade describes it this way:

> A patriarchal bargain is a decision to accept gender rules that disadvantage women in exchange for whatever power one can wrest from the system. It is an individual strategy designed to manipulate the system to one's best advantage, but one that leaves the system itself intact.
>
> (Wade 2010)

Many celebrities—singers, models, actresses, socialites—generate a great deal of wealth by doing little other than making themselves attractive to men. Ironically, internalizing domination can be self-serving—and when a majority of dominated subjects accept domination, the relations of domination are perpetually reproduced.

We've focused on women as dominated subjects here, but insofar as all societies include multiple hierarchies and asymmetrical relations of power, *we all submit to domination* simply by being a part of a social structure—any social structure. Some of us resist in small ways, but most of us actively comply with the hopes of improving our station within the system by playing by its rules. It might serve our interests, however, to occasionally reflect on who benefits most from the existing relations of power, who benefits least, and how the relations of domination are reproduced. For instance, who benefits most from the social system in which young adults are strongly encouraged or required to take on a great deal of loan debt and submit to the demands of their professors

Figure 5.2 "Cruel Culture" (© 2011 Malcolm Evans, reproduced with permission)

for four years in pursuit of an undergraduate degree? Banks benefit by reaping interest on the loans, and professors benefit by getting a salary and through the prestige that comes with a university post. But are students reaping equal rewards by submitting to these relationships of domination? These are important questions, because revealing the often invisible relations of domination is perhaps the first step to denaturalizing them.

One final caveat: we must guard against rushing to judgment about whether subjects in particular social positions are dominated. Because the future is unpredictable and since one's interests are relative to one's desires and complicated social relations, it is rarely obvious whether a set of practices or social relations are dominating. Some subjects may experience as oppressive what others experience as liberating (see, for instance, Figure 5.2). Throughout the modern period, European imperialists oppressed indigenous peoples in various colonies across the globe, and they legitimated their oppression by claiming, for instance, that they were "liberating" the "primitive savages" and helping them become more "advanced." Judging whether a group is oppressed by imposing our own particular ideas about what is "liberating" may itself be a means of domination.

6

How Society Works: Habitus

Most of the key concepts discussed in this book—such as socialization, domination, legitimation, authority—are broadly used by scholars. Almost all social theorists, sociologists, and cultural anthropologists for the last two hundred years have utilized these concepts in one way or another; they are common fare. By contrast, the concept of *habitus* is much less broadly utilized. (Note: the plural of habitus is habitus; readers must determine whether the word is singular or plural from context.) This concept can be found here and there in western philosophy and social theory, and anthropologist Marcel Mauss reintroduced it in the early twentieth century, but it was importantly picked up and significantly revised by sociologist Pierre Bourdieu and his disciples in the second half of the twentieth century. He revised this concept in order to address what he saw as some of the weaknesses of traditional sociological accounts of how social order is reproduced over time. It should be clear that the root of habitus is "habit," and the concept does indeed concern human habits. One's habitus is the result of socialization, and is related to the fact that one develops habits linked to one's social class. For Bourdieu, these habits work—independently of an individual's conscious intentions—to reinforce or reproduce social hierarchies.

To understand the concept of habitus and to situate it in the context of Bourdieu's thought, it will be necessary to back up and explain what Bourdieu was using the concept in part to criticize. So before we get to a full explanation of what Bourdieu means by habitus, we will need to consider what he was fighting against: the concept of *meritocracy*.

Meritocracy

By definition, a meritocracy is a society in which people get what they earn, deserve, or *merit*. Usually a meritocracy is contrasted with a type of society in which rights and privileges are assigned by birth, rather than by merit. This oversimplifies things quite a bit, but in medieval Europe there were primarily three social classes: royalty (kings, queens, etc.), nobility (lords, ladies, etc.), and serfs. In this system each class had radically different rights and privileges, and the classes were in a relationship of exploitative domination: for the most part, the royalty and nobility lived off of the work of the serfs. In addition, one's class was assigned at birth, and social mobility—specifically *upward* mobility—was denied. If one was born a serf, one would remain a serf for life—there was no way to become royalty, no matter how hard one tried.

By contrast, or so the story goes, in a meritocracy one can be born poor, but if one works hard enough one can work one's way up to an elite level. Talk of meritocracy is usually linked to "rags-to-riches" stories: one can be born "dirt poor" but die a billionaire, if only one works hard enough. Alongside rags-to-riches stories is talk of personal responsibility: if one is not doing well in life, it is probably the result of one's own (lack of) effort, for which only oneself is personally responsible. In a meritocracy, one's social class (and the privileges that come with class) are determined not by birth but by one's merit and hard work. In principle, meritocracy allows for a great deal of upward (and downward) mobility.

Consider the American myth: although the United States began as a class-based society where race predetermined one's social status, those class assignments based on race have since been outlawed, and today African-Americans have risen to the highest classes in American society—the country has even had a black president. Although it began as a society in which class was based in part on race, today it has become a society in which class is based on merit. Anyone can become a millionaire or a president, if only one works hard enough.

So we have a distinction here between two types of society: one where class and privilege are assigned at birth, and one where class and privilege are based on merit and hard work. The problem, for a social theorist like Bourdieu, is that *meritocracy is a myth*. The American myth that alleges racism is over and anyone can get ahead if only she works hard enough is told without any attention whatsoever to the fact that wealth and income gaps between whites and blacks in America have actually *grown* rather than lessened in the last few decades, which is a serious problem for this myth (see Lui 2006)—and Bourdieu can offer a reasonable explanation of what this myth ignores.

We do not, in fact, live in a meritocracy, and never have. Although individuals are not locked into a class on the basis of birth, Bourdieu would argue that we are largely—although not entirely—locked into class on the basis of our habitus.

Habitus

Bourdieu defines habitus as follows:

> The conditionings associated with a particular class of conditions of existence produce *habitus*, systems of durable, transposable

dispositions, structured structures predisposed to function as structuring structures, that is, as principles which generate and organize
practices and representations that can be objectively adapted to their
outcomes without presupposing conscious aiming at ends or an
express mastery of the operations necessary in order to attain them.

(Bourdieu 1990, 53)

The discussion that follows is based in part on the same text the above defini-
tion is from, as well as his *Practical Reason* (1998) and *Language and Symbolic
Power* (1999), but most of all on his book *Distinction: A Social Critique of the
Judgment of Taste* (Bourdieu 1984).

Bourdieu's definition—and his writing style in general—is notoriously
opaque, but the basic elements are not too difficult to understand. First, when
Bourdieu mentions "structured structures" and "structuring structures," he is
suggesting something like the following (which we covered in a different way
in Chapters 3 and 4). Our society (a structure) is built out of (or structured
by) the classifications we use; our classifications constitute the blueprint we
use to build our world. In addition, subjects internalize, through the process
of socialization, those classifications—as well as the coordinated practices of
rights and responsibilities—we see in the world once it has been built. Sometimes Bourdieu calls the set of classifications our "matrix of perception," by
which he means the matrix of classifications through which we perceive the
world. In summary, we build a world with our classifications; we view the world
built through our matrix of perception; and in turn we ourselves are structured
by those classifications, and the rights and responsibilities connected to each.
We build the world, but then it builds us. It is important, however, to note that
according to Bourdieu the set of classifications one uses, or one's matrix of
perception, varies from class to class, even within the same society.

Second, what is important are *dispositions*. For Bourdieu, we all have dispositions socialized into us at a young age, and our habitus is that part of our
selves where our dispositions lie. Bourdieu says that these dispositions also are
produced by a particular class of conditions; what he means here is that we are
all socialized in different ways depending on the society or class in which we
were born. At the very least, then, we can clarify the definition of habitus in the
following way: *habitus is that part of oneself where one's matrix of perception lies
and where one's dispositions (or predispositions) sit, and all of this is the result of
a process of socialization that varies by one's society and class.*

We can draw examples from our predispositions about what is disgusting.
We tend to have "gut reactions" when we see someone eating something that
disgusts us. However, what is particularly significant about those gut reactions
is that they vary from place to place. Foods that are a "delicacy" elsewhere
might be "disgusting" here. In some societies, animals like fish and fowl are
presented at the dinner table with the head intact. Because of how socialization

takes place in those societies, that is "normal," although in the United States that may be considered "disgusting." Consider caviar: in the US, the response to caviar depends on one's social class. Those who grow up in blue-collar families are much more likely to respond to caviar with disgust ("Fish eggs? Sick!") than those who grow up in elite, wealthy families ("Caviar? Delicious!"). One's habitus in this case is linked not only to one's society in general, but also to one's particular class.

Dispositions is a rather broad term, and there are many things that Bourdieu would include under the term. Dispositions include:

- preferences or tastes,
- abilities to distinguish between subtle differences,
- ideas of success or life goals, and
- one's *practical sense.*

Preferences or tastes are fairly straightforward: what one prefers, likes, or dislikes depends in part on one's socialization into a particular class.

One key reason why tastes are linked to class is because people tend "to make a virtue out of necessity," as the saying goes. What the saying means is that people can see what they are forced to do as a result of their life circumstances as if it were both something they chose or desired and something virtuous. People who cannot afford "nice" cars might say to themselves: "all I want is a vehicle to get me from point A to point B—having an expensive car is a needless luxury." In doing so they are "making a virtue out of necessity" by taking what they cannot do and thinking of it both as something they don't want to do and as something that it would possibly be immoral to do.

We tend to think of taste as an extremely personal thing, but Bourdieu's research shows that it is not. The tastes of members of the working class do not vary greatly—rarely do they have expensive tastes. There is always some individual variation of course, but for the most part members of a class commonly share similar tastes. If tastes are the result of "making a virtue out of necessity," this is exactly what we would expect—at least when it comes to poorer classes—and that is precisely what Bourdieu's research finds. If someone is a "meat and potatoes" eater, that may not be "personal" so much as class-based—it might mean she grew up in a family that "preferred" those simple foods merely because pork chops and potatoes were what the family could afford.

The ability to distinguish between subtle differences is more complicated. The basic idea is that there are innumerable differences between things in the world, and what differences we are able to notice or draw attention to will depend on how we have been socialized. For instance, my father grew up in a blue-collar family, and classic American sports cars were important to him. Consequently, I was raised capable of telling the difference between 1967, 1968, and 1969 Chevrolet Camaros. These cars are different in lots of ways: colors, wheels, stripes, bumpers, etc. Which things are essential for determining which is a '67, which is a '68, and which is a '69? I know that Figure 6.1 depicts a '67 because it lacks turn signal lights on the side of the car; Figure 6.2 depicts a '68 because it *does* have the turn signal lights on the side; and Figure 6.3 depicts a '69 because it has a crease along the side

Figure 6.1 Chevrolet Camaro, 1967 (Creative Commons Copyright (cc) Nathan Bittinger)

Figure 6.2 Chevrolet Camaro, 1968 (Creative Commons Copyright (cc) Rex Gray)

Figure 6.3 Chevrolet Camaro, 1969 (Creative Commons Copyright (cc) RussBowling)

of the body, which starts just above the wheel well. This ability to differentiate the subtle differences between these three cars is part of my class habitus. Those socialized in classes different from my own may not be able to spot these differences.

Although my father grew up in a blue-collar family, he was sufficiently upwardly mobile that I grew up more or less in a middle-class home. As a middle-class white male who pursued a PhD, I developed a taste for "microbrews," which is relatively common for people with my social background and income level. I could do a blind taste test and tell the difference between a lager, an ale, a porter, and a stout. To someone who doesn't drink microbrews, however, the subtle differences (or not so subtle, actually, to my palate) will not be detectable. By contrast, I cannot tell the difference between a merlot, a shiraz, a cabernet sauvignon, and a zinfandel, but for those born into a wealthier class than I, the differences might be easier to spot. While a theorist like Bourdieu would not insist that the ability to distinguish subtle differences is always linked to class (many are linked to age difference, it seems), those abilities are *often* linked to class.

Ideas of success and life goals are also part of one's habitus. Growing up in an upwardly mobile family and having a father with a college education, I was taught (actually, it was merely assumed) that someday I would go to college—a college education was taken for granted as normal for someone in my social class. By contrast, I have extended family members who see going to college as undesirable or unlikely. I have cousins who do not have role models with a college education, and as such they are not sure they will be able to get into college, afford college, or complete college. Whereas it was merely taken for granted for my family, in their families it is on the outskirts of what is possible. For Bourdieu, life goals may also be the result of "making a virtue out of necessity": people who are unlikely to be able to afford to go to college may internalize their life possibilities and, as a result, view college as unnecessary and undesirable. Consequently, the reason why they may not go to college may have nothing to do with their intellectual ability, but everything to do with the internalization of expectations for members of their class.

> If French working-class youth did not appear to aspire to high levels of education attainment during the rapid educational expansion of the 1960s—and according to Bourdieu they did not—this was because they had internalized and resigned themselves to the limited opportunities that previously existed for their success in school.
>
> (Swartz 1997, 104)

Bourdieu sometimes talks about this using the phrase "the hysteresis effect," a term he appropriated from the hard sciences. It refers to an effect where elements in a system are slow to respond to changes in the system. For Bourdieu, we sometimes see the hysteresis effect in families with upward mobility: with new means they can afford to aspire to new life goals, but they may fall back on the life goals to which they were previously adjusted.

Practical sense is a broad term, and refers loosely to the practical ability to interact "appropriately" with others on an everyday basis. When we meet someone new and that person reaches out her hand and places it mid-air in front of us, we know exactly what to do: stretch out an arm, hold her hand in ours, and gently shake. There is nothing universal about a handshake, but because we are socialized from birth in our society to know how to respond to one, that action becomes a part of our practical sense. It is something that is second nature, and we do it without reflection and without thinking. In this way having a practical sense is like having a skill in sports. In the United States, children are taught how to play baseball, and this involves knowing how to hold a baseball bat, for instance. If one is right-handed, one must place the right hand above the left, at a certain spot near the base of the bat, and one is supposed to grip it tightly (but not too tightly). Over time, this ability becomes internalized as a part of one's practical sense. We do not have to consciously think about it if we pick up a bat—we grab it and naturally put our hands in the right spot.

The concept of practical sense can further be broken down to include at least the following:

- language, diction, or ways of speaking,
- ways of carrying one's body, or other bodily habits, and
- one's idea of what counts as "reasonable" or "common sense."

Language, diction, and ways of speaking would involve, for instance, things like accent, slang, or the ability to speak "proper" language in "proper" settings. One might hear the slang word "slut" from an individual with one habitus, but for an alternative habitus one might hear the phrase "flagrantly accessible woman." Those with a blue-collar habitus are more likely to speak loudly or boisterously, while those from wealthy classes are more likely to speak softly and with reserve. In the American South, people tend to use the word "y'all" (a contraction of "you all") for the plural form of "you," but in the American Midwest people tend to use "you guys" for the same thing. This last example is a regional distinction rather than a class-based one, but the point is the same: how one speaks will depend on how one's habitus is socialized.

Ways of carrying one's body and other bodily habits are also socialized into one's habitus. Just as blue-collar people will tend to speak more loudly than wealthy people, so wealthy people will tend to be more reserved with their body movements than blue-collar people. Wealthy people are unlikely to gesticulate wildly, or to high-five one another with energy, or have other sorts of fancy handshakes—all of which might be common for men in a blue-collar workplace. A similar notable point is that people from different regions and social classes will have different ideas about what counts as "personal space." Some people will tend to stand closer while talking and others will stand further apart—and these differences will often line up with class or regional differences.

The third part of one's practical sense includes one's idea of what counts as reasonable or common sense. In actuality, "common sense" is an oxymoron: what people take to be common sense varies from region to region and from class to class, in which case there is nothing "common" about it. What professors take to be common sense or reasonable will probably be rather different from what students take to be common sense (in fact, professors regularly lament their students' lack of common sense). One important consequence of this is that if two people are from different classes, they may both have common sense according to their own class, but may see the other person as lacking common sense—simply because their standards for what is commonsensical or reasonable are different from one another.

Because they are so clearly linked up with social classes, habitus—and their individual elements—can be markers of social boundaries. People like cheap beer not only because they are "making a virtue out of necessity"—they like it in part because it is a point of pride for members of their social group. Ordering a "Bud Light" at a bar can be like running up a flag—it sends a signal to other patrons that one is a member of a particular group—and groups are usually proud of their flags. "We're not spoiled rich pansies—we like *real* beer," or so they might say. I personally don't like cheap beer; I prefer micro-brews, and it is no surprise that this preference is extremely similar to other people in my social class. By drinking a Lagunitas India Pale Ale I can distinguish myself from "hoi polloi," who drink beers like Bud or Coors Light. If we looked for some objective qualities that make one beer objectively better or worse than another, we would be out of luck. A preference for *any* sort of beer is usually an acquired taste—an "objective" third party who had never had any beer would probably like neither choice. Why do we acquire tastes the way we do? Probably as a result of our class location. In summary, tastes both "make a virtue out of necessity" and serve as social boundary markers.

Of course, few people consciously reflect on their habitus, how it works, or how they got the tastes or ideas of common sense they have inherited. On the contrary, habitus is something that is thoroughly naturalized and taken for granted—it usually operates without people thinking about it. In part, this is what Bourdieu is talking about when he says that part of one's habitus is the ability to act "without presupposing conscious aiming at ends or an express mastery of the operations necessary in order to attain them." One's practical sense is internalized just as playing a sport is internalized: good baseball players do not consciously think "when the ball comes I need to move my two arms in unison so that the bat strikes the ball at an ideal location." In fact, if an athlete consciously thought about her actions this way, it would probably ruin her athleticism. She might not even be able to explain explicitly what she does to others. "You can't learn how to swim without jumping in the water," as the saying goes: it is something your body learns, not something your mind consciously comprehends.

So when Bourdieu says that one acts "without presupposing conscious aiming at ends or an express mastery of the operations necessary in order to attain them," he means that because of how habitus works people usually act in the world, often achieving their practical ends or goals, without actually thinking about what they are doing or what they want to accomplish.

Normalization, Discrimination, and Privilege

Much like so-called "common sense," what is taken to be "normal" (or a normal habitus) varies from community to community and from society to society—in which case these things are *not*, in fact, "common" or universally "normal." Even within the same society, different subgroups have variable ideas about what is "normal." What we have are societies where there are dominant and subordinate groups, and where each subgroup has its own idea of what is normal.

Usually the dominant group attempts to pass off its idea of what is normal as if it were universal. That is, they don't think, "this is what *we* think is normal"; they think, "this is simply what *is* normal." However, because they are the dominant group, they usually have some means of power at their disposal to enforce their idea of normalcy on others. Bourdieu suggests that there is an implicit *collusion* between members of a class—they work together or col-lude, although often without intentionally doing so. Most middle-aged, white, middle-class Americans think facial piercings and visible tattoos are abnor-mal, while some subgroups think that facial piercings and tattoos are banal or commonplace. However, because middle-aged, white, middle-class Americans are the dominant group in many cities in the country, those individuals with facial piercings or visible tattoos might be discriminated against, especially when it comes to finding work. People with my parents' habitus, for instance, would probably discriminate against job applicants with facial piercings when conducting job interviews, simply because they would find such things to be abnormal, "weird," or "unprofessional"—all the while ignoring the fact that such things are weird or unprofessional to *themselves and the dominant group*, not to everyone.

In every society there are various groups with different habitus, each dif-ferent from the others, but the dominant group lifts its own habitus up to the status of "normal," forgets that it is just one habitus alongside others, and unconsciously colludes to put in place regimes of privilege and practices of dis-crimination. Those in the dominant group, because they are dominant, usually have the power to exclude people with an alternate habitus from their social networks, circles of friends, and places of work. Very serious consequences can result from having a habitus different from the dominant one. Again, what is "normal" is not universally normal, but only what the dominant group takes to be normal—and which they can impose on other groups. This does not, of course, mean that in every society there is one clear dominant group and a number of obviously subordinated groups. Inter-relations in society are much more complex than that. Middle-aged, white, middle-class Americans are more or less clearly dominant in the Midwest, but much less so in New York City or Los Angeles. Facial piercings and tattoos probably do not stand out nearly as much in those cities as in conservative cities such as Indianapolis. In addition, even in cities like Indianapolis, there are probably pockets of the city where there are concentrations of people with a habitus different from the dominant one, and they may be able to impose as "normal" their own habitus *in those pockets* of the city. A Hasidic Jew would stand out in Indianapolis, but not in New York City, and there are pockets of New York City where Hasidism is even dominant.

The privilege and discrimination that result from having a habitus different from the dominant one can clearly be seen in Woody Allen's film *Small Time Crooks*, which, although fictional, presents a fairly realistic portrait of what happens when different habitus intersect. In the film, Woody Allen's charac-ter, Ray, launches a bank robbery scheme with some of his peers. They rent a shop next door to a bank and set about digging a tunnel from the basement of the shop into the basement vault of the bank. Ray's wife, Frenchy—played by Tracey Ullman—opens a cookie store in the shop in order to cover up the comings and goings of the characters drilling in the basement. Their attempt to dig into the vault turns out to be a dramatic failure, but Frenchy's cookie store becomes a hit. The success of the cookie store is so great that the group starts a number of franchises, and the failed thieves become millionaires practically overnight.

The most humorous parts of the film take place when this group of blue-collar thieves starts mixing and mingling with their new peers: the upper crust of New York City. They have radically different habitus, and stick out like a sore thumb among the wealthy class they are now a part of. Frenchy wants to acclimate to the new group, but feels so out of place that she hires a wealthy man named David—played by Hugh Grant—to give her lessons on how to behave "properly" around her wealthy new friends.

There is a scene in which Ray and Frenchy are getting ready for, and then throw, a party for their new peers, in which the differences in habitus are particularly clear. The party is being hosted in their new, upscale New York apartment, furnished with the best things their new money could buy. Of course, what counts as "best" to Ray and Frenchy, with their blue-collar habitus, is rather different than what counts as "best" to the people coming to the party.

Frenchy and Ray's idea of good food can be contrasted with the wealthy people at the party. To begin with, Frenchy wants to have what she perceives to be fancy foods. She has a strong desire to conform or acclimate to the habitus of her new peers, but because she doesn't yet have a wealthy habitus, she doesn't understand wealthy tastes quite correctly. She insists that the truffle shavings be thick (rather than fine, as the chef assures her they are supposed to be); she calls the escargots "snails;" and she pronounces the word crudités as crude-ites (rather than crue-de-tay). In addition, she insists that the table have "finger bowls" for finger washing at the table, despite the fact that her new chef strongly insists otherwise. By contrast, Ray—who doesn't care to conform to his new peers' habitus—thinks the menu for their party is disgusting. He makes a plea for cheeseburgers or spaghetti and meatballs, and refuses to try the escargot: "a snail leaves a little trail of scum in the yard when it walks" ("Not in France, they don't," his wife replies). Her husband accuses her: "You're so hoity-toity all of a sudden." At the party one of the guests asks for some Evian or Perrier brand water; Ray says they have anything she wants, but goes on to say that he prefers tap water himself, "because the fluoride keeps your teeth from rotting."

The tastes in clothing and décor are also radically different. The black suit Ray wears to the party has some sort of gold and black band around the collar, and Frenchy wears what the guests take to be a gaudy and absurdly shiny silver dress.

The difference in practical sense stands out in the bodily and verbal interaction between Ray and his guests. Although the new butler is at the door to greet guests, when the doorbell rings Ray runs up, practically elbows the butler aside, and greets the guests himself. Rather than greeting guests formally, as they expect, Ray says "how ya doin'?" and calls one woman "honey" and another "toots." At one point Frenchy addresses the other women at the party by informally calling them "girls." Perhaps the funniest moment of the party scene is when Ray starts telling jokes to the guests. "So guy says to 'im, ya know, what do ya do for a living? He says, 'I'm a mom-back.' What's a mom-back? He says, 'Ya know, I stand behind the truck—I say [waiving both arms back] mom-back, mom-back'" (that is, "come on back"—his job is to wave trucks onto loading docks). The woman he's talking to doesn't laugh, and Ray tries to explain it to her again, but she still doesn't laugh. The other guests in the circle awkwardly smile at him, and Ray says "I think it was too fast for her." When the woman he's talking to doesn't get his second joke, he gives her a light backhanded slap to the shoulder.

What do the wealthy people at the party think of Frenchy and Ray's behavior? When they are out of the room, the guests converse: "I can't believe this room. This takes bad taste to new heights." "This is excruciating." "Can you believe the two of them? I can't keep a straight face." "And what she's done with this apartment: the sheer flawless vulgarity of it all." "She's the definition of bad taste." There is no conspiracy, but this is obviously collusion.

We have here a clash of habitus. The blue-collar habitus of Frenchy and Ray could hardly be any more different from their new wealthy peers. This is the hysteresis effect in action: their habitus reflects previous socio-economic conditions, and it is extremely slow to adapt to new socio-economic conditions. We see a difference in preferences and tastes, the ability to distinguish between subtle differences, ideas related to life goals, language and diction, ways of carrying one's body (at no point do the guests at the party touch anyone other than to formally shake hands, while Ray is touching people all the time), and, ultimately, ideas of reasonableness or common sense. Because these two groups share a different habitus, the guests at the party seem to think Frenchy and Ray lack all common sense (which manifests itself to them as bad taste). Ray, by contrast, thinks *they* lack common sense (who wants to eat slimy snails?). The truth, of course, is that they have different senses, each taking their own to be "common."

Habitus and the Maintenance of Class in a "Meritocracy"

The problem, of course, is that when it comes to wealthy circles in New York City, one habitus is dominant over others. Ray and Frenchy will never be welcomed into this circle—they will be discriminated against by these "elites," and will never receive the privileges that "insiders" receive. Of course, the elites will be unlikely to see this as discrimination—they will see their "discrimination" as the careful use of common sense. Bourdieu claims:

Habitus are generative principles of distinct and distinctive practices—
what the worker eats, and especially the way he eats it, the sport he
practices and the way he practices it, his political opinions and the
way he expresses them are systematically different from the indus-
trial owner's corresponding activities. But habitus are also classificatory schemes, principles of classification, principles of vision and
division, different tastes. They make distinctions between what is
good and what is bad, between what is right and what is wrong,
between what is distinguished and what is vulgar, and so forth, but
the divisions [from one habitus to the next] are not identical. Thus,
for instance, the same behavior or even the same good can appear
distinguished to one person, pretentious to someone else, and cheap
or showy to yet another.

(Bourdieu 1998, 8)

The members of the wealthy class, or the dominant class in this case, see Ray
and Frenchy through the matrix of perception of their own habitus and, as
such, see them not only as different but as bad or wrong. Their exclusion of
such differences is therefore not seen (by them) as arbitrary, but as good and
right. Discrimination therefore functions under the mask of *rightness*.

For a social theorist like Bourdieu, one's class in a so-called meritocracy has
more to do with one's habitus than one's merit. Or, to put it slightly differently,
what counts as "meritorious" is often one's habitus.

Each class acquires a habitus that is well suited to a particular class position: blue-collar families train children who "fit" to blue-collar jobs and
white-collar families will train children who will "fit" to white-collar jobs,
and this will work largely independently of intelligence, work ethic, and so
on. No matter how hard Ray and Frenchy attempt to join wealthier classes,
they will never be included—their habitus will always be subject to the hysteresis effect and will therefore count against them, in the sense that their
habitus will always make them appear to members of wealthier classes as
lacking common sense or reason. Frenchy's attempt to "dress up" and look
nice for her party was unsuccessful—she didn't have the eye for subtle differences to pull it off. Or, to put it as Bourdieu does in the quote above,
what she saw as "distinguished" her guests saw as "vulgar." By contrast, the
least intelligent wealthy person may be included as an insider to elite circles because of her habitus. Wealthy people find jobs for those within their
network of family and friends—the least intelligent member of an elite class
could get "placed" in a job that would never be accessible to the smart-
est poor person in the world. This is not because elites have more intrinsic
merit than others, but simply because class habitus is counted as meritorious—
which is a privilege ultimately awarded on unfair grounds. As I noted above,
social domination through discrimination takes place as if it were right

and good, at least from the perspective of those who control jobs and other positions of status.

This sort of exclusion of people with an alternate habitus is linked up with a legitimation of their abandonment. Bourdieu argues,

> The Anglo-American ideology, always somewhat sanctimonious, distinguished the "undeserving poor," who had brought [poverty] upon themselves, from the "deserving poor," who were judged worthy of charity. Alongside or in place of this ethical justification there is now an intellectual justification. The poor are not just immoral, alcoholic and degenerate, they are stupid, they lack intelligence.
>
> (Bourdieu 1998, 43)

For Bourdieu this is doubly unfair to those with an alternate habitus: their social subordination is *created* by the way habitus works in the system (that is, they are *seen as stupid* because they have an alternate habitus, and are thus excluded from jobs or positions of privilege), but the system simultaneously *blames them* for their subordination (that is, it is generally assumed that they did not deserve jobs or positions of privilege *because* they were stupid).

It is for these sorts of reasons that Bourdieu and others argue that class difference can be reproduced over time without anyone intending it to be reproduced. Individuals are socialized into "self-perpetuating hierarchies of domination" (Swartz 1997, 6), and—because of how their habitus works—"actors *unwittingly* reproduce the social stratification order" (Swartz 1997, 7; emphasis added).

Those of us who live in a so-called meritocracy live in a world much more like the medieval social world than we think. Our social hierarchies are not assigned at birth and rigidly reinforced throughout life and without exception, but our social hierarchies are reproduced because of the class habitus we are socialized into from birth. Class movement isn't expressly forbidden and isn't impossible, but class differences are nevertheless largely maintained. We don't check people's literal pedigree in our society, but we do check their "habitus pedigree." The problem for Bourdieu is that the practical difference between these is minimal. Whether I cannot enter an elite class because I was born a serf or because I tell blue-collar jokes is ultimately immaterial—either way the social hierarchy is reproduced.

Habitus and Religion

How does habitus relate to those traditions we colloquially call religious? A full answer to this question will have to wait until Chapter 10, but at the very least we can say at this point that communities often have their own habitus, including those sorts of communities we call religious.

Because social concepts and categories almost always group together dissimilar things, it is usually impossible to find a set of common elements that every member of a category shares. Unlike most religious groups, Christians have historically defined themselves around a set of beliefs or doctrines, which sometimes makes it easier to find relatively common similarities. Protestants, for instance, tend to have a set of beliefs in common that distinguishes them from Catholics. However, as we noted in Chapter 2, it is not always the case that everyone who self-identifies as part of a Protestant group shares the same beliefs. This is particularly the case with evangelical Christians. Evangelical Christianity—a predominantly American form of Protestantism—has been notoriously difficult to define around a set of doctrines or beliefs because the different groups that self-identify as "evangelical" have had a lot of different beliefs that have changed or evolved over time. Julie Ingersoll, a scholar of evangelical Christianity, notes, "With each attempt at definition, there are inevitable groups that 'seem to be' evangelical but are ruled out, because of some view they hold or some practice they embrace" (Ingersoll 2003, 12). That is, if we line up people who self-identify as evangelical, or who seem to be evangelical, but then posit a definition based on what they seem to have in common, we inevitably end up excluding some of the ones we wanted to include.

It is for this reason that Ingersoll suggests that we should throw out the search for common doctrines: perhaps what is relatively common to evangelicalism is *not* doctrine but a shared habitus. Ingersoll writes (here she is in part quoting Barbara Wheeler):

> Wheeler suggests that observers of evangelicalism consider that "it is not doctrine or ancestry or warm feeling . . . but religious culture." Maybe, she continues, "the best definition of an evangelical is someone who understands its argot, knows where to buy posters with Bible verses on them, and recognizes names like James Dobson and Frank Peretti." Wheeler points to the distinctly evangelical religious dialect, leaders and celebrities, self-help groups, and Christian service providers (e.g., chiropractors and dentists), as well as the extensive material culture of music, tee-shirts, bumper stickers, books, and jewelry.
>
> (Ingersoll 2003, 13)

Ingersoll does not use the term habitus here, but we can see she is talking about the same thing: evangelical Christians have a very distinct dialect and set of tastes.

The evangelical dialect is particularly obvious—it has even been satirized by evangelicals themselves. The Bel Air Drama Department of the Bel Air Presbyterian Church (in Los Angeles, California) has an amusing video on YouTube called "Christianese" (available at www.youtube.com/watch?v=4H-29cJSuv8). The video is set in the format of a television commercial for audiotapes that teach foreign languages. It begins with a scene in which a young woman is with a church group, but doesn't understand the language and phrases the group is using (such as "delve into the Word," "the Lord just put it on my heart," "I stepped out in faith," and "grieve the Holy Spirit"). The narrator says, "Ever been part of a conversation with other Christians and you have no clue what they're saying? Well, no more! Announcing the tape series you've been waiting for: How to Speak Christianese." The narrator goes on to explain that this tape series, which you can listen to "in the privacy of your very own home," will explain what Christians mean when they use these unusual phrases—so that you can avoid the "unwanted embarrassment" that comes with feeling like an outsider. Of course this is an evangelical group satirizing themselves, but they are illustrating one of Bourdieu's key ideas: the way people talk—their diction or dialect—can serve as a social boundary marker that designates some people as insiders and others as outsiders. No doubt this evangelical group is pointing out the exclusionary nature of their diction with the hope of avoiding the exclusion that typically results, but in doing so they are making it obvious that even they recognize the boundary-marking nature of their way of talking.

So perhaps what is relatively common (although not completely common) to most evangelicals is not their doctrines or beliefs but, instead, their diction and their tastes in Christian music, novels, t-shirts, and so forth.

I have family members who have a white, middle-class, and evangelical Christian habitus. They include in their circle of friends not just people who think, talk, dress, and behave like them; they also want them to be what they call "good Christian people." What does that mean? At the very least it means that they want to be around people who share their Christian-inflected habitus. This is relevant for the parts of the country they live in, where evangelical Christianity is a dominant group, and their collusion has wide-ranging effects: if one does not share their evangelical Christian habitus, one will be excluded from certain social circles and job networks. In fact, just as having a visible tattoo or facial piercing might exclude one from some job possibilities, being unable to use an evangelical Christian vocabulary might similarly exclude one from job possibilities. "[One's] social sense is guided by the system of . . . signs of which each body is the bearer—clothing, pronunciation, bearing, posture, manners—and which, unconsciously registered, are the basis of 'antipathies' or 'sympathies'" (Bourdieu 1984, 241). That is, who one *sympathizes with* or has *antipathy toward* will depend on one's initial read of their habitus. Consequently, when a business owner implicitly wants "good Christian people" among her workers, she needn't explicitly say so or explicitly discriminate—it is just that those people with an alternative habitus will appear wrong, bad, vulgar, etc.—they will elicit antipathy rather than sympathy. On the one hand, when having the "right" habitus is implicitly counted as "meritorious," those with that habitus will experience a wide variety of privileges; those with a shared habitus will be included in the collusion. On the other hand, discrimination against those with an alternative habitus will happen naturally and invisibly.

We see this sort of privilege and discrimination in the experiences of a young woman named Gina Welch, author of *In the Land of Believers: An Outsider's Extraordinary Journey into the Heart of the Evangelical Church.* Welch is an atheist who went "undercover," so to speak, at televangelist Jerry Falwell's church in Lynchburg, Virginia; she wanted to see what evangelical communities were like from the inside, so she pretended to be an evangelical for a little over a year. At first it was difficult, in part because she did not understand the evangelical dialect. Eventually, however, she was able to master it:

> I had recently cleared the language barrier, finally unpacking idioms that had signified nothing to me when I first started at Thomas Road [Baptist Church]. Now I knew what it meant to speak in the flesh or the Spirit, I knew what it meant for the Lord to put something on somebody's heart.
>
> (Welch 2010, 114)

Prior to her achievement of an insider's status, she was pulled over by a Virginia highway trooper. The trooper unfortunately looked warily at her California driver's license and gave her a ticket:

> "I don't know what you're doing here," he said, ripping a ticket off his pad, "but we don't drive like that in Virginia."
>
> Years later I got pulled over running late for [church] one Sunday morning, going 80 coming into Lynchburg from Charlottesville. The trooper again looked at my California license warily and then asked why I was driving so fast. I told him, nerves buzzing, that I was late for church.
>
> "Don't be nervous," he said. "It's alright. Where do you go to church?"
>
> I mentioned Thomas Road [Baptist Church], explained that I drove down on Sundays and Wednesdays. Recognition smoothed his features like a cool cream. "You come down every week . . . " he said, smiling and shaking his head in wonder.
>
> He asked me nicely to slow down, then let me go.
>
> (Welch 2010, 99)

It would be inappropriate to make too much of merely two experiences (and Welch admits this), but it is worth noting that this is precisely what we would expect to see if this trooper was an evangelical Christian similar to the ones at Thomas Road Baptist Church: once learning she was an insider (an evangelical) rather than an outsider (a Californian), the trooper registered sympathy rather than antipathy for her and let her go—she was admitted into the collusion.

Subjects do not necessarily "merit" sympathetic treatment by those in the same religious community, but they receive it all the same. And when one religious group is the dominant group in a particular region, their unconscious extension of sympathy to those with a similar habitus and unconscious discrimination against those with a different habitus results in that religious group being indirectly but effectively installed as the ruling group. This can take place even when these subjects are state employees; in a sense, evangelical Christianity becomes the established state religion when employees of the state (like the trooper above) have an evangelical habitus. The discrimination against other religious groups—that is, those religious groups with an alternative habitus—will happen unconsciously and unwittingly. In such cases, religious domination through discrimination takes place as if it were right and good, at least from the perspective of those dominant religious practitioners who are in positions of power.

7

How Religion Works: Legitimation

> [R]eligion is something eminently social. Religious representations are collective representations that express collective realities.
>
> Émile Durkheim, *The Elementary Forms of Religious Life* (2001, 11)

Legitimation and Manufacturing Consent

A great deal of social reproduction takes place via the cycle of socialization. As noted above, presumably the first person who wore pants did so just because he or she individually liked pants. However, wearing pants has become a fictitious necessity: my parents were taught that they had to wear pants, they taught me to wear pants too, and I'll teach my children that they have to wear pants. Through the process of socialization, social practices reproduce themselves over time.

Socialization doesn't always "take," however, and often people begin to ask "why?" Every once in a while a child asks her parents, "Why do I have to wear pants?" The first answer to the "why" question is usually "because that's just the way things are." This often works, because people conveniently ignore that when it comes to social constructions, this is completely false: things *are not* just the way they are; things are how we have made them. Wearing pants has become second nature to me; I couldn't imagine going to work without pants. But again, there is nothing at all natural about this—many societies throughout time haven't required individuals to wear pants. Insofar as the practice has become naturalized here, it has also become a fictitious necessity.

What happens when "that's just the way things are" doesn't suffice as an answer? What happens when individuals probe further and require further justifications? This is when societies turn to what scholars call "legitimation." Legitimations offer some sort of justification for conformity to a practice, and they often involve appeals to what the gods or sacred texts say. "Why can't I?" "Because the Bible says so."

A related technical term for what is going on here is "manufacturing consent." People don't always want to do what they are told, but one can manufacture their consent by convincing them that they must, that it's inevitable that they comply, or that there will be supernatural consequences if they do not. When societies can successfully manufacture consent, people are easier to control, since they'll voluntarily do whatever society wishes of them. "Why should we do this?" Responses such as "you'll go to hell if you don't" might persuade people it is in their best interests to comply with social expectations.

This emphasis on how discourses ("discourses" is a technical term for "ways of talking") can be used to legitimate practices or manufacture consent to social order requires us to switch from focusing on what discourses *mean* and instead focus on how they are *used* or what they *do*. This approach requires us to think about the *social effects* of the way people talk, rather than the apparent meaning of their words. The social function of legitimations may have little or nothing to do with the literal meaning of the words used. For instance, in the US it is a popular practice for people to place "I support the troops" stickers on their cars. However, few of the people I know who have such stickers actually do much of anything to support American troops in any tangible way; I suspect that "I support the troops" stickers function to discourage people from criticizing America's foreign wars—no one has to literally "support the troops" for the rhetoric on the stickers to serve this social function. Again, to explain how such rhetoric works we must focus on what the words *do* more than what they *mean*.

Because of this focus on the social effect of religious talk, religious stories, religious rituals, and so on, the primary questions we ask will not be "What do they say?," "What do they mean?," or "Do they really believe it?" Instead we will ask, when reading a text, for instance, "Who is trying to persuade whom of what in this text? In what context is the attempt situated, and what are the consequences should it succeed?" (Lincoln 2006, 127). That is, we'll focus on what may or may not be *accomplished* by what is said.

Throughout the history of Western civilization there have been many who have suggested that religious legitimation is absolutely necessary for social order. Philosophers like John Locke and Jean-Jacques Rousseau suggested that people would not be moral unless they believed in hell: they argued that morality would not work unless people believed that a god would send them to hell when they died unless they acted morally. Consequently, Locke and Rousseau argued in their political writings that atheism should be illegal: atheists will not obey the law because they have nothing to fear in the afterlife. In retrospect, their worry was obviously misplaced; empirical evidence demonstrates that those who identify as atheists usually do obey the law. However, there is no doubt that some people do act morally at times out of a fear of eternal punishment, so the point remains: religious legitimations can justify certain social or moral norms when people question them. In sum, the social order can be maintained when it is questioned or criticized through the use of religious legitimations. "God says so" or "God will punish you if you don't" are only the most obvious and straightforward examples of religious legitimation. As we will see below, social reproduction sometimes requires much more complex forms of legitimation or justification; manufacturing consent can be a messy process.

While legitimations might seem like intentional manipulations, this is not necessarily the case. Few scholars in religious studies argue that people intentionally manipulate others with talk about gods. On the contrary, appealing to gods comes naturally to people who are raised in communities where those sorts of appeals are normal. If one thinks God is good and sexism is bad, one will naturally come to the conclusion that God must be opposed to sexism. If someone is faced with sexist behavior and responds by saying, "God wouldn't approve of that," it is unlikely that that person is trying to intentionally manipulate her audience. Rather, saying this will come automatically and will seem like common sense, even though it is still a legitimation. As Bruce Lincoln puts it, "it is often the case that those who would persuade others [by means of legitimation] *are themselves most persuaded of all*" (Lincoln 2007, xv; emphasis added).

In addition, most social theorists are ambivalent in their assessment of legitimation. On the one hand, legitimation maintains social order, which usually serves the interests of the population within a community. If we all did what we wanted all the time without any respect for social norms, we would have chaos—and few people's interests are served when chaos reigns. On the other hand—and as we noted in Chapter 5—social order often involves domination or exploitation. Less than two hundred years ago white people in America thought it was entirely appropriate to buy and sell people with dark skin. When others objected, white people often pointed to passages in the Bible that spoke favorably of slavery in order to justify it; because slavery is discussed a lot in the Bible, it was a very useful tool for legitimation of the practice. Legitimation can be used for a wide variety of purposes, some of which we might value today and some we might consider unjust.

What is the difference between a legitimation and a religious legitimation? For Peter Berger (see Berger 1967, 29ff), a legitimation is religious when it involves some sort of superhuman or supernatural element. If one asks one's boss, "why do I have to do this," and one's boss says, "because it is in your contract," that is a justification designed to get one to comply. For Berger, that's a legitimation, but not a religious one. If one's boss went on to say, "because you'll go to hell if you don't," then it is a religious legitimation, because it involves an appeal to something beyond the human realm. Similarly, Lincoln writes,

> religious claims are the means by which certain objects, places, speakers, and speech-acts are invested with an authority, the source of which lies *outside the human*. That is, these claims create the appearance that

their authorization comes from a realm beyond history, society, and politics. . . . Among these resources figures prominently one that is both a prize and a weapon in such struggles: the capacity to speak a consequential speech and to gain a respectful hearing. With religious claims, the attempt is made to naturalize (indeed, to supernatural-ize) this capacity, thereby placing it—and some people's hold on it—beyond the possibility of contestation.

(Lincoln 1994, 112; emphasis original)

What Lincoln is suggesting here is that once one's claims are "supernatural-ized," so to speak, when they appear to derive from divine forces beyond the human realm, they gain authority. Appeals to gods, if convincing, carry more authority than appeals to oneself as an individual.

However, as David Kertzer notes in his discussion of rituals, this sort of distinction between "religious" rituals and "non-religious" rituals (such as nationalist rituals) is not all that useful. Many of the claims that we wouldn't necessarily call "religious" involve an appeal to sources that lie "outside the human," as Lincoln puts it. For instance, we don't normally refer to "universal human rights" as "religious," but discourses on "inherent dignity" and "inalien-able rights" treat them as if they were universal morals built into the fabric of the universe, or as if they existed independently of human agreements—in which case perhaps they're not so very different from so-called "religious" claims. Societies are full of legitimations and rituals of all sorts, and the ones we refer to as "religious" function precisely in the same way as the so-called "non-religious" ones—there is no substantial difference between the two when it comes to the way they work. For this reason I side with Kertzer when he claims that "such a distinction is more a hindrance than a help in understand-ing" how culture functions (Kertzer 1988, 9). Consequently, we will follow Kertzer here: there appear to be insufficient reasons to emphasize a distinction between religious and non-religious legitimations, and, on the contrary, it will prove useful to compare them and study them side-by-side.

Cultural Toolboxes and the Maintenance of Social Order

It is useful to think of a culture as a "toolbox" with a wide variety of "tools" inside. "[C]ulture . . . [is] a profuse repertoire of discourses and practices, that is, what other authors have labeled a 'tool kit,' or a 'surfeit of cultural mate-rial'" (Hammer 2009, 10). These "tools" are what we use to legitimate the social order. Kertzer notes that we do not usually invent these sorts of tools. On the contrary, for the most part we inherit them. "Most often, people participate in ritual forms that they had nothing to do with creating. Even where individuals invent new rituals, they create them largely out of a stockpile of pre-existing symbols" (Kertzer 1988, 10).

A cultural toolbox can include all of the following types of tools, to take the example of the American nationalist cultural toolbox:

- *Concepts, norms, and values*—freedom, equality, "the American way," civil liberties, patriotism, "life, liberty, and the pursuit of happiness," "In God We Trust"
- *Traditions, rituals, and practices*—July 4th celebrations (including fireworks, barbecues, etc.), inauguration ceremonies, pledge of allegiance, playing the national anthem at baseball games
- *Myths and stories*—George Washington cutting down the cherry tree, the ride of Paul Revere, Johnny Appleseed, the story about how dropping "the bomb" in World War II was unfortunate but absolutely necessary to end the war, the myth that America is the "land of opportunity" and a "meritocracy"
- *Texts*—the Declaration of Independence, the Constitution (including the Bill of Rights)
- *Icons*—the eagle, the statue of liberty, the Washington memorial, the Empire State building, Uncle Sam, Lady Liberty
- *Figures*—Thomas Jefferson, George Washington, Benjamin Franklin, Abraham Lincoln
- *Ideologies*—"manifest destiny," "common sense."

Most of these tools have an almost universal privileged or authoritative status in America; this is what makes them useful for legitimating the social order. Since the American constitution is authoritative in America, people will appeal to it to justify certain things. However, since the American constitution does not carry any authority in China, it will not be used there to legitimate or maintain the social order. The application of such tools is limited to the reach of their authoritative status.

It is important to note that competing groups within a single society generally use the same cultural tools. For instance, a speech writer for the Democratic candidate for president would use the type of American nationalist cultural tools listed above—perhaps she might throw in a quote from former American President Thomas Jefferson to support her candidate's views. Jefferson is an authoritative figure who carries a weight in America that someone like the former British Prime Minister Winston Churchill would not. However, speech writers for the Republican candidate will use *the same set of tools*. In any particular culture, people generally use the same cultural toolbox—it is just that they use the tools in different ways. When Christians argue among themselves, they generally appeal to the same text: the Bible. However, it is clear that different Christians have used the Bible in different ways: two centuries ago some American Christians appealed to the Bible to legitimate slavery, and other American Christians appealed to the Bible to oppose slavery. The same is true of all so-called sacred texts such as the Torah, the Qur'an, etc. The way the tools in a cultural toolbox are used is always highly variable.

In order to be more specific about how the tools in cultural toolboxes are used, we will look at how they can reflect and reinforce the three general elements of societies we saw in Chapter 5: (1) insider/outsider boundaries, (2) social positions and social hierarchies, and (3) social roles, moral norms, and behavioral codes.

Social Boundaries

First, *elements of cultural toolboxes can be used to reflect and reinforce social boundaries*. Perhaps the most obvious examples of this are flags: nations use flags to identify themselves. Most ships on the open ocean are required to bear flags of their nation of origin. The Canadian flag on a ship tells the world: "this is a Canadian ship." Catholics are sometimes known for wearing a crucifix on a chain around their neck; this says to the world: "I'm a Christian." Similarly, evangelical Christians are known for having fish symbols on their car, such as the one in Figure 7.1. This symbol also tells the world: "I'm a Christian." By contrast, some atheists and evolutionists who oppose conservative evangelical Christianity have appropriated this symbol and tweaked it a bit, so that it looks like a fish evolving by growing legs (Figure 7.2). This tells the world that the owner of the car identifies as an insider in another group, and a group that is opposed to the Christian group. In short, this symbol tells the world: "I'm outside conservative Christianity and I'm inside the evolutionist camp." In response, the conservative Christians have taken this symbol and manipulated it as in Figure 7.3. This tells the world: "I'm a Christian and I think the

Figure 7.1 Jesus fish.

Figure 7.2 Darwin fish.

Figure 7.3 Jesus fish eating a Darwin fish.

Darwinist groups are stupid." Note that all of these symbols mark an individual as an insider or a member of a certain group, and simultaneously opposes him or her to another group. From our perspective, what these symbols "mean" is less important than what they do: *they mark insider/outsider boundaries.*

Much of the Lotus Sutra—a famous Mahayana Buddhist text—is about how wonderful the sutra is, a focus that draws insider/outsider boundaries. That is, much of the sutra tries to convince the reader that followers of this Mahayana sutra are better off than followers of *other* Buddhist sutras. The text even suggests that the preaching contained in the book is the "greater vehicle" to enlightenment, as compared with all the "lesser vehicles" of other Buddhist communities. The people who follow other traditions "fail to understand" (Watson 2002, 26), and one famous historical figure named Shariputra (who was long since dead when the Lotus Sutra was written) is even portrayed as saying that he misunderstood the truth until he heard the "greater vehicle" in the Lotus Sutra:

> How greatly I have been deceived! . . .
> Formerly I was attached to erroneous views,
> acting as teacher to the Brahmans.
> But the World-Honored One [i.e., the Buddha], knowing what
> was in my mind,
> rooted out my errors and preached nirvana.
> I was freed of my errors
> and gained understanding of the Law of emptiness [i.e., the teaching of
> the Lotus Sutra].
>
> (Watson 2002, 27)

The Lotus Sutra is full of stories about magical things that happen when people read or hear sutra: music starts playing out of nowhere, robes rise off of the ground and dance in the air, and even towers covered with jewels rise out of the ground. In fact, the superiority of Mahayana Buddhism over all other Buddhist communities seems to be the central theme of the book. In short, *the stories in the Lotus Sutra draw insider/outsider distinctions between different Buddhist groups, and mark one as superior to the others.*

Rituals too can mark insider/outsider boundaries. For instance, the Catholic church requires all members to go through what they call "first communion." Communion, also called the "Eucharist," is one of the central ritual practices of the Catholic church. However, not everyone can participate in communion—individuals can only do so after they have gone through an initiation process. The initiation process involves taking classes on the doctrines of the church, confessing one's sins to a priest, etc. The final part of the initiation is the ritual celebration of one's "first communion." This ritual is designed to mark an individual as a full insider in the Catholic church, with all the rights and responsibilities of a full member. Prior to that ritual initiation, there are things one cannot do—in particular, one cannot take communion. People who are not Catholic and have not gone through the ritual do not have the rights of a full member—if they attended a Catholic church they would not be allowed to participate in the Eucharist (unless they hid their identity as outsiders). In summary, the central function of the ritual is marking one as an insider to the community, rather than an outsider. Again, from our perspective, what is important is less what the first communion ritual "means"—if we asked a Catholic priest he would probably tell us it meant something relating to Jesus' body and blood—and more what the ritual "does": *it marks some individuals as insiders.*

In *The Elementary Forms of Religious Life*, Émile Durkheim (2001) argued that what was fundamental to religion is that it unites all people in a community, giving them a sense of solidarity with one another. On the one hand, this is in part clearly true: people do get a sense of belonging when they participate in a communal tradition. On the other hand, social theorist Tim Murphy rightly notes that Durkheim's point is too simple: group membership is about *differentiation* as much as unity:

> even a casual survey of the history of religions shows that [Durkheim's insistence on unity] is, at best, a half truth. Insofar as religions unite one group, they do so by *differentiating* its members and its memberships from other groups. Difference, not unity, is the dominant trope in the history of religions.
>
> (Murphy 2007, 137)

In addition, not only do religious traditions demarcate insiders from outsiders, but there is almost always a value judgment in the distinction: "*By definition,* that which the one sees as holy, the other sees as evil" (Murphy 2007, 138; emphasis original). The people with the Darwin fish are not just dividing themselves from conservative Christians; they are criticizing conservative Christians. The stories in the Lotus Sutra do not just draw lines between different forms of Buddhism; they are designating one group as the superior and the others as inferior. These are not neutral insider/outsider distinctions, but asymmetrical valuations.

Social Hierarchies

The second point of focus is that *elements of cultural toolboxes can be used to reflect and reinforce social hierarchies and social positions.* For example, there are multiple creation stories in what is called the ancient Hindu tradition. One of them, from the Rig Veda, describes a "primal man" (a giant person with god-like qualities), who was killed and whose body was divided up to make the world.

11. When they divided up [primal] Man,
Into how many parts did they divide him?
What was his mouth? What his arms?
What are his thighs called? What his feet?

12. The Brahman was his mouth,
The arms were made the Prince,
His thighs the common people,
And from his feet the serf was born.

(Goodall 1996, 14)

This is not just a story about the creation of the world; it is a story that legitimates a certain class structure. The differences between mouth, arms, thighs, and feet are not just differences. On the contrary, they are hierarchical: the mouth is at the top, and the feet are at the bottom. Similarly, the Brahman (the priestly class) were made out of the mouth, so they are at the top of society. The serfs (the servant class) were made out of the feet, so they are at the bottom of society.

> Here, as in all such cases, the duties and privileges of the various social classes ... are justified ("explained") by reference to their bodily [associations]. . . . Warriors fight because of their association to the arms, chest, heart, and lungs (where energy and courage are located), while the lower classes run errands, produce food, and generally support their class superiors because of their proximity to feet, legs, and abdomen.
>
> (Lincoln 1991a, 174)

We should not understand this story as merely reporting on how the world was really created (in any case, we are approaching claims about gods from a sceptical perspective); instead we should understand this story as suggesting how the world *should* look. That is, it is not a "description" or a "map"; it is a "prescription" or a "blueprint." The author is telling us who should have the most authority in society and who should have the least. In addition, the story depicts the social order not as created by humans, but as created by divine beings. Challenges to the social hierarchy are therefore challenges to the divine order of things. So, if we focus on what this story "does" rather than what it "means," we will see the following: *this story reflects and reinforces a certain social hierarchy*; it naturalizes or makes a fictitious necessity out of an arbitrary social order.

In the Lotus Sutra there is a short narrative about an eight-year-old girl (called the "dragon girl") who achieved Buddhahood very quickly. Of course, her quick Buddhahood was the result of having heard the "greater vehicle" to enlightenment in the Lotus Sutra rather than a lesser one from some other

Buddhist tradition. However, the author of this story has to deal with the fact that in most Buddhist traditions at the time, it was believed that women were inferior to men and could not achieve enlightenment—at least not until they were reincarnated as men in a future life. In the dialogue, a man says to the dragon girl,

> this is difficult to believe. Why? Because a woman's body is soiled and defiled, not a vessel for the Law. How could you attain the unsurpassed bodhi? . . . [A woman] cannot become a Buddha. How then could a woman like you be able to attain Buddhahood so quickly?
>
> (Watson 2002, 86)

The narrator answers the objection by completing the story: "At that time the members of the assembly all saw the dragon girl in the space of an instant *change into a man*" before fully completing the process of Buddhahood" (Watson 2002, 86; emphasis added). The story therefore does not challenge the idea that women cannot attain Buddhahood. Instead, the story gets around it by saying that she was able to turn herself into a man and *only then* achieve Buddhahood. Rather than challenge the gender hierarchy, the story *reflects and reinforces as legitimate the superiority of men over women*.

As historian Fay Botham notes in *Almighty God Created the Races* (2009)—a history of Christian segregation—prior to America's Civil War, Christians commonly legitimated the slavery of Africans by pointing to a story in the first book of the Bible. In Genesis, God tells a man named Noah that he is about to send a flood in order to wipe out all evil, but instructs Noah to build an ark—that is, a large boat—and fill it with his immediate family and non-human animals of all kinds; that way they will be saved from drowning with the rest of the world. After the flood, Noah builds a vineyard, makes some wine, and gets blackout drunk. The next morning his son Ham walks into Noah's tent, finds him laid out naked on the floor, and then leaves to tell his brothers—Shem and Japheth—about their father's condition. Shem and Japheth take a blanket into the tent and cover their father, all the while turning their eyes aside in order to avoid looking at him. When Noah wakes up and finds out that Ham saw him naked, he becomes very angry—for reasons that are not entirely clear in the story—and curses his son, saying that Ham and his descendants will be slaves to his brothers and their descendants (see Genesis 9:25–27). Thus in the American South, when people challenged the legitimacy of slavery, white Christians would point to Genesis, claim that Africans were descendants of Ham, and conclude that of course they were justified in enslaving them—not only was slavery a morally acceptable practice, but it was supported right there in "God's word." Because the Bible was universally revered as authoritative in the US at the time, and because this was popularly received as an acceptable interpretation, *this story functioned to legitimate a racial hierarchy between whites and blacks.*

After the Civil War, slavery was abolished. However, a racial hierarchy persisted, in part through Jim Crow laws and segregated social arrangements. Segregation laws prohibiting whites from marrying blacks were enforced well into the twentieth century. When challenged, some white Christians legitimated segregation by pointing to another passage in Genesis. According to Genesis 11, a group of people gathered together in an attempt to build a tower that would reach all the way to the gods in the heavens. God appears to think they are becoming too powerful, and decides to put a stop to it:

> The LORD came down to see the city and the tower, which mortals had built. And the LORD said, "Look, they are one people, and they have all one language; and this is only the beginning of what they will do; nothing that they propose to do will now be impossible for them. Come, let us go down, and confuse their language there, so that they will not understand one another's speech." So the LORD scattered them abroad from there over the face of all the earth, and they left off building the city. Therefore it was called Babel, because there the LORD confused the language of all the earth; and from there the LORD scattered them abroad over the face of all the earth.
>
> (Genesis 11: 5–9)

This story was widely interpreted in the middle of the twentieth century as saying that this was the origin of the separation of different races across the world—it was *God himself that divided the races and scattered them across the earth*. As such, to allow whites and blacks to mingle or marry would be to reverse what God had done. The view that "God had created separate and distinct races and intended them to remain that way" was for a long time accepted as common sense among white Christians in the US (Botham 2009, 107). Again, *they used passages from the Bible to reflect and reinforce a hierarchical separation of whites and blacks*.

Rituals too are often used to reinforce social hierarchies. A common example is seating patterns. Lincoln draws attention to these in his book, *Discourse and the Construction of Society*. He notes how medieval feasts had seating arrangements that reflected the social hierarchy—each man had a seat in relationship to the king or noble that reflected his distance from the top of the hierarchy. "The map of the [dining] hall is thus also a map of society, in which persons of different rank and standing were assigned to different loci along a north–south axis" (Lincoln 1989, 79). He similarly notes (132) how his own family dinner table was organized to reflect the social hierarchy (see Figure 7.4).

This seating arrangement reflects two hierarchical relations, including both a gender hierarchy and an age hierarchy. On the one side there are males, and on the other side are females. But each side is additionally divided by age: the

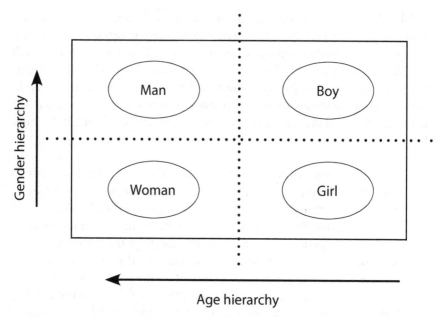

Figure 7.4 The heteronormative family table (adapted from Figure 8.2 of *Discourse and the Construction of Society,* © 1989 Bruce Lincoln)

younger are on one side and the older on another. This accords with my own experience: every big Thanksgiving dinner I have attended has had a separate children's table, distinct from the adults' table. In addition, the seat on the end is almost always occupied by the oldest male present—I have never seen a woman of any age sit on the "throne" end of the table. Similarly, throughout the history of the Christian church, it has often been the case that the seating in the church was divided by sex (a practice the early Christians appropriated from Jewish synagogues). In addition, churches have also divided seating by race. In summary: *ritual seating patterns reflect and reinforce social hierarchies.* By sitting where they are invited to sit, individuals learn who they are and where they sit in relation to others within the social hierarchy.

Assigned Behaviors

The third and final point of focus is that *elements of cultural toolboxes can be used to reflect and reinforce assigned behaviors: social roles, moral norms, behavioral codes, and so on.* This is perhaps the easiest to understand—Aesop's fables provide a great example. There is almost always a "moral to the story." Readers learn, for instance, from "The Tortoise and the Hare" that "slow and steady wins the race."

There are many Buddhist texts about different places in which you can be reincarnated for various moral or immoral actions. One text says that liars and people who hate their family will go to a hell in which "they are split like wood with burning saws" (Lopez 2004, 6). People who start forest fires are sent to a hell in which they are perpetually burned (6–7). Murderers are sent to a hell of fire so hot that even their bones melt (7). Thieves are sent to a hell in which they are forced to "drink molten copper" (8). Not all evil is punished so painfully, however. People who have evil thoughts about stealing but don't actually steal are reincarnated as ghosts that can only eat feces, phlegm, and vomit, and people who are cruel are born as ghosts that can only eat "worms, insects and beetles" (11). By contrast, positive thoughts or deeds are encouraged with the promise of being reincarnated in better circumstances. People who give away houses will have palaces in their future life, and doctors who help the sick in the present life will be safe from illness in the next (14). Since the text is also sexist, it suggests that a woman who is not too emotional and who hates her womanhood can improve her station by being reborn as a man in the next life, while a man who commits adultery with other men's wives could be demoted and reborn as a woman (15). Another text, however, promises a much harsher punishment for adulterers; they will be reborn in a hell in which

> the wardens seize the sinners and place them in a forest of knife-like leaves. The sinners look up to the tops of the trees and see beautiful, well-groomed women. As soon as the sinners see the women, they start climbing the trees. The leaves on the trees are as sharp as knives. They slice off the flesh and pierce sinews until every part of the body is cut away. When the sinners arrive at the tops of the trees, they see the women down on the ground. . . . The sinners look upon them and, with hearts full of lust, start climbing down the trees. . . . When the sinners are on the ground, the women are back on top of the trees. This cycle continues for an infinite hundreds of thousands of millions of years.
>
> (72–73)

Much like parents threatening their children with the claim that "Santa Claus won't come this Christmas if you lie," we can imagine parents reciting these hell narratives to their children, in order to teach what behaviors their community believes to be moral: "don't steal, or you'll go to this hell" or "don't cheat, or you'll go to that hell." *The telling and re-telling of these narratives reflect and reinforce certain moral norms or prescribed behaviors.*

Maintaining or Challenging the Social Order?

While we have focused on how the elements of a cultural toolbox can be used in support of social reproduction, it is important to note that they can also be used to challenge an existing social order. The elements of a cultural toolbox can be used to support the status quo *and* to challenge the status quo. As sociologists Peter Berger and Thomas Luckmann argue, "The experts in legitimation may operate as theoretical justifiers of the status quo; [but] they may also appear as *revolutionary* ideologists" (Berger and Luckmann 1967, 128; emphasis added). There is nothing about the tools in a cultural toolbox that predetermines how they can be used—they can be turned toward a variety of different ends. Cultural tools are *easily recycled* for "new political purposes," and "new political forces eagerly rummage through the preexisting body of religious rituals and symbols" to find those that will work for them (Kertzer 1988, 45).

Similarly, Lincoln suggests that myths:

> may be instrumental in the ongoing construction of social borders and hierarchies, which is to say, in the construction of society itself. As such, myth has tremendous importance and is often a site of contestation between groups and individuals whose differing versions of social ideals and reality are inscribed within *the rival versions of the myths they create.*
>
> (Lincoln 1991a, 123; emphasis added)

That is, different groups can tell different versions of the same myth (or practice different versions of the same ritual, etc.) in order to accomplish *different* social ends. As a result, "Studies of myth . . . ought to be attentive to the multiple competing voices that find expression in differing variants, and to the struggles they wage in and through mythic discourse" (Lincoln 1991a, 124). By telling persuasive stories that depict the world the way they think it should be, groups can fight and defeat other groups without raising a fist or shooting a gun. *Myths and rituals are often best understood as bloodless battlegrounds for social power.* Kertzer insists that the same is true of rituals:

> Rituals do change in form, in symbolic meaning, and in social effects; new rituals arise and old rituals fade away. These changes come through individual creative activity. People, in short, are not just slaves of ritual, or slaves of symbols, they are also molders and creators of ritual. It is because people create and alter rituals that they are such powerful tools of political action.
>
> (Kertzer 1988, 12)

The elements of a cultural toolbox do not have a fixed use; they are often capable of being recycled by individuals who take them up and give them new life. "Every culture has its own store of powerful symbols, and it is generally in the interests of new political forces to claim those symbols as their own" (42–3). Anthropologist Marshall Sahlins points out that concepts, signs, or words—which we usually think of as having stable uses that are outside our power to change—are necessarily subject to change when they are put to work in specific contexts: "*in action* . . . cultural categories acquire new functional values" (Sahlins 1987, 138). There is nothing to guarantee that a word is used in exactly the same way each time it is repeated, and without such a guarantee, it automatically follows that to repeat a word is necessarily to put it at risk of change. Just as cars will break down the more we drive them, so words will change meaning the more we use them in new contexts. The same general rule applies to all elements of cultural toolboxes. If cultures are capable of evolving, or if cultural tools are capable of being recycled and reused in new ways, it follows that they can be used to challenge rather than reinforce the status quo.

In addition, not only can the use of cultural tools change, but so can the particular *selection* of which tools will be utilized. There is always a great deal in the repertoire of a tradition, and not all of it can be used at once. What elements from a cultural toolbox people choose to utilize will depend not on the tradition itself, but on what they desire their communities to look like. Notably, the idea that tradition reflects the past is misleading; the selective uses of tradition reflect what people want for their future.

Kertzer points out that a number of rituals were used by American revolutionaries to challenge rather than reinforce the status quo (i.e., America's status as a colony of England). They made effigies of King George III and burned them, had funerals for them, and buried them (Kertzer 1988, 161–2). He suggests that these rituals may have been more effective—because more attention-grabbing—at generating negative sentiments toward the King and England than did the signing and distributing of the United States' constitution. He calls these "rituals of revolution," and it is clear that they have a great ability to challenge rather than reinforce the social order.

Let me offer two other examples. In America, most heterosexual Christian weddings end with the minister announcing the married couple to the audience like this: "I now present to you Mr. and Mrs. Craig Martin." In a small but substantial way, this reinforces the subordination of a woman's social position to a man's. Not only is he mentioned first and she second, but her name disappears. It is as if she as an individual becomes nothing more than an attachment to her husband. In much of the history of Western culture, this has actually been the case: women have often been little more, socially speaking, than fashion accessories to their husbands' careers. In order to challenge this social subordination of women to men, when my wife and I got married we asked the minister not to do this, so he announced us in this way: "I now present to you Craig and Erica." In this way we were attempting to tweak the ritual in order to challenge the status quo, rather than reinforce it. (It is worth noting that we still placed my name first, which is still subtly patriarchal.)

Second, it is a ritual in North America for a man to ask a woman to marry him, rather than the other way around. Again, this is an odd sexist practice if we are aiming at gender equality. As a result, when I proposed to my wife I told her that I was not, by asking her to marry me, agreeing to marry her—I asked that she propose to me as well. So, a few weeks after I proposed, she reciprocated by proposing to me in return (I said "yes"). Again, in this way we were attempting to tweak a social practice in order to challenge the status quo, rather than reinforce it.

There is nothing unusual about this. Tools such as hammers can be used for hammering or pulling out nails, but they can also be used for purposes for which they were never intended: one could use a hammer as a doorstop, or even use a screwdriver as a hammer. How the available tools in a cultural toolbox will be used depends in part on tradition—people will tend to use them in the ways they have always been used—but when circumstances change they can turn the tools to entirely new uses, or even reactivate old tools that have not been used for a while.

In summary, the tools in our cultural toolbox can be used to reflect and reinforce social boundaries, hierarchies, and prescribed behaviors, but they can also be used in order *to challenge and reshape* these things.

Religious Essentialism

Having a cultural toolbox is like having a box of Legos. With a box of Legos one could build just about anything. There's nothing intrinsic to the blocks themselves that predetermines how they will be used. One could build a car, a plane, a hat, a cat, or whatever. Similarly, the elements of a cultural toolbox can be used to maintain (or challenge) all sorts of different types of society. The elements of the Christian cultural toolbox have been used both to support violence and to oppose violence. The elements of the Islamic cultural toolbox have been used both to maintain sexism and to challenge sexism. The elements of the Hindu cultural toolbox have been used both to maintain the elite privileges of the priestly class and to challenge the elite privileges of the priestly class. No matter how such cultural tools have been used in the past, someone will probably use them in new ways in the future. In short, *there are no essences to be found in a religious tradition's cultural toolbox.*

One reason why it is hard to see this is that it conflicts with a naïve "belief system" theory of religion many people hold. As we noted in previous chapters, people often take religion to be about "beliefs," and then assume that the actions or behavior of religious practitioners is caused by their stated beliefs. On the "belief system" theory we tend to think of beliefs as the essence of a religion, and assume that the essence unfolds in the same way for all religious practitioners. This is not only false as a theory of religion, but it is a dangerous theory as well: it wrongly leads people to think that if the Qur'an says Muslims should kill infidels, that means all people who say they "believe" in the Qur'an will kill infidels. This is clearly not true. Malory Nye puts it well in his discussion of how defining religion as a "belief system" slides into an explanatory account:

> What is happening here is, in fact, that this idea of belief is being used not merely as a definition [of religion], but as an explanation. That is, religious belief becomes an explanation in itself: our absence of understanding what a person from another religion is doing or thinking leads us to fall back on our basic knowledge of their beliefs. Thus we assume that a Hindu is acting a certain way because s/he 'believes' in reincarnation, and a Muslim in another way because s/he believes in Allah. Such an explanation may or may not be correct—but what it does is rule out a number of other possible explanations.
>
> (Nye 2008, 117)

It may be the case that reported beliefs directly inform practitioners' behavior some of the time, but often the reverse is true: people's stated beliefs are legitimations that reflect and reinforce an already existing set of behaviors, practices, or agendas. The naïve theory of religion supposes that practices and behaviors follow directly from beliefs, but in fact "beliefs" are often invoked secondarily.

In *Politics, Law and Ritual in Tribal Society*, Max Gluckman discusses an African nation in which the citizens believed that whoever became king of their nation was awarded supernatural powers after going through a ritual that instantiated him as king; it was believed that these supernatural powers were so great that the king could control even the weather. However, because he was thought to be capable of controlling the weather, "the king was held responsible for what we would call 'natural' disasters, and rebellion against him was warranted in the national interest" (Gluckman 1965, 165). That is, sometimes after a natural disaster the citizens would rebel and overthrow the king for causing or failing to prevent the disaster. The naïve theory of religion would approach this sort of story and assume that the people obviously have to rebel because of their beliefs—as if the day after the disaster they said to themselves, "well, we don't want to do it, but our belief system says we've got to overthrow the king." But Gluckman rightly points out that the "belief" didn't work this way. Gluckman writes, "in practice rebellion was probably waged by a prince as leader *of a discontented faction*" (emphasis added; 165). That is, the people didn't feel the need to rebel every time a natural disaster happened, but only when a rebellion *was already brewing*. People were not at all forced by their stated beliefs to depose a king after a natural disaster; rather, discontented groups who *already opposed the king* sometimes used natural disasters to legitimate the rebellion they wanted to launch for independent reasons. It is not that their beliefs determined their rebellion, but rather that their rebellion already in the works was legitimated by an appeal to their beliefs.

If we set aside the naïve theory of religion as a "belief system," according to which stated beliefs always determine practitioners' behaviors—like an essence that unfolds from the inside out—it is much easier to see that beliefs and doctrines are usually in a very complex relationship with behaviors and practices, and that people who share a cultural toolbox may in fact do very different things with the tools inside. Rather than try to discover an essence to a religious tradition by looking at its cultural toolbox (like trying to prove that Christianity is intrinsically a violent religion because Jesus said "I came to bring not peace but a sword"), we can better understand the social effects of myths, rituals, and other elements of cultural toolboxes if we consider the critical questions listed above *in particular historical contexts*. In this particular historical context, who is trying to persuade whom of what by brandishing this element of the cultural toolbox? What are the consequences should the attempt succeed? Is domination being reinforced or challenged? Answers to these sorts of questions will bring into relief a wide variety of things we would not otherwise notice.

8

How Religion Works: Authority

Authority and Projection

Appeals to authority are found in all cultural traditions. When people ask the "why do we do it this way?" question and demand an answer, the answers offered—designed to legitimate or manufacture consent to social order—are almost always linked to locally authoritative figures, texts, icons, symbols, and so on. We say "locally authoritative" because none of these things are authoritative for all societies in all times and places. What is authoritative here may not be authoritative there, and what is authoritative now may not have been authoritative then.

There are at least three types of authority. First, there are authoritative *things*: texts, rituals, practices, and so on. The US constitution is clearly an authoritative text in the United States. The Bible is an authoritative text for Christians. Zazen—a type of meditation—is an authoritative practice for Zen Buddhists.

A second type of authority is linked to religious *figures* or social *positions* above one in a social hierarchy. For instance, the Dalai Lama is an authoritative figure for Tibetan Buddhism. The pope is an authoritative figure for Catholicism. The president is an authoritative figure in the United States. For those who claim to be adherents to these traditions, the actions or commands of these authoritative figures have a special, important, or sacred status. US citizens aren't expected to follow what the president of Iran says, but they are expected to respect the authority of the American president. The same goes for authoritative figures in religious social hierarchies.

The authority of figures in a social hierarchy is almost always maintained by some set of visual markers or social practices. In the military, subordinates have to salute superiors; in addition, every military person wears insignia that designates her place in the social hierarchy and whether she bears authority over others. US presidents do not have authoritative status as president until they pass through a swearing-in ceremony. One minute before being sworn in, Barack Obama was *not* president; one minute after, he *was* president. This sort of ritual is not just window dressing—it is fundamental to establishing a figure's authority. When President Kennedy died in 1963, his vice president—Lyndon B. Johnson—knew that he wouldn't carry the authority of a president until he was sworn in. Consequently, on the plane ride from Dallas, Texas (where Kennedy was shot) back to Washington, DC, Johnson was sworn in. In addition, he had Kennedy's widow—Jackie Onassis—witness the swearing-in ceremony. Johnson was smart—he knew that once this was announced upon his arrival in DC before the cameras, it would solidify his position as the new president (see Kertzer 1988, 57ff). Similarly, the pope's hat is not worn just for fashion reasons, but to mark his place at the top of the social hierarchy.

A third type of authority—the most important type, arguably—involves *absent* authority figures. Examples of absent authority figures would include gods, saints, bodhisattvas, and other types of divine or dead figures. Gods and goddesses, Jesus, the Buddha, Krishna, and similar figures are different from the former type of authoritative figures because they are, in some important way, absent. If one has the right connections, one could call up the current Dalai Lama, pope, or US president, and ask them what they think about particular social or moral issues. By contrast, one can't call up Jesus and ask him what he thinks. If one attributes a view to the Dalai Lama that he doesn't hold, he can challenge it or contest it; he can always hold a press conference and publicly declare: "I did not say that!" Absent authority figures cannot do so. The so-called "founding fathers" of the United States are authoritative figures, but they are long since dead and therefore absent. If one says they were in support of separation of church and state or against separation of church and state, there is pretty much nothing they can do about it—they are absent and cannot object.

Authoritative texts, insofar as their authors are absent, are very similar to absent authority figures: people can offer interpretations of a text, but if the author is gone, the text is open to continual interpretation and reinterpretation. Neither dead figures nor authoritative texts can contest the views attributed to them. For this reason we can consider absent authority figures and authoritative texts side by side in what follows.

Because absent authority figures and texts with missing authors cannot contest the views attributed to them, they are more open to what scholars call "projection." In a sense, projection is just like ventriloquism: when ventriloquism takes place, a ventriloquist projects her voice onto a dummy—making it seem as if her voice is actually coming from the dummy. Similarly, religious practitioners will often project their own views on absent authoritative figures or authoritative texts, which they effectively use as dummies. These absent authoritative figures make good dummies precisely because they're absent—they are not around to contest the words being put into their mouths.

Why would someone project their views on an authoritative figure? The answer is simple: these figures carry more authority than most other people do. If John Doe tells Jane Doe that she should support gay rights, she probably wouldn't much care—John Doe is nobody of importance. However, if Jane is a Buddhist and John can convince her that the Buddha would support gay rights, that would carry a lot more authority. If she is a Muslim and he could convince her that Allah or Muhammad would support gay rights, that would carry a lot more authority. In short, most religious practitioners are nobodies— but their words can be made to carry a great deal of authority if they can successfully put their words into the mouth of an absent authority figure.

That projection takes place is undeniable. The figures of the Buddha and Jesus provide us with perhaps the best examples. In the Buddhist tradition, an indefinite number of sutras (i.e., teachings) are attributed to the Buddha. The Lotus Sutra, for instance, begins with the following narration: "At that time the World-Honored One [i.e., the Buddha] calmly arose from his samadhi [i.e., a type of meditation] and addressed Shariputra, saying: 'The wisdom of the Buddhas is infinitely profound and immeasurable'" (Watson 2002, 1). The rest of the sutra is narrated as a conversation between the Buddha and his audience. However, the text is almost definitely dated at least a few centuries after the Buddha died. There are thousands of similar sutras; they were written after the Buddha died, but pretend to offer the actual words of the Buddha himself.

In *The Invention of Sacred Tradition*, Olav Hammer and James Lewis point out that almost all religious traditions falsely attribute texts to absent authority figures. "Why does nearly every religion have spurious traditions and misattributed texts?" (Hammer and Lewis 2007, 4). Their own answer is that attributing texts to a founder or other ancient figure "confers legitimacy to religious claims and practices" (Hammer and Lewis 2007, 4). Their book offers evidence that this sort of falsification has happened in Scientology, Mormonism, Christianity, Zoroastrianism, Judaism, and various forms of paganism.

> The authority gained by projecting one's tradition into a legendary past . . . can serve several purposes. . . . [In part], inventing one's history enables religious innovators to shape the tradition of which they are part by ascribing at times radically new ideas to ancient, founding figures.
>
> (Hammer and Lewis 2007, 6)

That is, innovations are passed off as if they were ancient, thereby giving them an air of authority they might not otherwise have had.

Consider the example of Jesus: not only do many scholars believe that many of the words attributed to Jesus in the New Testament did not originate with him, but it is clear that throughout history various "interpretations" of those words in the New Testament have involved projection. About a hundred years ago, Albert Schweitzer (1910) wrote a book called *The Quest of the Historical Jesus* in which he surveyed a series of nineteenth-century biographies of Jesus. What did he find? They all reflected nineteenth-century values. More recently historian Jaroslav Pelikan (1985) wrote a book called *Jesus through the Centuries* in which he surveyed views of Jesus from the first century to the present. Stephen Prothero (2003) wrote a book called *American Jesus: How the Son of God became a National Icon* in which he surveyed the views of Jesus from the beginning of the United States to the present. Olav Hammer (2009) edited a volume on *Alternative Christs* that surveyed a wide variety of visions of Jesus outside so-called orthodox Christianity.

All of these works find that in every time period, people remake Jesus in ways that reflect the social, moral, and political concerns of their own age. Glancing at only a few examples will "show how the interests of each epoch are echoed in emerging alternative Christ themes" (Hammer 2009, 280). To offer just one instance, Jesus has often been co-opted for Marxist and socialist projects. Lyman Abbott, a socialist Christian writer from the late nineteenth century, provides us with a clear example of projection in his *Christianity and Social Problems.* There Abbott explains that slavery gave way to feudalism in the Middle Ages, and that feudalism gave way to capitalism in the modern period. Under the capitalist economic system, there arose a sharp class distinction between capitalists and laborers. What should Christians make of this state of affairs? "The general effect of Christ's teaching, and of human development under its inspiration, is to abolish the class distinction between capitalist and laborer, as other class distinctions have been abolished" (Abbott 1899, 163). Although he has already told his reader that the class distinction between capitalists and laborers *did not exist* until the modern period, he projects this Marxist position onto a first-century Jesus. To be fair to Abbott, we should note that he deploys the strategy of projection not to serve his own selfish interests or to bring about some sort of repressive social control—he seems genuinely to intend to bring about social effects that would relieve some of the burdens of poverty. Nevertheless, his interpretation is obviously projective. Abbot's interpretation of Jesus tells us more about his Marxist values than it does about Jesus himself.

Take a few minutes to surf the web, or go down to a local bookstore, and see how many different books you can find about Jesus. There are books that portray Jesus as a communist, and there are books that portray Jesus as a capitalist. There are books that portray Jesus as against gay rights, and there are books that portray Jesus as supporting gay rights. Whatever social, moral, or political position one can find, someone has probably written a book saying that Jesus would support that position. Logically speaking, Jesus simply could not have held all these positions—and perhaps not any of them, since they all concern nineteenth, twentieth, and twenty-first century issues, and Jesus lived in the first century. That Jesus has been made to support so many contradictory social positions is proof that *projection has to be taking place at least some of the time.*

Return-to-Origins Narratives and False Universalism

Projection often takes a very specific form, which scholars call a "return-to-origins" narrative. A return-to-origins narrative involves positing a "pure" origin of a religious tradition, which was followed by a "corruption" of the original message. The narrative is used to authorize one's own position as "pure" while portraying one's opponents' position as "corrupt." Much of the propaganda produced by the Protestant reformers took this shape: they insisted that Jesus' original message was perfect, but that when the Catholic church formed, the church leaders distorted Jesus' message to serve their own interests. By contrast, Protestants claimed their views were closer to Jesus' original message than the Catholics' distortions or abominations. The problem, of course, is that the Protestants were, to some extent, simply projecting their own view onto the "origin" they claimed to be returning to.

In the US, we see return-to-origins narratives in discussions of the so-called "founding fathers," as well as debates about the meaning of the constitution (the people who favor going back to the constitution's "original meaning" literally call themselves "originalists"). Consider Peter A. Lillback's book, *George Washington's Sacred Fire* (2006). Frustrated with the common claim that Washington was a deist rather than a Christian, Lillback sets out to demonstrate conclusively that Washington was, in fact, a believing Christian. Lillback is up front about the fact that this is a concern precisely because people tend to reinvent the past to reflect their interests:

> [o]ne of the interesting proofs of the significance of George Washington in American history is that we read into him what we want to see. To a secularist, Washington was a secularist. To a Christian, Washington was a church-going believer. It is natural that people want to make Washington in their own image.
>
> (Lillback 2006, 26)

Why does Lillback care? As a Christian himself, he wants the US to get back to its Christian origins:

> [w]here a nation began determines its destiny. . . . If we look carefully at Washington's words, it is clear that [he was ignited by] a "sacred fire" [of faith]. Throughout the rest of this book, we will continue carefully to consider his words. And as we do so, we believe they will

fuel the "sacred fire of liberty" and *continue to illumine the path to America's future.*

(emphasis added; 35)

As is clear, Lillback's interest in Washington is not out of a concern for the past but out of a concern for the future. And, as a Christian himself, he *wants* to find a Christian Washington, so that he can call America to return to Lillback's preferred "origin."

It is clear that many of Lillback's readers feel similarly. Consider the following reviews from the book's Amazon.com page (spelling and punctuation all original):

- George Washington was a man of honor and this book brings that out. We need another President like him.
- All these haters because it has conservative points of view? Guess what, our founding fathers were more conservative than all but a handfull of republicans. We're becoming a "sissy version" of what we once were.
- [Washington's] devout belief in Divine Providence as it relates to the founding of this nation was unshakable. An inspiration to anyone who has even just one patriotic bone in their body.
- Makes you want to be involved in taking America back from the lying looting thugs!!
- Our contempary congress should take a clue from him.
- Good for the kids to read inorder for them to know why America was founded and why we need GOD back in our country.

For these readers the book serves as a useful moral guide and a return-to-origins narrative—for them, the US has gotten away from its authentic, Christian origins, modeled by Washington, and we must turn away from our corrupt detours and return to Washington's ideal.

One other unique form of projection takes place when people make the claim that "all religions" teach the same moral code; we can call this "false universalism." What happens is that people take their own particular moral code, project it onto all religions, and claim to have found it there. If all religions make the same claims, they must be true, right? Although the historical record reveals that there are always *some* similarities in moral codes across world cultures, there is much more difference than there is similarity. In addition, even though a moral rule like "don't murder" appears to be more or less universal, what counts as murder varies from culture to culture. Yes, murder is prohibited everywhere, but what counts as murder in one country might be considered self-defense in another, and killing women or slaves might be called murder in some cultures but considered legal in others. Once we look at the details, the prohibition of "murder" is universal in name only, and the actual moral codes differ widely from context to context. However, by ignoring the very real diversity across world cultures and projecting one's view onto them, one can pass off one's view as universally authoritative.

In his self-help book, *The Power of Now*, Eckhart Tolle does precisely this. He claims to have discovered the teachings in his book by surveying the world's religions: "When I occasionally quote the words of Jesus or the Buddha . . . I do so not in order to compare, but to draw your attention to the fact that in *essence* there is always and has been only one spiritual teaching, although it comes in many forms" (Tolle 1999, 9). By claiming he has discovered the "essence" of all religious teachings, he's asserting a universal authority for his own particular ideology. However, if we carefully compare his ideology with the teachings of the historical figures he cites, we'll quickly see that he's projected, not found, his view in other cultures—his universalism is a false universalism.

Authoritative Figures as Mirrors

Most people have seen a Rorschach inkblot, such as is shown in Figure 8.1. This is how Rorschach tests are supposed to work: the idea is that a psychologist will show an inkblot to a patient and ask her what she sees—her answer

Figure 8.1 Rorschach inkblot (© 2011 Kathleen Roepken, reproduced with permission)

is, theoretically, supposed to shed light on what's going on in her unconscious mind. If one says, "I see myself stabbing my mother to death with a knife," then the psychologist has probably discovered something interesting about one's unconscious desires. What the patient "sees" in an inkblot theoretically tells us more about the patient than it does about the inkblot itself.

Similarly, much of what religious practitioners say about absent authoritative figures tells us more about *them* than it does about the authoritative figures themselves. If a Buddhist practitioner claims that adherence to the message of the Buddha demands that we give equal rights to gays and lesbians, this probably tells us a lot more about *the practitioner's views* than about the Buddha himself. When people ask themselves "What would Jesus do?," their answer is pretty much always the same as the answer to the question "What do *I think* I should do?" The same goes whether we're talking about the Buddha, Jesus, Allah, Avalokiteshvara, Krishna, or whomever.

One group of social scientists created a set of studies to test this claim (Epley *et al.* 2009). They surveyed Americans, asking them to report their perceptions of the political views of others, specifically on topics such as abortion, same-sex marriage, the death penalty, affirmative action, etc. They asked participants' own views, and then asked them to estimate the views of millionaire Bill Gates, then-president George W. Bush, the "average American," and God. Not surprisingly, individuals' own views most correlated with their reports of God's view. Statistically, whatever the individuals thought was morally correct was closest to their reports of what God thought. That is, it appears that *God served as a mirror for their own views.*

Not satisfied with this result, the researchers went a bit further. In a follow-up study, after their initial survey of participants they asked participants to read persuasive policy statements arguing a view on affirmative action contrary to what the subjects first reported. Then they polled the subjects a second time, and they found that some participants' views on affirmative action had shifted. In addition, they also found a correlation between participants' changing views and their report of God's view—that is, *when the participants' views changed, they also attributed that same change to God.* Again, it appears that God served as a mirror for their own views. The researchers concluded that although the "Jewish and Christian traditions state explicitly that God created man in his own image," it rather appears to be the other way around (21533).

Is projection intentional? That is, do religious practitioners *intentionally manipulate* their audiences by projecting their values onto authoritative figures? It would be naïve to suggest that projection is *never* intentional, but it seems unlikely that it is intentional most of the time. In fact, it appears that most people are unselfconscious and unreflective about the rhetoric they use. Interpreters develop what Pierre Bourdieu calls a "practical sense," which allows them to intuit the stakes of religious debates and negotiate them by responding in ways that both reflect their prior assumptions and serve their future interests (see Chapter 6). For Bourdieu, one's practical sense is "second nature," and, as such, arguments are executed naturally, without hesitation, and without conscious reflection.

From the assumptions that the Bible is good and that sexism is bad, it is a short leap to the conclusion that the Bible must be opposed to sexism. Similarly, other interpreters can easily come to alternative conclusions if their practical sense is predisposed to different assumptions: "God made men and women fundamentally different, so wouldn't it follow that God wants men and women to have different social roles?" From this assumption it is a short leap to the conclusion that the sexist social roles prescribed in some parts of the Bible rightly reflect the way God intended the world to function optimally. While some might argue that this is an overly cynical view, there is no other way to account for the great number of fundamentally opposed "interpretations" that can come out of a single figure or text. In any case, this way of accounting for the differences in interpretation need not assume that devotees manipulate their traditions knowingly or intentionally—most of the time projection is performed *unreflectively*.

Authority and Audience

To be more precise, we must note that "authority" is not some magical property that simply resides in a figure or a text. When we say that things, people, or absent figures are authoritative, we do not want to imply that there is something special about them in and of themselves. The Torah is not an authority by itself—it is authoritative only for a community that recognizes it as authoritative. There are billions of people in the world who do not hold the Torah to be an authoritative text, and it probably means little to them. The Torah's authoritative status is not rooted in the Torah itself, but in the community that gives it a sacred status.

Because authority is not intrinsic but rather conferred by a community, it can best be understood as a relationship between three elements. Consider textual authority: the authority of a text is an effect produced by a triangular relationship between (1) a text, (2) its interpreters, and (3) various audiences. In addition, for projection to function successfully, interpreters must mystify or obscure their role in that triangular relationship. Audiences must *misrecognize* the meaning given by the interpreter as residing in the text itself—the active contributions of the interpreter to the "meaning" of the text have to remain hidden. In other words, projection works only when an audience cannot tell that projection is taking place. I can manipulate you by projecting my words onto the figure of Buddha only if you cannot see that that is what I am doing—if you knew I was projecting, you would stop listening to me. Most of the time, it seems, projection *does* remain invisible. Interpreters of sacred texts

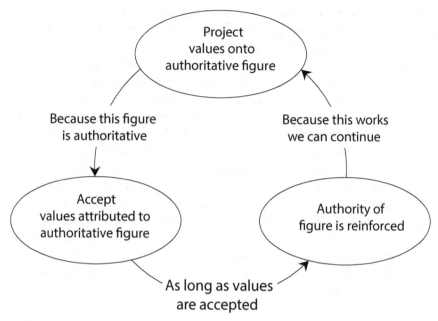

Figure 8.2 The circular relation between authority and projection (© 2011 Valissa Hicks, reproduced with permission).

are usually better than magicians at hiding their sleight of hand. As a result, in a sense "authority . . . is primarily in the hands of those who control the texts" (Rothstein 2007, 27). When an audience's behavior can be directed by a skillful interpreter who invisibly manipulates a text the audience reveres, the authority of the text is simultaneously the authority of the interpreter.

In addition, there is a circular relationship here between projection and authority. People project their values onto Jesus or Buddha, for instance, only if those figures are widely hailed as authoritative. However, doing so perpetuates within the community the idea that they should listen to what Jesus or Buddha has to say. The strategy of projection reinforces the authority of whatever is subjected to projection (Figure 8.2). Even if a Marxist's interpretation of Jesus persuades her audience to support socialism, *the audience still thinks it is following Jesus* rather than Marx, and as such Jesus' authority is further naturalized.

Selective Privileging

One of the difficulties that comes with using authoritative figures or authoritative texts is that sometimes they say more than you want them to say. For instance, texts like the Bible or the Qur'an sometimes resist projection, simply because there might be parts of them that contradict the message you want to project onto them. When interpreters run up against passages in their authoritative text they don't like, they tend to select and privilege other parts of the text. In fact, we all pick and choose what we like from our cultural traditions and ignore what we don't like—which is why those fans of George Washington mentioned above might want to focus on Washington's possible Christian faith but will probably ignore the fact that he was a slave owner.

Michael Cook points out how this often works with modern Muslim interpreters of the Qur'an. He notes that religious practitioners are interested in authoritative texts because of what contemporary relevance they can be made to have:

> The text needs to be interpreted because, having been composed a long time ago . . . it now contains much that is at first sight obscure, irrelevant, or disconcerting. This means that the commentator has a tendency to approach the text with the presuppositions and concerns of his own time, and may seek to realign the meaning of the text accordingly. Rarely is he concerned to answer a strictly historical question of the form: "Never mind what this means to us now, what exactly did it mean to them then?"
>
> (Cook 2000, 28)

From a scholarly standpoint, looking at how a text was understood in its original context is completely different from looking at how a text has been recycled over time in other contexts. Because religious practitioners want to make old texts relevant for their own times, they will privilege those parts of the texts that are easier to fit to their own presuppositions, or those parts of the texts onto which they can most easily project their own views.

Cook shows how this is the case with interpretations of the Qur'an on the question of tolerance. What does the Qur'an say about whether Muslims should tolerate people in other communities? Cook points out that it actually says *multiple* things. On the one hand, there is what Cook calls the "sword verse":

> wherever you find the idolaters, kill them, besiege them, wait for them at every lookout post; but if they turn [to God], maintain the prayer, and pay the prescribed alms, let them go on their way, for God is most forgiving and merciful.
>
> (Abdel Haleem 2004, 116)

According to this passage, people who worship other gods (which are merely idols, according to the Qur'an) should be killed unless they convert. There is, however, a qualification in the same section for Jews and Christians, who are called "the People of the Book": "Fight those of the People of the Book who do

131

not [truly] believe in God and the Last Day, who do not forbid what God and His Messenger have forbidden, who do not obey the rule of justice, until they pay the tax and agree to submit" (Abdel Haleem 2004, 118). Apparently, idolaters are to be slain, but Jews and Christians will only be required to pay a tax or a fine—although if they do not pay they should be fought by Muslims. However, Cook rightly points out that "these two verses do not represent the full range of Koranic statements bearing on the question" (Cook 2000, 35). In an entirely different section of the Qur'an we find this passage, which Cook calls the "no compulsion" verse: "There is no compulsion in religion: true guidance has become distinct from error, so whoever rejects false gods and believes in God has grasped the firmest hand-hold, one that will never break" (Abdel Haleem 2004, 29). According to this passage, the difference between truth and falsehood is obvious, so there is no sense in forcing people to join Islam. Cook points out that the "sword verse" is the one privileged by Muslims who are militant about Islam. By contrast, for most contemporary Muslims—who are not militant—the "no compulsion" verse is "literally a godsend, scriptural proof that Islam is a religion of broad and general toleration" (Cook 2000, 35). One famous interpreter of the Qur'an, Sayyid Qutb, utilized the "no compulsion" verse to demonstrate that Islam was the original religion of toleration. Despite the fact that Qutb was himself a militant, he insisted that "[f]reedom of belief . . . is fundamental to human rights, and it was Islam that first proclaimed this value" (Cook 2000, 35). Even a militant can interpret the text in a liberal fashion. Whatever the text says about toleration depends in part on what the reader wants it to say—there is often enough ambiguity that one can wrestle out of it the message one wants.

The Bible is very much the same. In the Bible the Israelites' god tells them to conquer a number of cities filled with idolaters, and to kill every living thing in those cities. That is, they are not to show mercy even to women or children, as some ancients wanted to do:

> when the Lord your God gives them over to you and you defeat them, then you must utterly destroy them. Make no covenant with them and show them no mercy. Do not intermarry with them, giving your daughters to their sons or taking their daughters for your sons, for that would turn away your children from following me, to serve other gods. Then the anger of the Lord would be kindled against you, and he would destroy you quickly. But this is how you must deal with them: break down their altars, smash their pillars, hew down their sacred poles, and burn their idols with fire.
>
> (Deuteronomy 7:2–5)

In a nearby passage the Israelites' god tells them to beware psychics and false prophets:

> If prophets or those who divine by dreams appear among you and
> promise you omens or portents, and the omens or the portents
> declared by them take place, and they say, "Let us follow other gods" . . .
> you must not heed the words of those prophets or those who divine by
> dreams; for the Lord your God is testing you. . . . But those prophets
> or those who divine by dreams shall be put to death.
>
> (Deuteronomy 13:1–5)

Palm readers and fortune tellers should beware—the Bible says they should be
put to death.

These sorts of rigorous demands are present in the New Testament as well.
To begin with, in the Sermon on the Mount Jesus insists that his followers must
keep following the laws prescribed in the Hebrew scriptures; in fact, he says
they have to follow the law *more closely* than they have been. Jesus explicitly
states, "whoever breaks one of the least of these commandments, and teaches
others to do the same, will be called least in the kingdom of heaven" (Matthew
5:19). So, according to Jesus, those demands made on the ancient Israelites—
such as the demand to kill idolaters—are still in place.

In addition, Jesus makes absolute oppositions between following him
and every other commitment one might make—and there are serious consequences for falling on the wrong side. In the gospel of Luke, Jesus says his
followers must hate their family members: "Whoever comes to me and does
not hate father and mother, wife and children, brothers and sisters, yes, and
even life itself, cannot be my disciple" (Luke 14:26). In the gospel of Matthew,
Jesus says: "I have come to set a man against his father, and a daughter against
her mother, and a daughter-in-law against her mother-in-law; and one's foes
will be members of one's own household" (Matthew 10:35–6). Throughout
the gospels Jesus makes it clear that if one does not follow his teachings,
there will be a severe penalty: "You that are accursed, depart from me into
the eternal fire prepared for the devil and his angels" (Matthew 25:41). One
of Jesus' teachings in Matthew is that one should avoid not only adultery but
also lust—so much so that it is better to cut one's eye out rather than commit
an act of lust:

> You have heard that it was said, "You shall not commit adultery."
> But I say to you that everyone who looks at a woman with lust has
> already committed adultery with her in his heart. If your right eye
> causes you to sin, tear it out and throw it away; it is better for you to
> lose one of your members than for your whole body to be thrown
> into hell.
>
> (Matthew 5:27–29)

Jesus' lustful followers have a choice, then, between hell or losing an eye.
Jesus did not come to be a friend; on the contrary, he says, "Do not think that

I have come to bring peace to the earth; I have not come to bring peace, but a sword" (Matthew 10:34).

However, whether Christians privilege these violent passages in the Bible or something much more amenable to contemporary values—like the "love your neighbor" passages—will depend on what Christians want the Bible to say. Many people claim to take the Bible as "literally" true in all respects, but none of them hate their father or mother, and none of them have cut off pieces of their body (although there was a famous rumor that circulated in ancient Christianity that Origen—one of the church fathers—cut off his genitalia because he believed they were causing him to lust). Instead, even people who claim to take the Bible as "literally" true actually choose to privilege more agreeable passages and ignore these more difficult ones, as *all* religious practitioners do.

An open letter to the conservative Christian radio talk-show host "Dr Laura" circulated on the internet a few years ago, and it highlights very clearly and humorously an example of selective privileging. The anonymous author of this letter states the following (which I quote in full):

> Dear Dr Laura,
>
> Thank you for doing so much to educate people regarding God's law. I have learned a great deal from your show, and I try to share that knowledge with as many people as I can. When someone tries to defend the homosexual lifestyle, for example, I simply remind him that Leviticus 18:22 clearly states it to be an abomination. End of debate.
>
> I do need some advice from you, however, regarding some of the [other] specific laws and how to best follow them.
>
> a) When I burn a bull on the altar as a sacrifice, I know it creates a pleasing odor for the Lord (Leviticus 1:9). The problem is my neighbors. They claim the odor is not pleasing to them. Should I smite them?
>
> b) I would like to sell my daughter into slavery, as sanctioned in Exodus 21:7. In this day and age, what do you think would be a fair price for her?
>
> c) I know that I am allowed no contact with a woman while she is in her period of menstrual uncleanliness (Leviticus 15:19–24). The problem is, how do I tell? I have tried asking, but most women take offense.
>
> d) Leviticus 25:44 states that I may indeed possess slaves, both male and female, provided they are purchased from neighboring nations. A friend of mine claims that this applies to Mexicans, but not Canadians. Can you clarify? Why can't I own Canadians?

e) I have a neighbor who insists on working on the Sabbath. Exodus 35:2 clearly states he should be put to death. Am I morally obligated to kill him myself?

f) A friend of mine feels that even though eating shellfish is an abomination (Leviticus 11:10), it is a lesser abomination than homosexuality. I don't agree. Can you settle this?

g) Leviticus 21:20 states that I may not approach the altar of God if I have a defect in my sight. I have to admit that I wear reading glasses. Does my vision have to be 20/20, or is there some wiggle room here?

h) Most of my male friends get their hair trimmed, including the hair around their temples, even though this is expressly forbidden by Leviticus 19:27. How should they die?

i) I know from Leviticus 11:6–8 that touching the skin of a dead pig makes me unclean, but may I still play football if I wear gloves?

j) My uncle has a farm. He violates Leviticus 19:19 by planting two different crops in the same field, as does his wife by wearing garments made of two different kinds of thread (cotton/polyester blend). He also tends to curse and blaspheme a lot. Is it really necessary that we go to all the trouble of getting the whole town together to stone them? (Leviticus 24:10–16). Couldn't we just burn them to death at a private family affair like we do with people who sleep with their in-laws? (Leviticus 20:14)

I know you have studied these things extensively, so I am confident you can help.

Thank you again for reminding us that God's word is eternal and unchanging.

Your devoted disciple and adoring fan.

What this author clearly points out in this satirical letter is that Dr Laura selectively focuses on the passages on male sexuality while blatantly ignoring the surrounding passages. Whether or not Jews or Christians focus on the heterosexist passages probably depends not on something intrinsic to the text but rather on the norms or political preferences of their own community. Selective privileging permits one to sort through authoritative texts and find what one wants to find.

Challenging Authority

Regnant authorities are often subjected to challenge, particularly when they are being utilized to legitimate social agendas that work against some group's interests. There are at least three different ways one could challenge a regnant authority:

1 one can point to competing authorities,
2 one can offer internal critique, or
3 one can offer external critique.

First, one could challenge authority simply by calling into question the self-evident privilege accorded to that authority, especially when there are *competing* authorities. Why, for instance, should I follow Jesus rather than Zoroaster? Why should I follow the New Testament rather than the Zend Avesta? Are there good reasons for following one god rather than another?

The philosopher Jean-Jacques Rousseau was one of the best at pointing out some of the problems with appealing to authority. In one of his books we can hear his own voice coming out through one of his fictional characters, who says the following:

> I considered all the different sects that reign on earth and accuse each other of falsehood and error, and I asked, "Which one is right?"
>
> "Mine!" answered everyone. "Only I and those who agree with me think rightly; everyone else is mistaken."
>
> "How do you know that your sect is the right one?"
>
> "God said so."
>
> "And who told you that God said so?"
>
> "My minister. He knows. He told me to believe it, and I do. He assures me that those who say anything different are liars, so I do not listen to them."
>
> (Rousseau 1983, 271–2)

However, insofar as ministers disagree with one another, which ones should people trust? Rousseau's character goes on to challenge his imagined debate partners, and they respond:

> "God himself has spoken; listen to his revelation."
>
> "That is another matter. God has spoken! What an impressive statement! To whom has he spoken?"
>
> "To men."
>
> "Then why have I heard none of his words?"
>
> "He has told other men to report them to you."
>
> "I understand: it is men who will tell me what God has said.
>
> I would rather have heard God himself; it would have been no more difficult for him, and it would have protected me from being misled."
>
> "He protects you from it by proving that his spokesmen were really sent by him."
>
> "How does he prove that?"

"By miracles."

"Where are those miracles?"

"In books."

"Who wrote those books?"

"Men."

"And who saw the miracles?"

"Men who attest to them."

"What! Always human testimony! Always men who report to me what other men have reported! How many men there are between God and myself!"

(Rousseau 1983, 273)

Rousseau's conclusion is that determining which authorities to trust tends to depend not on evidence (because the evidence is always handed down by other authorities), but rather on accident of birth: if one is born in a Christian country one will probably trust the Bible, and if one is born in a Muslim country one will probably trust the Qur'an. For Rousseau, accident of birth is not a very reliable way of determining which religious traditions are true.

Rousseau's critique calls authorities into question on the basis of the fact there are so many of them: why would we trust some and not others? This is a serious challenge to taken-for-granted authorities. How does one really know one is not worshipping the wrong god? And, perhaps, how does one know there are any gods at all?

The second type of challenge to authority is what scholars call *internal critique*. Internal critique involves the identification of tensions or contradictions *within* a figure's message or *within* the message of a particular text or collection of texts. In the Bhagavad Gita, for instance, the god Krishna says "I exist in all creatures," but then goes on to say the opposite: "all creatures exist in me, but I do not exist in them" (Miller 1986, 67, 83). Which is it? Does he exist in all creatures or does he not? There are many such contradictions or tensions in the Bible as well. In Genesis 1, God creates non-human animals before he creates humans, but in Genesis 2 God creates a man before he creates non-human animals. In the New Testament, the gospels disagree on which day Jesus died on the cross. One story in the gospels claims that Jesus once went into the Jewish temple and threw out the moneychangers; however, one of the gospels claims he did this at the beginning of his career as a teacher, while the other three say he did it the week before he died. Both the gospel of Matthew and the gospel of Luke recount Jesus' genealogy, and not only are they very different when they get deep into his forefathers, but they cannot even agree on who his grandfather was. These criticisms are examples of *internal critique*, since they all point to some tension or contradiction *internal to* a particular text or body of texts.

The third type of challenge to authority is what scholars call *external critique*. External critique involves weighing the value of a text or a figure's message against some external criterion. Internal critique would compare, for instance, one part of a text to another part within the same text, whereas external critique would compare the text to something outside the text altogether. Hector Avalos provides us with a stark example of external critique of the Bible. Avalos points out all of the following:

- The description of the creation of the world in the Bible is contradicted by almost all forms of modern scientific inquiry (Avalos 2009, 50; Avalos 2007, 17).
- At some points the Bible recommends genocidal practices, which is clearly morally wrong by modern standards (Avalos 2009, 50).
- Much of the Bible is patriarchal in its orientation and recommendations, and patriarchy is clearly morally wrong by modern standards (Avalos 2007, 18).

In each instance the critique is external: Avalos appeals both to scientific research and ethical norms *outside* the Bible to critique the Bible. Every once in a while external critique is simply dismissed by religious practitioners; if a group believes the Bible is entirely divine, then the patriarchal stuff in there must be right, even if it appears wrong to others (if that is their view, internal critique is more likely to gain traction, since internal critique points out contradictions *within* the text itself).

Responding to Challenges

How do people respond to challenges to their sacred authorities? On the one hand, they could simply dismiss or ignore the challenge. In fact, this is probably what most people do. How does one know it is right to follow the Buddha as opposed to Muhammad, or Ahura Mazda as opposed to Yahweh? Most people ignore the objection and take it for granted that the authorities they have inherited from their parents are the most trustworthy ones.

However, if religious practitioners want to take more seriously criticisms of their authorities, how might they respond? A common response is wishful thinking. Let me offer just one example. When I was a freshman in college I took an introductory course on the Bible, and was introduced to the fact that there are two conflicting accounts of Goliath's death in the Hebrew scriptures (cf. I Samuel 17 and II Samuel 21). Undaunted by what I took to be only an *apparent* contradiction, I quickly raised my hand and suggested that perhaps it was possible that "Goliath" was a common nickname for big and tall men in ancient Palestine; if that were the case, there may have been many Goliaths running around back then, and different accounts of the death of Goliath were not really contradictory but simply the accounts of two *different* Goliaths. Such speculation, of course, originated not in my informed knowledge of ancient

Near Eastern languages, cultures, and practices (I had no informed knowledge of these matters), but in my *wish* that these stories did not conflict with one another. I resolved the contradiction with *wishful thinking*—in my mind they were not contradictory because I did not want to believe they could be contradictory.

Wishful thinking is a typical response to these sorts of challenges to authority. If one *wants* to believe that the Bible is perfect, my speculation that there were two Goliaths might be persuasive—despite the fact that there is no justification for this interpretation other than that we *want it to be true* (that is, there is no historical evidence whatsoever for this reading of the text). If one *wants to believe* that Jesus should be trusted over Muhammad, or that the Zend Avesta should be trusted over the Bible, Rousseau's objections are unlikely to make a dent in one's wishful thinking.

Another response to external critique could be partial *rejection*: many religious practitioners simply reject part of their tradition as outdated, outmoded, or just plain wrong in some respects. For instance, I once met a theologian who said that he accepted Jesus' ethical teachings, but rejected Jesus' claims about the fact that the end of the world was near. Since this sort of rejection is partial, practitioners can save the authoritative figure or text in general.

Finally, we should consider a very specific type of rejection: the *refusal to extrapolate*. What is extrapolation? Extrapolation consists of taking a specific principle, idea, or rule in a text and attempting to fit it to an alternative context. Extrapolation asks: "perhaps this text meant this for them, but they lived in a different context—how can we make this relevant for our own context?" One example of extrapolation is provided by the ways in which Shari'a law (the body of Islamic jurisprudence) is interpreted with respect to rules about fermented drinks. Shari'a law forbids the consumption of fermented drinks made from grapes and dates. However, it says nothing explicit about the consumption of vodka or rum. In order to see the injunction as also applying to vodka or rum, one must extrapolate from a principle assumed to be present in the rule. For instance, one could argue that what is essential to the rule is the prohibition of foods or drinks that have incapacitating effects on one's body and mind. Although it doesn't mention vodka in the injunction, vodka is one such drink that has incapacitating effects. As a result, one could *extrapolate* that the injunction should cover vodka in addition to wine made from grapes.

Unlike extrapolation, which attempts to make some part of a text relevant in an alternative context, a *refusal to extrapolate* attempts to undermine any possibility of extrapolation. Rather than say "how can we make this relevant for our own context?," the refusal to extrapolate attempts to show something like the following: "the context in which this text was written was so different from our own context that there is nothing in it that is relevant for us any longer." This mode of interpretation links the text so radically to its context of authorship that any attempt to draw contemporary relevance is foreclosed. In sum, the refusal to extrapolate says: "this part of the text is past its expiration date."

One might think that the refusal to extrapolate challenges the authority of the text, but it does not. Although the refusal to extrapolate suggests that some part of a text may no longer be applicable, given that circumstances are rather different from those of the original audience, this mode of interpretation separates out some part of the text as irrelevant or no longer applicable, *in contrast with* the other parts of the text that *are still relevant* and still applicable. The text retains its authority, but some parts of it apply only in certain circumstances. This interpretive move is necessary for those who do not want to dismiss the applicability or authority of a text altogether. For instance, many people are willing to dismiss the authority of the text: some people are free to say, "I don't care what the Qur'an says about sex, marriage, gender, homosexuality, or whatever—I derive my moral norms on these matters from other sources." Those who perform a refusal to extrapolate typically do so because they cannot say this. In effect, their position is usually the following: "the Qur'an is still an important authority; it is just that this small part of it is no longer applicable." In adopting this position they get to have their cake and eat it too—the text remains authoritative and parts of it remain applicable, but they can reject those parts they are uncomfortable with. In summary, the refusal to extrapolate deals with challenges to the authority of a text by rejecting one part of the text as out of date, while simultaneously upholding the authority of the text in general.

Authority Is Complicated

In conclusion, authority is an extremely complicated matter. Although religious practitioners frequently hold particular figures or sacred texts as authoritative, that doesn't mean they follow their authorities in any simple or straightforward manner. On the contrary, authorities are often subjected to projection, selective privileging, partial rejection, the refusal to extrapolate, and so on. Knowing who or what some group holds as authoritative tells us *almost nothing* about them—further investigation into how religious groups use or manipulate the authorities they hold dear is necessary to understand religious practitioners. Bible scholar William Arnal is perhaps correct when he suggests that understanding "the historical Jesus"—that is, the actual Jesus behind the myths, legends, and interpretations—is completely irrelevant for understanding the historical development of Christianity:

> The ultimate goal of historical Jesus studies is to uncover the origins of Christianity itself, to reconstruct the Jesus who is assumed somehow to lie behind this movement as its root *cause*. . . . [However],

ultimately, the *historical* Jesus does not matter, either for our understanding of the past, or our understanding of the present. The historically relevant and interesting causes of the development and growth
of the Christian movement will be found, not in the person of Jesus,
but in the collective machinations, agenda, and vicissitudes of the
movement itself.

(Arnal 2005, 76–7; emphasis original)

That is, Arnal's claim is that understanding Christianity does not really
require us to understand who Jesus really was, but how the figure of Jesus—
as an absent authority—was recreated and recycled over and over in various
historical contexts. On this view, the reinventions of Jesus are more important
than Jesus himself. The same goes for all religious traditions: the "origin" of
a religious tradition is largely irrelevant. Religious traditions are subject to
ongoing recreation and evolution, and focusing our studies on their "origin"
is as misguided as trying to measure the height of an oak tree by looking at
an acorn.

9

How Religion Works: Authenticity

Need it be said that determining the criteria for what is or is not "authentic" is always problematic?

Jean-François Bayart, *The Illusion of Cultural Identity* (2005, 78)

All that is solid melts into air.

Karl Marx and Friedrich Engels, *The Communist Manifesto* (1998, 38)

In 1553, in the city of Geneva, the theologian Michael Servetus was put to death by being burned at the stake. What had he done to be sentenced to this horrible fate? Was he a murderer? A rapist? A thief? He was none of these things: Servetus was put to death for suggesting that the doctrine of the trinity—the belief that the Christian God, Jesus Christ, and the Holy Spirit are all united as one being—was untrue.

What is the trinity? In the sixteenth century, the three largest branches of Christianity in western Europe (the Catholic Church, the Lutheran Church, and the Reformed Church) all held that God, Jesus, and the Holy Spirit were united in one being. The official doctrine was that all three were divine, but that couldn't mean that their church worshiped three different gods— somehow these figures were three and one at the same time. The city of Geneva (where the Reformed Church was in league with the city authorities) convicted Servetus of a capital crime for calling this belief into question. His doubt—and his attempts to persuade others—made him a heretic: someone who claimed to be Christian but really wasn't.

John Calvin, one of the founders of the Reformed Church, requested that the sentence of stake-burning be commuted to beheading, but the city refused. On the 27th of October in the year 1553, Michael Servetus was tied to a stake and burned to death.

Why does Servetus's fate matter to us in the twenty-first century? Servetus's story is just one example of an issue that still has incredible relevance to how religion is used today: the way that the internal unity or internal conformity of a religion is defined and enforced. Or, put another way, it is how people answer this question: Who is like me? Who is really Christian? Or Jewish? Or Hindu? Because of how the Reformed Church in Geneva answered this question—who was *really* Christian and who was not—Michael Servetus was killed. Alleging that someone is *not really* Christian is a game that sometimes has, quite literally, grave consequences. Although we will focus in this chapter on the example of Christianity, this question applies to all cultural traditions.

Who Is a True Christian?

It is not surprising that some of the people who self-identify as Christians don't always get along with other people who identify themselves as Christians. The same is true for any tradition: there are pagans who disagree with pagans, Muslims who disagree with Muslims, and Scientologists who disagree with Scientologists. When there are disagreements between different Christians—especially when the stakes are high—it is not unusual for one group to say about the other: "they're not really Christian." What are we, as scholars, to make of these sorts of claims? How could we go about figuring out who is and isn't actually a Christian? The problem seems to be that every Christian group has their own criteria that they use to determine their group boundaries.

For example, early in the twentieth century, a group of Christians rallied around what they called the five "fundamentals" of Christianity—which is where the term "fundamentalism" comes from. They claimed that one is not a Christian unless one believes that Jesus was divine, that Jesus' mother was a virgin, that Jesus' body rose from the dead, that the Bible was historically accurate in every one of its claims, and that Jesus' death on the cross covers the debt of sin. At the other end of the spectrum, the "death of God" theologians of the 1960s and 1970s identified as Christian, but completely rejected the idea that God existed. One of their battle cries was "God is dead; long live Jesus Christ!" For them, "God" was an authority figure no longer of use to the Christian tradition, which was actually about the message of liberation and compassion spread by Jesus of Nazareth. There are even some churches in North America for people who identify as atheist Christians.

So we have two different groups, both of which self-identify as Christian. But where the one group thinks that belief in God, the virgin birth, the resurrection, etc. are necessary for Christian identity, the other thinks belief in God is dispensable—and may even be harmful—for Christians who want to get at the true heart of Christianity, which is compassion and justice. Meanwhile, most contemporary evangelical Christians think a "born again" personal experience is central to Christianity, many Catholics believe that participation in the Catholic mass is satisfactory, and others identify as "culturally Christian" because they grew up in a Christian community and celebrate Christian rituals and holidays, even though they reject all of Christianity's supernatural beliefs. *Almost every group that identifies as Christian uses different criteria for group membership.*

So, as scholars, what do we do? How do we define the borders of a religion? (Obviously we are coming close to some of the issues discussed in Chapter 3; that is, how do we determine membership in category or classification?) One possible solution is to create what scholars call a "stipulative definition."

A stipulative definition is a working definition that helps to narrow down a complicated set of data for a limited purpose. For instance, a scholar might say something like this: "*For the purposes of this book*, we are using the term 'Christian' to refer to those groups who believe that Jesus is the messiah." Think about it this way: if one were writing a book on "country music," one would have the problem of delimiting what exactly would count as "country music." Would one include John Lee Hooker, Bob Dylan, Neil Young? Would one include the modern, electric-guitar-driven, pop-oriented country, or restrict it to acoustic guitars and traditional instruments? Would one include the indie rock sub-genre "alt-country"? How would one separate country music from folk music? Or from rock music, blues, or bluegrass? Different people use the term differently, and there is no definition that one could give that would fit with all of the different uses out there in the world. But one could give a stipulative definition: "*For the purposes of this book*, when we say 'country music' we are referring to music that has the following features...."

When scholars set out a stipulative definition of a cultural tradition like "Christianity," their stipulative definition never matches up perfectly with all of the different uses of the term employed by those who self-identify as Christian. Stipulative definitions are useful from an outsider's, scholarly perspective, insofar as they help one limit the scope of one's research: "I'm just going to study what *I'm* calling 'Christian,' not every single thing that's ever been called 'Christian.'" However useful, such stipulative definitions don't tell us anything about how insiders define themselves or what Christianity *really* is.

Since stipulative definitions do not claim to define what something really is, they won't help us provide an answer to the question "Who is a true Christian?" And, in any case, Christians who make claims about who is a true Christian probably don't care about stipulative definitions—the leaders of the city of Geneva were not suggesting that Michael Servetus didn't fit their stipulative definition of "Christian," they were saying that he was *not a real Christian*. And, if we as scholars simply accepted their definition, that would implicate us in their perspective and their politics (just as accepting one definition of "wetlands" over another would implicate us in certain political power plays, as we saw in Chapter 1). To understand what is going on in these sorts of identity claims we will have to consider how they are tied to power relations.

Authenticity Claims as Rhetorical Power Plays

For centuries, religious practitioners have claimed a special power or special authority for their own beliefs and practices by claiming that they have the real or authentic ones. This sets up a binary opposition between "the real" or authentic and "the unreal" or inauthentic—between an "us" and a "them." The contrast between "authenticity" and its opposite lines up with all the other pairs of words that people use to distinguish what they think is real from what they think is false or illegitimate:

right/wrong
good/bad
true/false
real/fake
orthodox/heretical

It is important to note that these are not neutral distinctions; the words on the left have positive associations, and the words on the right carry negative associations. When we apply these labels, something more than mere description is happening: we are making a rhetorical power play, a value judgment, a claim about which are good and which are bad.

We see the same sort of strategy with words in many things we do in our culture, even ones not typically labeled as "religious." During the 2008 US presidential election campaign, some members of the Republican Party talked a lot of talk about "real Americans" or "the real America." One of John McCain's strategists, Nancy Pfotenhauer, even made reference on CNN to "the real Virginia," basically meaning those parts of Virginia that agreed with her and her candidate. Every once in a while, when I am facing off with scholars who don't share my views, I might say that their work is "not *really* scholarly." The rhetorical or persuasive effect of the claim to authenticity is basically the same: "My practices or views are authentic—*the right ones*—and these others are inauthentic—*the wrong ones.*"

What people usually do not do in such cases is provide an argument for or defense of their claim. In fact, the claim that one's own group is authentic usually gets brought out when the person or group making the claim doesn't have a good argument—people resort to what practically amounts to name-calling when they do not have any substantial justification for what they are saying.

Authenticity rhetoric can do two different things. On the one hand, as we have seen, it can be used to award a special authority to one's own group: "We are the good group; we have the right interpretation and the real truth. They are the bad group: corrupted, fallen, and false." By claiming that their own group is "authentic," people assert their authority or superiority over others who disagree with them.

On the other hand, authenticity rhetoric can be used to distance oneself from others who claim to be like you, and maybe even claim authority over you. It is clear why Christians or Muslims might want to use this tactic when talking about the Crusades or Al-Qaeda. By claiming that the Crusaders were not really Christian or that Al-Qaeda is not really Muslim, they get to distance themselves from those other groups. If I say "they are not really scholars"—simultaneously implying that I *am* a true scholar—I am actually saying something like this: "I call myself a scholar and they call themselves scholars, but *I'm not like them.*" In one of his essays, Bruce Lincoln offers a definition of what historians of religion ought to be doing, and says that anyone who falls outside that definition—particularly those who use their academic work to promote a religious tradition—should not be identified as a historian, and then sardonically adds that they might rightly be called a "cheerleader, voyeur, [or] retailer of import goods" (Lincoln 1996, 227). The implication is clear: "cheering on religion and writing a history of religion are not the same—do not confuse what I do with what those cheerleaders do."

Certainly, this is to some extent understandable—people who self-identify as Muslim are usually very different from one another in many respects. Identifying someone as a Muslim does not tell us very much about her—she could be conservative or progressive; she could be sexist or a feminist; she may support Shari'a law or may oppose it. Similarly, identifying someone as a Christian may not tell us much about her, either—she may or may not believe in the trinity; she may or may not go to church every Sunday (or any day, for that matter); she may or may not believe in the separation of church and state. She *probably* believes in God and Jesus, but even that is not certain—the "death of God" theologians mentioned above claimed that the authority of God was an obstacle to realizing the love of Christ. As we saw in our earlier discussion of essentialism, we make a mistake when we lump together all who identify as Christian or all who identify as Muslim, as if they all shared the same views or practices. It's a common mistake, but a mistake nonetheless.

So this strategy of talking about "real Christianity" is a handy rhetorical device for (1) claiming that your own views or practices are superior to those of others, or (2) separating or distancing yourself from others. This helps us understand how these claims function, but nothing about whether or not they are true. Is there any way we, as scholars, could decide between competing authenticity claims? Probably not.

Defining Authentic Christianity: Mission Impossible

The Ontario Consultants on Religious Tolerance host a website called religious tolerance.org. On one of their pages, they consider what methods one might use to find out which religion is the "true" religion. One possible method is to "pray to God and ask to be enlightened." Apart from the fact that it is unclear which god one would pray to, they note "[t]his method appears to be unreliable. When people pray to God for enlightenment, most seem to conclude that their own religion and faith group is the true one" (Ontario Consultants on Religious Tolerance 2007). When people use the tools of their own religious tradition for answers, they typically end up validating their own tradition. There seem to be no reliable ways to decide between different claims about who does or does not have the true form of a religion. Every group brings its own set of priorities and values, and in the process remakes that religion, ever so subtly, for themselves.

Let's look at an important example: the beginning of "orthodoxy" in the early Christian community. A review of the writings of early Christians shows that there were many different groups who considered themselves followers of Jesus in the first few centuries, and they generally had very different ideas about who Jesus was and why he was significant. It is for this reason that scholars sometimes talk about early "Christianities" in the plural, rather than just early "Christianity." There does not seem to have been one "true" Christianity since the beginning; all the evidence points to the fact that there were *always* several branches of Christianity.

Elaine Pagels outlines the wide variety of forms of early Christianity in *The Gnostic Gospels*. Pagels demonstrates that some early Christians believed that Jesus literally rose from the dead, but other Christians thought that the idea was "extremely revolting, repugnant, and impossible"—these Christians apparently believed that a symbolic interpretation of the "resurrection" was far superior to the idea of a zombie-Jesus coming back from the dead (Pagels 1979, 5). Some early Christians believed that there was one god and only one god, but other Christians believed this to be utter nonsense—for the latter group it appeared obvious that although there might be a supreme god, there were other "demigods" (or lesser gods) out there as well (Pagels 1979, 44). Some early Christians believe that God the Father and Jesus the Son were male, but that the Holy Spirit was neutral, whereas other early Christians believed that the Holy Spirit was female or a "mother" (Pagels 1979, 62ff). Some early Christians claimed that Jesus literally suffered and died on the cross before rising from the dead, but other Christians insisted that Jesus was a spiritual being incapable of suffering or dying, and only appeared to have suffered and died on the cross (Pagels 1979, 87ff). This one book provides us with quite a few examples, but there are many more to be found in history. In sum, *there were many different groups that identified as "Christian" from the very beginning.*

Why did these different groups not just use the Bible to sort out who was right and who was wrong? Simple: because there was no Bible. The early Christians had hundreds of stories (some spread by word of mouth and some written down), collections of sayings, letters, testimonies, prophecies, and other documents that were circulating throughout their communities in the Roman

Empire. Today they are easy to find, although in the past many of them had been suppressed. A good collection of primary sources from early Christianity (such as Bart Ehrman's *After the New Testament* [1999]) will include, for instance:

- The Gospel According to the Ebionites,
- The Secret Book of John,
- The Gospel of Truth,
- The Wisdom of Jesus Christ,
- The Gospel of Phillip,
- The Gospel of Thomas,
- The Gospel of Peter,
- The Proto-Gospel of James,
- The Infancy Gospel of Thomas.

Some of these texts were lost (or suppressed) for some time, but recovered at a later time. The study of these books reveals themes and narratives that have completely reshaped how scholars think about the early Christian church. Although much of their content is the same as or similar to what we find in the New Testament gospels, some of it is differs considerably. In the Infancy Gospel of Thomas there is a story about how Jesus as a toddler murdered a boy who stumbled into him by accident: "a child who was running banged into his shoulder. Jesus was angered and said to him, 'You shall go no further on your way.' And immediately the child fell down dead" (Ehrman 1999, 256). When Joseph (his father) confronts him, Jesus insults him: "You have acted very stupidly.... Do not vex me" (Ehrman 1999, 256). In the Gospel of Peter, Jesus appears as a giant after he rose from the dead, being carried by two other giants: "[The soldiers] then saw three men exit the tomb; two supported the one, and a cross followed them. The heads of the two reached up to the heaven, but the one they supported with their hands stretched beyond the heavens" (Ehrman 1999, 246). Other weird things happen; for example, the cross starts talking to the soldiers. In the Gospel of Thomas, Jesus says that he will turn Mary—it's unclear which Mary he's talking about—into a man: "I shall guide her so that I will make her male, in order that she also may become a living spirit, being like you males. For everyone woman who makes herself male will enter the Kingdom of Heaven" (Ehrman 1999, 244).

Of course, the fact that there were lots and lots of Christian texts circulating created conflicts between different groups, especially when they disagreed about which ones should be regarded as the most authoritative texts. This conflict was brought to a head when an early Christian leader named Marcion (110–160 CE) established a specific set of documents as authoritative: he rejected most of the documents circulating at the time, and created the first official Bible. Marcion included in his Bible an edited version of the Gospel of Luke and ten letters attributed to the apostle Paul, but rejected all of the other texts that were available to him—including all of the Jewish Scriptures, which Christians later called the Old Testament. Marcion insisted that Jesus' god was not the same god described in the Old Testament—that god was just a demigod—and that the Old Testament was so different from the teachings of Jesus that they could not be reconciled. It is not that he did not believe in the god of the Old Testament, or even that the god of the Old Testament created the world. On the contrary, the fact that the god of the Old Testament created the world was a mark against him: "Why, [Marcion] asked, would a God who is 'almighty'—all powerful—create a world that includes suffering, pain, disease—even mosquitos and scorpions? Marcion concluded that these must be different Gods" (Pagels 1979, 33).

This was not well received by many of Marcion's contemporaries. The early church father Irenaeus of Lyons stated in no uncertain terms that Marcion and those like him "cause the death of many, through the good name [of Jesus] spreading their evil doctrine, and through the gentleness and mercy of this name presenting the bitter and malignant poison of the serpent" (Grant 1997, 96). Out of their shared hatred of Marcion, a coalition of other Christians mounted an attack and created their own Bible. One of the earliest lists of authoritative texts—which dates to the second century, probably not long after Marcion—is called the "Muratorian Canon." Irenaeus himself (in the second century) and Origen (in the third) each had their own unique canons. According to the historian Eusebius, who wrote in the fourth century, the people of his own day were still debating which texts to include. Eventually a consensus was formed among a majority of Christians, and Marcion lost—in part because the dominant coalition was better at enlisting the support of the emperors—so that the "standard" Christian canon, or set of authoritative documents considered exclusively as "scripture," was relatively established for most (but not all) who identified as "Christian." This canon included a lot of writings that Marcion rejected, including the Old Testament, four gospels, Paul's letters, several other letters (such as those attributed to James and to Peter), and a few odds and ends (such as Revelation). However, even this collection of scriptures wasn't entirely stable. When the Protestant Reformation happened, many Protestants rejected some of the Old Testament that the Catholics had held as authoritative for centuries. Martin Luther wanted to throw out even more, such as the Epistle of James; but this was too controversial for his contemporaries and he had to relent.

In summary, there have been many different groups throughout history that call themselves "Christian," and many of them have had a different Bible. Is there an objective way to determine whether Marcion's or the Roman Catholic Church's or Luther's Bible is the authentic one? How could we justify saying one group was right and the others are wrong? Who is to say that Marcion's form of Christianity, now forgotten, was not "the real" Christianity?

Defining Authentic Hinduism: Mission Impossible

We encounter a different set of problems when it comes to looking at attempts to define "authentic" Hinduism. In *Rethinking Hindu Identity*, D.N. Jha shows how most modern definitions of Hinduism suffer from serious errors.

First, some Hindu thinkers point to the subcontinent of India as the basis for Hindu identity. On this view, "Bharata"—the native name for the land of India—grounds Hindu identity, just as some Israelis view the land of Israel as the basis of their identity. The land is claimed to be the essence or foundation of Hinduism, and thus the people *from* Bharata are the only ones who rightly bear a Hindu identity and deserve to live there. This view is built in part on a return-to-origins narrative that fabricates a golden age of Indian or Hindu culture:

> In this . . . format India, i.e., Bharata, is timeless. The first man was born here. Its people were the authors of the first human civilization, the Vedic [civilization] . . . The authors of this civilization had reached the highest peak of achievement in all arts and sciences, and they were conscious of belonging to the Indian nation, which has existed eternally.
>
> (Jha 2009, 10)

This view is espoused by the modern Hindu nationalist movement; the agenda of this movement involves—in part—expelling Muslims from India because their race and culture is understood not to have come from ancient Bharata; because they did not come from India and are not Hindu, they don't belong in India. This definition of Hinduism is a power play: if "we" have our origins in ancient Bharata, but "they" have their origins elsewhere, then they should leave. As Jha points out, this view "legitimates the . . . perception of national identity as located in remote antiquity, accords centrality to the supposed primordiality to Hinduism and thus spawns Hindu cultural nationalism" (14).

The problem with this view, however, is that the existence of a pure, eternal, and unchanging Bharata is a fiction. Jha demonstrates that the borders or boundaries of Bharata continually changed over time, as is evident upon consideration of ancient Indian texts. Just as the boundaries of the United States have expanded, retreated, and expanded again over time—from the original thirteen colonies to the present—so did "Bharata" move. There is no one location that always was and is Bharata. Consequently, this definition of Hinduism is not only a form of cultural chauvinism, it is also based on a return-to-origins fiction that scholars can show to be false.

Another way Hindu nationalists define Hinduism is to say that there has always been a unique "Hindu" culture or religion in India, and that unique culture is the core, essence, or foundation of the identity. One problem with this is that the ancient peoples who lived on the continent we now call India did not use the word "Hindu" to refer to their culture. On the contrary, the word was first used by outsiders—usually Arab Muslims who came to India—and they tended to use the term in a way that had a "geographic, linguistic, or ethnic connotation" (15). That is, when outsiders first used the word "Hindu," they were sometimes referring to a location ("Hindus are the people who live in this region"), sometimes a language ("Hindus are the people who talk this way"), and sometimes a racial or ethnic group ("Hindus are the people who live here but aren't Arabs"), but not a particular, distinct culture. In addition, Jha notes this is further complicated by the fact that Indians themselves never "describe themselves as Hindus before the fourteenth century"—that is, not only did outsiders not refer to a "Hindu religion" or "Hindu culture" in ancient India, but Indians themselves did not use the term *at all* before the fourteenth century (17), and didn't adopt the term commonly until the nineteenth century. Thus the idea that there has been an eternal, unchanging, and obviously identifiable "Hindu" religion or culture from the beginning of Indian civilization turns out to be just as false as the idea that there has always been one "Bharata."

A third way of defining an authentic Hindu identity has been based around the Vedas, ancient Indian texts that are sometimes thought to serve as a "foundation" for Hinduism, just as the Bible is assumed to serve as a "foundation" for Judaism or Christianity. Some "scholars of religion . . . define Hinduism as 'the religion of those humans who create, perpetuate, and transform traditions with legitimizing reference to the authority of the Vedas'" (Jha 2009, 21, quoting Smith 1989, 13–14). Those who take this approach "referred nostalgically to the earliest period of Indian past as one of 'Vedic harmony'—a period where people were 'ruled according to the principles of the Vedas and India enjoyed 2000 years of uninterrupted peace, tranquility and prosperity'" (Jha 2009, 2, quoting Misra 2004, 37). That is, they invented a return-to-origins narrative that placed complete, faithful adherence to the Vedas at the origin. However, claiming the existence of "Hinduism" on the basis of a continual adherence to the Vedas also contradicts the historical evidence: the evidence shows that the Vedas were often authoritative in word but not deed (that is, people said they followed the Vedas but clearly did not), and sometimes not even in word (that is, many Indians did not even accept the Vedas as authoritative). Later "Hindu" texts that are supposedly based on the Vedic tradition, such as the Upanishads and the Bhagavad Gita, actually *criticize* the Vedas. The historical evidence demonstrates that so-called Hindu "sects have not had the same attitude toward the Vedic corpus, and even the texts of specific sectarian affiliations often express contradictory views about it" (Jha 2009, 25).

The historical and archaeological evidence shows that there have been a wide variety of racial, ethnic, and cultural groups in India, and there are no unique commonalities to be found among them all. Why then posit a unified identity where none exists? Jha makes it clear why Indians might have invented the fiction of an eternal unchanging "Hindu" identity. "The demonization of Muslims was a prominent theme" in the nineteenth-century literature on Hindu identity (3). The rise in importance of "Hindu" identity in this literature was clearly linked to anti-Islamic sentiment: many Indians who wanted to expel Muslims from the country argued for expulsion on the basis of the claim that Muslims were infiltrating and infecting the purity of India or Hinduism. If Muslims did not descend from the original ancestors of Bharata, if they were not identified as "Hindu," or if they were not practicing the original religion of the Vedas, then they did not belong in India. In the end, the fabrication of a timeless Hindu identity appears to have been a power play born out of racial, ethnic, and cultural hatred of some Indians toward Muslims in their midst. Thus these definitions of "Hinduism" are very similar to the claims of racist Americans that black people should "go back to Africa"—they are the rallying cries of an exclusivist political platform.

Authenticity and Essentialism

The problem here is one of essentialism. The search for a "true Christianity" or a "true Hinduism" behind the labels is problematic not only because essences are invisible—if they exist at all—but also because the hermeneutics of suspicion ask us to set aside belief in invisible things for the purposes of our study. In addition, as we noted in Chapter 4, in place of essences what we inevitably find is that categories (1) group together dissimilar things and (2) identify things that are constantly shifting and changing.

First, there is not obviously one "thing" called Christianity because, in practice, the term collects together a lot of different groups of people that do not have one set of things in common. Any review of the historical record proves this to be the case.

Second, there is not obviously one "thing" called Christianity because those things that fall under the category are constantly evolving and changing. "You cannot step in the same river twice" applies to Christianity too—given all of the available evidence, those forms of culture we call Christianity have shifted, swirled, and changed. "Popular cultures and popular religions are not in any way immobile: they undergo evolutions, transformations, and even metamorphoses" (Bayart 2005, 66). Specifically, change over time

> arises because religions, like 'cultures' more broadly, have no essential components that are inherently stable over time: old doctrines are replaced by new ones, existing rituals die out in favor of ritual innovations, and organizational structures are transformed. Innovations

arise when the selection of religious elements from the repertoire changes, when existing elements are discarded or new elements are introduced.

(Hammer 2009, 11)

That is, change over time takes place because the tools in the cultural toolbox are discarded, rearranged, or replaced by new tools. None of these tools appear to be essential, and no single tool is used in identical ways over time, in which case no "essence" to Christianity among the various tools (and their uses) can be found:

[f]or many, religion is a "given," with religions such as Christianity and Islam often being viewed as static [or] eternal. . . . In practice, however, religious organisations and religious cultures are as subject to change and influence as any other human activity.

(Nye 2008, 52)

Every widely used cultural label collects together much more variety than similarity: many people who call themselves Hindus have different ideas about what makes a Hindu; many people who call themselves Buddhists have different ideas about what makes a Buddhist. We might want to put our finger on some particular form of a cultural tradition and say it's the "real" one, but because essences are invisible—again, if they exist at all—all that we as scholars have access to are their stories, their narratives, or their claims to authenticity. Rather than take sides with one political group's definition over another's, perhaps we should instead change the question. Rather than ask what is "authentic" or what is this group's "essence," perhaps we should instead ask the following sorts of questions. Who is making an authenticity claim? What do they stand to win in this context if their claim is received as persuasive? What could they lose if it is not? What competing authenticity claims are in place? And who holds the social, political, or legal power to enforce their definition of authenticity?

Focusing on the Competition

Identity claims are competitive. Not only do people oppose their identity to other identities, but competing groups within the same tradition will use a single identifier in different ways. As philosopher Chiara Bottici notes, "[t]he problem is that there is not a single 'self' that can tell the whole story. . . . [I]n the case of groups, we do not have just one, but many living bodies with many different stories of recognitions [or identifications] to tell" (Bottici 2007, 241). If words make worlds, then groups only exist because they are created by humans:

In the case of social entities such as nations, classes and states, we are not dealing simply with abstract notions, but with socially constructed beings: it is because there are narrating bodies [i.e., groups that make identifications] that behave *as if* such beings existed, that they do *actually* exist.

(241)

However, "in group identities, there is no single narrating body that can tell the whole story"—simply because groups are always divided among themselves and divided from outsiders about how they imagine their group identity—"therefore, it can always be the case that *there is no common story at all*" (244; emphasis added). For Bottici, there can never be one account of a group identity because those groups themselves are created by the way they are imagined by both insiders and outsiders, and not only might insiders and outsiders have different ideas, but, additionally, insiders are almost always divided among themselves. As we noted in Chapter 3, a social fact is still a "fact" as far as it is recognized by a community—but if a community is split on their use of an identification, then there are no secure "facts" to be had about that identity.

Religion scholar Aaron W. Hughes makes the same point in his discussion of how some scholars misguidedly search for an essence to "Islam." Is it essentially peaceful? Is it essentially violent? Hughes argues that these searches are misguided; such an approach cannot provide "a proper understanding of something called Islam precisely because no such thing can exist. Despite appeals to the contrary by either practitioners or scholars of the tradition, Islam, like any other religious tradition, is a series of sites of contestation" (Hughes 2007, 54). That is, there is no "thing" called "Islam," there is just a series of contested and variable claims about what "Islam" is. Similarly, Jean-François Bayart says that it is impossible to find essences behind authenticity claims: "Hard as I have looked, so far I have seen only *processes* of forming cultural or political identities" (Bayart 2005, 85; emphasis added). That is, there appears to be no authentic essence to be found, only the *process of competing groups claiming authenticity*. As a result, we cannot study "Islam" itself—since perhaps it doesn't exist—although we *can* study all those different groups that make claims about what Islam really is or is not. For Bayart, "there is no such thing as identity, only operational *acts of identification*" (92; emphasis added).

Once, during a class discussion about how identities are assigned by communities, a student asked me whether she was Catholic. She had been baptized, had received first communion, and had been confirmed, but she didn't really believe in any of the Catholic doctrines anymore. Was she still Catholic?

In "Rites of Institution" (an essay in *Language and Symbolic Power*, 1999), Pierre Bourdieu points out that identities work collectively. Acts of identification do not take place in a vacuum. Hermits do not need to make strong identity claims—and even if they did, who would hear them? Only people who are active in groups need to make identity claims that define themselves and others. For Bourdieu, "rites of institution" or "rites of passage" are one of the means by which a community can render an identity *publicly* recognized. For example, when a person is knighted, he is *instituted* as a knight in the eyes of others. When a president is sworn in, she is *instituted* as a president in front of a group of citizens who acknowledge her new identity. For Bourdieu, these identities would not work or would not function without some public recognition. A self-proclaimed president has none of the powers of a president if no-one recognizes her as president. At one point in the fifteenth century three different people all claimed to be the true pope of the Catholic Church at the same time. However, none of the three could garner everyone's recognition—each one's authority as "pope" extended only as far as he was recognized.

Replacing the question "Is my student Catholic?" with something like "*Who* identifies her as Catholic, before what audience, and for what reason?" helps us to see that naming or identifying is an action or a process that always takes place between at least four elements. We should not ask "Is she Catholic?" Rather, we should ask this four part question:

1 *who* is identified by
2 *whom* as
3 *what*, and
4 with what *social effects*?

So, in this case, we could say that (1) my *student* is identified by (2) some *churches* as (3) *Catholic*, and (4) with the effect that she is *entitled to the privileges* associated with that identity, such as the right to take Holy Communion or confess to a priest.

However, we could also say that (1) my *student* is identified by (2) *herself* as (3) *not Catholic*, and (4) with the effect that those people she tells that to will *disassociate* her from the local community that self-identifies as Catholic.

Similarly, we could say that in 1775—immediately before the American Revolution—(1) *King George* was identified by (2) *the white people living on the east coast of North America* as (3) *king* of their territory, and (4) with the effect that *his decisions were recognized* as authoritative for their community.

We could also say that in 1777—immediately *after* the start of the American Revolution—(1) *King George* was identified by (2) *certain white people living on the east coast of North America* as (3) *not king* of their territory, and (4) with the effect that they *did not recognize his decisions* as authoritative for their community and felt justified in mounting an armed resistance.

We could add that in 1777, (1) *the people living in England* identified (2) *King George* as (3) *king of the white people living on the east coast of North*

America, and (4) with the effect that *he was able to mobilize England's army* in an attempt to regain military control of the east coast of North America.

So the question "Was King George *really* the king of America in 1777?" is an unhelpful question—it would be better to ask *who* identified him as *what* and *who did not,* and *with what effects.*

Another student once told me that he was one-eighth Native American, and asked whether this made him *really* Native American. I asked what box he checked on his college application, and he said that he had checked "Native American" because this made him eligible for additional financial aid. So I told him that (1) *he* was identified (2) by his *college* as (3) *Native American,* and (4) with the effect that he was *eligible for certain financial scholarships.* Of course, in other contexts, particularly public contexts in which Native Americans would suffer discrimination or even be subject to violence, he might serve his own interests by identifying as white instead of Native American. The question "Is he *really* white or *really* Native American?" is not useful. From the perspective of a hermeneutic of suspicion, there are perhaps no essences to be found, only authenticity claims in progress; what matters is not what he "is" but who identifies him as what and with what effects.

Conclusion

What we have argued in this chapter is that the work of sorting out who is *authentically* a member of a group and who is not cannot be done from an academic perspective because essences do not make themselves available for scholarly study. In addition, authenticity claims typically function as rhetorical power plays between groups in competition and can be analyzed as such. We should replace questions about *authenticity* with investigations into *the process of identification*: who claims identities for themselves or others, who recognizes those identities, and what consequences, benefits, or penalties follow from that identification.

Michael Servetus identified himself as a Christian, but John Calvin and the authorities in Geneva did not—and those authorities had the power to enforce their definition. The consequence of their refusal to recognize him as Christian was that they were legally permitted to burn him at the stake. Rather than trying to determine who was right and who was wrong, it is perhaps more helpful to focus instead on the ways in which a great deal of social power is at stake when we perform acts of identification.

10

Case Study: What Would Jesus Do?

The phrase "What would Jesus do?" became widely popular in the United States in the 1990s among evangelical Christians, who would wear bracelets and related paraphernalia bearing this motto. Interestingly, this is not a new Christian phenomenon: the phrase was first popularized in Charles Sheldon's novel, *In His Steps*, which first appeared as a serial novel in 1896. In the book, a minister challenges the members of his church to join him in a pact of sorts, according to which they will devote themselves for one full year to living as they believe Jesus would. They commit to asking themselves daily what Jesus would do if he were in their situations, and promise to follow through on their answers.

This novel is of interest because in it we can find almost all of the elements we have covered in this book: classification, social stratification, domination, habitus, legitimation, authority, authenticity claims, and so on. In this chapter I will provide a reading of this novel, showing how the social and cultural theory I have proposed can shed light on a specific text.

Charles Sheldon's *In His Steps*

The story takes place in a town called Raymond, somewhere in America's Midwest, and centers around the activities of the members of the First Church of Raymond, a Protestant Christian Church. It begins as the minister at the church, Henry Maxwell, is preparing his Sunday sermon on a passage in the New Testament about following in Jesus' steps. While he is working, a sickly and "shabby-looking young man" characterized as a "tramp" comes to the door, asking for help finding a job (Sheldon 1899, 2). Reverend Maxwell claims he knows of no jobs and quickly dismisses the tramp, returning to his sermon.

During the next Sunday morning's church service, just after Maxwell had completed his sermon, the tramp returns. He interrupts the service as it is closing, walks up the center aisle to the pulpit, and turns around to address the church members. He tells them that he recently lost his job, his wife recently died, and that is daughter is staying with another family until he can find work. However, he implicitly criticizes them for offering him no help, despite their apparent commitment to following in Jesus' steps:

> But I was wondering . . . if what you call following Jesus is the same thing as what He taught. What did He mean when He said, "Follow me"? The minister said . . . that it was necessary for the disciple of Jesus to follow His steps, and he said the steps were obedience, faith, love, and imitation. But I did not hear him tell just what he meant that to mean, especially the last step. What do Christians mean by following the steps of Jesus? I've tramped through this city for three days trying to find a job and in all that time I've not had a word of sympathy or comfort except from your minister here, who said he was sorry for me and hoped I would find a job somewhere. . . . [W]hat I feel puzzled about is, what is meant by following Jesus? Do you mean that you are suffering and denying yourselves and trying to save lost humanity just as I understand Jesus did? . . . Somehow I get puzzled when I see so many Christians living in luxury and singing, "Jesus, I my cross have taken, all to leave and follow Thee," and remember how my wife died in a tenement in New York City, gasping for air and asking God to take the little girl too. Of course I don't expect you people can prevent every one from dying of starvation, lack of proper nourishment and tenement air, but what does following Jesus mean?
>
> (10–12)

The tramp seems to assume that following Jesus would include, at least in part, helping poor or jobless individuals such as himself. As such, the key to the tramp's speech is his implicit suggestion that these people are claiming to be Christians, claiming to be following in Jesus' steps, but that in reality they are living in luxury while many people outside this church—such as himself—are starving. He implies that they are hypocrites (that is, *inauthentic* Christians). However, in the middle of his comments to the church, he passes out on the floor. The minister takes him into his house and hires a doctor to look over him, but within the week he dies.

The death of the tramp makes a remarkable impact on Maxwell. The next Sunday he tells his church that "much that the man said was so vitally true" (16), and asks them to volunteer to "pledge themselves earnestly and honestly for an entire year not to do anything without first asking the question, 'What would Jesus do?' And after asking that question, each one will follow Jesus as exactly as he knows how, no matter what the results may be" (17).

About fifty members of the church stay after the service to meet and discuss the pledge (although the number who take the pledge later grows to around one hundred; 98). They begin the meeting with a prayer and then go on to consider how they will go about answering the question, "What would Jesus do?," since the answers may not be obvious. Protestant Christianity was formed in part on the basis of the slogan *sola scriptura*, which means "scripture alone," so it is surprising that their first consideration is, in fact, not to turn to the Bible in order to answer these questions. Instead, Maxwell claims, "There is no way that I know of . . . except as we study Jesus through the medium of the Holy Spirit" (20). That is, they decide to *pray* to their god and ask what they call the Holy Spirit to speak to them. The members of the church mention that there is bound to be disagreement—it is unlikely that every member will be in full agreement about what Jesus might do in any particular context or situation. Maxwell agrees, but suggests that their answers will not be too varying: "The standard of Christian action cannot vary in most of our acts" (21). Maxwell goes on to add, however, that they must be "free from fanaticism on one hand and too much caution on the other. If Jesus' example is the example for the world, it certainly must be feasible to follow it" (21–2).

In addition, although they do not say so in this first meeting, it becomes clear throughout the novel that the members of this church are implicitly guided by the ideals of honesty (81, 88) and selflessness, especially the latter. They seem to insist repeatedly throughout the novel that their actions should be guided by the welfare or suffering of others, rather than their own interests. This calls for, in many cases, a great deal of self-sacrifice on their part—and they view the avoidance of self-sacrifice as a terrible sin. At one point Maxwell uses the words "self-denial and suffering" to describe the ideal at which they are aiming (70).

It is worth noting that the interests of others include not only material interests (i.e., the hunger and joblessness of the tramp), but also what they would view as "spiritual" interests (i.e., they are concerned with the salvation of souls through the personal conversion to Christianity, without which they believe an individual will go to hell).

Edward Norman, editor of the local paper, is one of the individuals who enters this pact by taking the pledge. His first response is to take all tobacco and liquor advertisements out of the paper, as he believes that Jesus would not support the sale of these products. In addition, he decides to remove all stories about boxing matches, although it is unclear whether this is due to an objection to boxing itself or the gambling that often goes along with boxing matches. He also removes salacious accounts of local crime, as well as all gossip columns. The Sunday edition of the paper is permanently cancelled, as he believes Jesus would rest rather than work on the Sabbath.

The attempt to run the paper as Jesus might is not well received by others on the paper's staff. His assistant predicts that these changes "will simply ruin the paper. . . . Why, it isn't feasible to run a paper now-a-days on any such basis" (26). Although Norman is fully willing to face the risks, his assistant's prediction eventually turns out to be right—subscriptions wane and the paper almost goes bankrupt later in the novel.

Alexander Powers, a superintendent at the local railroad machine shop, implements his pledge in two ways. First, he decides to take a store room at the company and convert it into a break room for the laborers:

> I am going to fit it up with tables and a coffee plant in the corner. . . .
> My plan is to provide a good place where the men can come and eat
> their noon lunch and give them, two or three times a week, the priv-
> ilege of a fifteen minutes' talk on some subject that will be a real help
> to them in their lives.
>
> (44–5)

What Powers means is that he intends to invite Reverend Maxwell to give mini-sermons to the laborers during their lunch break in the room Powers has provided them. The second way of implementing his pledge involves tattling on his company for illegal activity. What happens is that an envelope containing information related to his company's illegal business was accidentally put in Powers' mailbox at work, and he opens it before noticing that it was not addressed to him. He discovers his company's violation of a number of "Interstate Commerce Laws" (47), and decides that what Jesus would do would be to report the violations to the government. Powers does so, simultaneously resigning from his position at the railroad machine shop. For Sheldon, this appears to be a perfect example of self-sacrifice in the name of honesty.

Rachel Winslow, a young woman with an apparently amazing voice, is slow to decide what Jesus would do in her situation. At first she is made an offer from a traveling opera company, which, although it would have made her wealthy and famous, she turns down because accepting the offer would have made a selfish rather than selfless use of her singing talents. She explicitly states, "I am completely convinced . . . that Jesus would never use any talent like a good voice just to make money" (51). She's not quite sure what she wants to do with her talent, but in the short term she decides she will help out with some local revival meetings.

The revival meetings are led by Mr. and Mrs. Gray, who have set up a tent for Christian services in a section of Raymond called "the Rectangle" (these are referred to as the White Cross tent meetings in the novel, although it is unclear where the name "White Cross" comes from). The Rectangle is a part of town near many of the factories and machine shops, and where a number of bars and pubs can be found. Though it is never explicitly said, readers get the impression that many laborers leave work at the factories and shops and head directly to the bars in the Rectangle. Since the characters see these patrons of bars as unsaved—and therefore going to hell—they find the Rectangle to be the perfect place to hold the tent services. As Rachel puts it, "It is in a part of the city where Christian work is most needed" (65). Therefore Rachel lends her talent to the Grays, and according to the narrator, her voice brings drunks out of the bars and into the tent meeting much like sirens draw sailors to their deaths: "Several windows near by went up. Some men quarreling in a saloon stopped and listened. Other figures were walking rapidly in the direction of the Rectangle and the tent" (68). Because of her talent, the tent quickly filled up and began "to run over" (69).

Virginia Page is an heiress sitting on a million dollars (which was an exorbitant amount of money in the 1890s). She has to decide what Jesus might do with the money she's inherited, but of course has difficulty: since Jesus was relatively impoverished according to the New Testament, there is no model as such provided for what he might do with wealth. "There could be no one, fixed, Christian way of using money. The rule that regulated its use was unselfish utility" (109). She eventually decides to use half of her money to endow Norman's newspaper, in order to prevent it from sliding into bankruptcy as he turns it into a "Christian" newspaper (127). The other half of her money she decides she will put to use by building some sort of lodging houses or schools for women in the Rectangle, and she intends to partner with Rachel in order to provide these women with a music program of some sort (146–8).

By contrast, Madam Page—Virginia's grandmother—will have nothing to do with the "What would Jesus do?" pledge. She is described as a woman of "wealth and social standing" (53), and it seems to follow that she is more concerned with her reputation among her peers than her Christian faith. In fact, she practically insults Rachel, explicitly describing the pact as "foolish," "impossible," and rooted in "false emotion" (57): "I felt confident at the time that those who promised [to take the pledge] would find out after a trial and abandon it as visionary and absurd" (56).

Virginia's response to her grandmother's challenge is put thus: "Do you mean . . . that we cannot possibly act as Jesus would, or do you mean that if we try to, we shall offend the customs and prejudices of society?" (57). Virginia implicitly makes a distinction between two choices: one can follow Jesus or one can follow society; she makes it clear that her grandmother is selfishly choosing society over Jesus. Madam Page is unmoved; she responds with condescension, and suggests that Rachel will see the truth of the matter soon enough.

Another member of the pact is Milton Wright, a man who owns a number of stores. Prior to making the pledge he was the sort of man who ran his business "from the standpoint of 'Will it pay?,'" but subsequent to the pledge he is "compelled to revolutionize the whole method of business" (85–6). He sets aside profit as a goal of his business, and decides that any money he makes will be put to use "for the good of humanity" (87). In addition, he decides that he will view his employees as "souls to be saved" (87).

The plot of the novel develops at first as a series of vignettes focusing on these individuals (and a few others), but later the storyline coalesces around a group effort. Maxwell decides that they should join forces in order to end the licensing of alcohol sales in their town (or, as they refer to it, "license"). Indeed, "[t]he destruction of the saloon is *the* theme of *In His Steps*" (Boyer 1971, 65; emphasis original). Not surprisingly, they see the Rectangle at the center of their efforts. Maxwell's concern about the saloons—a concern he sees as guided by the Holy Spirit—leads him to preach "against the saloon" one Sunday morning. The sermon is timed in relation to upcoming town elections:

> The regular election of city officers was near at hand. The question of license would be an issue in that election. . . . Was not the most Christian thing they could do to act as citizens in the matter, fight the saloon at the polls, elect good men to city offices, and clean the municipality?
> (Sheldon 1899, 100–1)

Maxwell's sermon serves to ignite the fervor of those who had made the pact, and the "tension" in the group reaches its "highest point" (101). Following the sermon, Donald Marsh—the president of a local college—talks to Maxwell and they decide to publicly campaign as a team against license for the upcoming election. They enlist Edward Norman, of course, who supports the movement against license in his newspaper.

Around the time that the group campaign against license begins, Virginia takes a special interest in a "homeless, wretched creature" (118) named Loreen at the Rectangle. Virginia's carriage is on its way to the tent meeting at the Rectangle when Loreen, drunk, comes reeling out of a saloon. Loreen had previously converted at the tent meetings, but apparently had reverted to her old ways. Virginia decides to take Loreen, in her drunken stupor, back to her own house in order to take care of her there. Virginia's house, of course, is also Madam Page's house, and Madam Page vehemently opposes this plan of action—not because it was against her faith, but because it was against "her social code of conduct" to bring into her home "the scum of the streets" (120). Virginia, however, stands up to her grandmother: "we call ourselves Christians. Here is a poor, lost human creature, without a home slipping into possible eternal loss, and we have more than enough. I have brought her here and shall keep her" (120). In addition, Virginia rejects Madam Page's concern with her social reputation: "Society is not my God. . . . I do not count the verdict of society as of any value" (121).

The first half of the novel (the book can easily be divided into two parts, each part having a relatively self-contained plotline) comes to a climax on the day of the elections. The narrator of the story claims that the Rectangle "boiled and heaved and cursed and turned its worst side out to the gaze of the city" (131). At the same time, an intense tent meeting was held that went on for hours. As they exit the tent, around ten in the evening, the Rectangle appears to be rioting. A rumor has been circulating that license had been defeated in the election—which later turns out to be false (137–8)—and Maxwell and Marsh are attacked by the crowd, which begins throwing stones, mud, and other "missiles" (135). As Maxwell and Marsh make their way through the crowd—followed by Virginia, Rachel, and Loreen—the Rectangle becomes "drunk and enraged" (135). From a saloon window a "heavy bottle" is thrown that hits Loreen, who immediately collapses (135). In seconds she dies, "and the next moment her soul was in Paradise" (136). The narrator notes, however, that "this is only one woman out of thousands killed by this drink devil" (136).

The church members respond by indirectly blaming themselves for her death. They believe themselves to be responsible because if they had opposed license at an earlier point her death could have been prevented. However, "the Christian conscience had been aroused too late" (139). Nevertheless, these sentiments of guilt serve to spur the community to redouble their efforts against license and the saloons, despite their loss in the elections.

The plotline of the novel lacks obvious direction and is a bit rambling, so this place is as good as any to halt summary and begin an analysis.

Analysis: Class and Habitus

Before beginning an analysis I should point out that while we can never know for certain what a person's intentions are, based on what we know of Sheldon's biography—he was a minister of a church and his stated views were similar to those of the characters in the novel—we can assume that Sheldon probably intended for the central characters to be read as exemplary; that is, it is unlikely that he is satirizing late nineteenth-century Christian social movements or anything like that. We can reasonably assume that Sheldon speaks through the voice of the narrator and the voice of some of the "heroes" in the plot, including Reverend Maxwell and Edward Norman.

When this novel first appeared, American society in general was primarily organized not by any Christian categories but by capitalist ones, and therefore it is no surprise that those capitalist categories appear in the novel. There is a clear divide between the *labor class* and the *professional class*. For instance, Marsh explicitly uses the phrase "a class of professional men" (Sheldon 1899, 103) to describe the class to which he and Maxwell belong. Maxwell explicitly uses the language of class when he goes to preach mini-sermons to the laborers at the railroad machine shops during their lunch break. First, he thinks of them as "working men" (45, 46), and notes that he is actually *afraid* to speak to them because of their difference from him. "He actually felt afraid of facing these men ... [who were] so different from a Sunday audience he was familiar with" (45). When Powers introduced Maxwell to the workers, he "spoke very simply, like one who understands thoroughly the character of his audience" (46).

This comment should remind us of Bourdieu's critique of capitalist ideology: "The poor are not just immoral, alcoholic and degenerate, they are stupid, they lack intelligence" (Bourdieu 1998, 43). Sheldon is presenting the members of the working class not only as different, but as possibly intellectually inferior; as Bourdieu rightly insists, this offers members of wealthier classes a reassuring sense of superiority.

Sheldon goes on to differentiate Maxwell further from these laborers: "Like hundreds of other ministers he had never spoken to any gathering except those made up of people of *his own class* in the sense that they were familiar, in their *dress and education and habits*, to him" (Sheldon 1899, 46; emphasis added). Sheldon is describing, without using Bourdieu's vocabulary, this class' *habitus*. They dress differently from Maxwell, they have a different educational level, and they have different *habits*—the last term is, obviously, the root of the word "habitus." Sheldon goes on:

> [Maxwell] had the good sense on this his first appearance not to recognize the men as a class distinct from himself. He did not use the term 'working men', and did not say a word to suggest any difference between their lives and his own.
>
> (46)

That is, their lives *are most definitely different* from his own—he even calls them "a class distinct"—but he had the "good sense" not to draw attention to this fact.

One key element of habitus is language, diction, or way of speaking. This is another way that Sheldon separates out the wealthier classes from the working class. Throughout the novel the people from the church or from Maxwell's class do not speak with an accent of any sort, but the laborers or the characters from the Rectangle almost always do. At one point some characters in the Rectangle say things such as "Who's de bloke?" and "De Fust Church parson," while a drunken man says "Trow out de life line 'cross de dark wave!" (74). These people are members of "a class distinct" or an alternative habitus not only because of their jobs (as working men), their dress, their education, their "habits," but also because of their manner of speaking.

What sets this class apart from Maxwell's class more than anything else, however, is apparently the consumption of alcohol in the saloons at the Rectangle. The Rectangle, for Sheldon, is tantamount to hell. When Loreen stumbles out of a bar to be picked up by Virginia, they have an interesting exchange of words. When Virginia first grabs her, Loreen screams at her: "You shall not touch me! Leave me! Let me go to hell! That's where I belong! The devil is waiting for me. See him!" (116). At that point Loreen points to the bartender in the saloon she just exited. Of course, Virginia persuades Loreen to come with her, but it is clear that the saloons and the Rectangle are to be understood as hell on earth.

Sheldon uses startling rhetoric to separate the working class who patronize the saloons from the wealthy Christians. Consider the vocabulary Sheldon uses to make up chains of associations in Table 10.1. Sheldon himself, through the voice of the narrator, implies a cosmic dualism: "The end of the week found

Table 10.1 Charles Sheldon's rhetorical language.

The good side	The bad side
"life of purity" (97)	the Rectangle as "festering sore" (77)
"good men" (101, 104)	"the evil" (77)
"a class of professional men" (103)	"drunken, vile, debauched humanity" (97)
"clean city life" (105)	saloon as "an enemy, not only to the poor and
"professional men" (105)	tempted, but . . . to the church itself" (100)
"organized righteousness" (106)	"hell of drink" (101)
"best men" (107)	saloons as "crime-and-shame-producing insti-
"decent citizens" (107)	tutions" (101)
"clean, honest, capable, business-like" (107)	city officials who support license are "a corrupt,
"noble" (107)	unprincipled set of men, controlled in large
"good citizens" (107)	part by the whiskey element, and thoroughly
"cleansing our city" (107)	selfish" (103)
"purify our civic life" (107)	"horrible whirlpool of deceit, bribery, political
"lovers of right, purity, temperance, and	trickery, and saloonism" (104)
home" (107)	"slums" (105)
"long needed reform" (107)	"whisky-ridden city" (105)
"civic righteousness" (108)	"rum and corruption" (105)
"lovers of Jesus" (109)	"cowardly and easily frightened" (106)
"good" (155)	"whisky men" (107)
	"corrupt city government" (107)
	"rule of rum" (107)
	"shameless incompetency" (107)
	"worst enemy known to municipal honesty"
	(107)
	"evil forces" (108)
	"coarse, brutal, sottish lives" (109)
	"saloon devil" (110)
	"slaves" (110)
	"horror" (110)
	"poor creatures" (110)
	"devilish drink" (110)
	"greatest form of slavery now known to Amer-
	ica" (110)
	"whisky forces" (111)
	"aggressive" (111)
	"hatred" (111)
	the saloon as a "deadly viper, hissing and coil-
	ing, ready to strike its poison" (111)
	"earthly hell called the saloon" (116)
	the saloon as "enemy of the human race" (154)
	"bad" (155)
	"vileness" (157)
	"the devil" (157)

the Rectangle struggling hard between *two mighty opposing forces*. The Holy Spirit was battling with all His supernatural strength against the saloon devil which had so long held a jealous grasp on its slaves" (emphasis mine; 110). Or: "The Holy Spirit and the Satan of rum seemed to rouse up to a desperate conflict" (132). For Sheldon, one class is literally divine and the other class is literally evil and demonic. Sheldon is, in fact, *literally demonizing* the working class. As the narrator notes at one point, "Jesus is the great divider of life. One must walk either parallel with Him or directly across His path" (130). There is no doubt which side of the divide the working class falls on. To put it in Bourdieu's terms, this absolute distinction between classes seems to be a key feature of the matrix of perception of Sheldon's class—he views the world through this binary distinction.

One commentator suggests:

> In broad outline, we are confronted with an urban 'WASP' [white Anglo-Saxon Protestant] middle class—professional men, managers and minor entrepreneurs, together with their comfortable wives and daughters—which finds itself deeply fearful of, yet simultaneously fascinated by, the burgeoning immigrant working-class population which is crowding into the cities.
>
> (Boyer 1971, 67)

In addition, as Bourdieu's account of habitus notes, those who share a habitus will see those with an alternative habitus not only as different—and possibly as something to be afraid of—but as lacking reason and common sense, or even as vulgar or bad. This is borne out in Sheldon's novel. We can see from the list of associations in Table 10.1 that the working class is not only *different* from the wealthy Christians, but also evil, debauched, shameful, coarse, brutal, sottish, vile, and—in short—bad.

This dualism is complicated by the fact that for Sheldon's form of Christianity, the goal is not to discriminate against the working class but to convert them to Christianity. That is, presumably Sheldon wants his intended audience—other Christians—to reach out to those on the wrong side of this class divide and to help bring them over from the dark side. (The language of "good side" and "dark side" may seem unscholarly, but this is exactly the sort of language Sheldon uses; see, for example, his metaphorical use of the language of "darkness" on page 161). However, Sheldon makes it clear that coming over to the good side is incompatible with the habits of the dark side. For instance, when Loreen, after having been saved, reverts to visiting the saloons, Virginia's thoughts were as follows: "She simply saw a soul that had tasted of the joy of a better life slipping back again into its old hell of shame and death" (115). It appears that any alcohol consumption is necessarily on the dark side, and—as Jesus is the great divider—one must choose a side; one cannot both be Christian *and* drink.

On the other hand, being within the wealthy class is not in and of itself redeeming. Madam Page stands out as the paradigmatic hypocrite, as she chooses the standards of society and her reputation among the same over the standards of the church. Maxwell identifies these hypocrites and targets them in a to-do list he makes for himself: "2. Preach fearlessly to the hypocrites in the church no matter what their social importance or wealth" (70). However, this group of hypocrites is still "in the church," still shares his habitus, and can be separated out from the "sinful people in the Rectangle," which he targets in an altogether separate item on his to-do list (70).

In summary, Sheldon's matrix of perception seems to involve a threefold classification for his society:

1 The authentic members of his church and class who make the "What would Jesus do?" pledge.
2 The inauthentic members of his church and class who hypocritically refuse to make the pledge.

---

3 The working class ("a class distinct") who patronize the saloons at the Rectangle.

The gap between his class and the working class appears to be much greater than the gap between those who made the pledge and the hypocrites: the hypocrites are subjected to substantial criticism, but never the demonizing invective directed at the third group. If the hypocrites were really on the wrong side of the line above—that is, if they were considered as demonic as the working class men who drink at the Rectangle—then we would see efforts on the part of the members of the pact to reach out to them. However, we do not. When Powers sets up a space for Maxwell to preach to the people at the railroad, it is *only for* the working class, not for the other members of management—apparently the other members of management, insofar as they share Maxwell and Powers' class, need not be subjected to evangelism. Similarly, Rachel's and Virginia's efforts at the Rectangle are directed solely at the working class and homeless members of the Rectangle. Sheldon seems to be focused narrowly on class difference above all other differences, which contributes to the demonization of the working class alone. While one might think that the difference between "true Christian" and "non-Christian" (as Sheldon defines these) might be central, instead the central difference relevant to the novel is economic class.

Would Sheldon's novel have reinforced or challenged the status quo in 1896? I think any rigorous answer to this will necessarily be divided. On the one hand, Sheldon seems to *intend* to challenge the status quo. The sale of alcohol was clearly legal in most parts of the United States at that time, and Sheldon's novel is aimed at encouraging hypocritical Christians who support license (or who indirectly support it by failing to challenge it) to change their behavior on this issue (we will say more on this below). However, on the other hand, Sheldon's novel not only reflects the class divisions of late nineteenth-century capitalism but seems to teach readers that the division is one with a cosmological significance. That is, many of Sheldon's readers doubtlessly came away with the impression that the class distinction is not unique to capitalism, but runs throughout time and the universe: it is not a *capitalist* distinction—it is perhaps the very distinction between good and evil.

The readers of Maxwell's class who are persuaded by Sheldon's novel learn that the members of a class distinct from their own are not only different, but evil. As we saw above, according to Bourdieu,

> habitus are also classificatory schemes, principles of classification, principles of vision and division, different tastes. They make distinctions between what is good and what is bad, between what is right and what is wrong, between what is distinguished and what is vulgar, and so forth, but the divisions [from one habitus to the next] are not identical. Thus, for instance, the same behavior or even the same good can appear distinguished to one person, pretentious to someone else, and cheap or showy to yet another.
>
> (Bourdieu 1998, 8)

What results from this sorting out of society into good and bad classes? Groups will award privileges to members of their own class and will discriminate against those of another class, who they may see as lacking reason or common sense, or who they may see as merely stupid. Because of this, class hierarchies can be reproduced automatically and without people intending them to be reproduced. A system of class habitus can reinforce the status quo in much the same way that a cultural toolbox can legitimate the status quo. It was for this reason that Bourdieu saw that "meritocracy" is a myth—people may "get ahead" in life because of their habitus more than because of their intelligence, effort, or work habits. One's habitus can count as "meritorious," independently of one's ability.

In fact, this is *exactly* the lesson that Sheldon's novel teaches. There is a great deal of collusion between the members of the wealthier class. Fred Morris was a newspaper reporter who took the "What would Jesus do?" pledge, although he worked for a newspaper other than Edward Norman's. When he decided that Jesus wouldn't work on Sundays, he was fired from his job at the other paper. However, because of his connections through his class and his church, Maxwell introduces him to Norman, who offers him a job on the spot. What is interesting is that Norman offers him the job prior to learning anything of Fred's merits, *other than his Christian identity*:

> I can give you a place . . . I want reporters who won't work Sundays. And what is more, I am making plans for a special kind of reporting

which I believe young Morris can develop because he is in sympathy with what Jesus would do.

(Sheldon 1899, 85)

It is fascinating that the language of "sympathy" is exactly the language Bourdieu used: "[One's] social sense is guided by the system of . . . signs of which each body is the bearer—clothing, pronunciation, bearing, posture, manners—and which, unconsciously registered, are the basis of 'antipathies' or 'sympathies'" (Bourdieu 1984, 241). For Bourdieu, one's sympathies and antipathies are extended to others on the basis of whether they share one's habitus. It is therefore no surprise to see Norman extending a job to a reporter who shares his way of speaking about Jesus, who shares his habitus, and who therefore shares his sympathies. Later in the novel Norman makes a to-do list similar to Maxwell's: "10. . . . [Jesus] would probably secure the best and the strongest Christian men and women to cooperate with Him in the matter of contributors [to the paper—i.e., reporters and others writing stories]. That will be my purpose" (Sheldon 1899, 155). As Bourdieu suggests, through the normalization of the dominant habitus, privileges will be extended to individuals who share the dominant habitus, and discrimination will result for those with an alternate habitus. Here Norman explicitly says that he intends to implement a form of religious discrimination in the workplace: he intends to hire people who are Christians like himself. This could not be more clear as an example of collusion. However, there is an element of divine legitimation for this principle of discrimination—it is not only what he intends to do, it is what *Jesus* would probably do.

Bourdieu predicts that, because of the way habitus work, social hierarchies will reproduce themselves over time. It appears that readers persuaded by Sheldon's novel—at least those of Maxwell's class—will learn the lesson that they should extend privileges to those who share their habitus, and discriminate against those with a working class habitus. In addition, the discrimination receives a divine legitimation; those with an alternative habitus are not only seen as bad, vulgar, or stupid (remember: Powers had to speak "simply" to his laborers), as Bourdieu suggests, but also evil, debauched, shameful, coarse, brutal, sottish, and vile (to choose just a few of Sheldon's adjectives). To hire people with such a habitus would doubtlessly be seen as unreasonable, and therefore the gap between the wealthy classes and the working class is likely to be unbreached. Despite Sheldon's apparent intention to encourage those of his class to reach out to those on the dark side, the overall message is that they are not worthy as peers and do not merit jobs until they assimilate to his class's habitus.

To the extent that Sheldon's readers are members of the dominant class—that is, people who hold positions of privilege and power—his book and its demonizing message seem more likely to have the effect of widening the class gap than closing it.

The characters of *In His Steps* are obsessed by thoughts of an immigrant working class of whose existence they are keenly aware, but from whom they feel totally cut off. So deep is this obsession that it generates extreme anxiety at the prospect of actual encounters with the unknown social group.

(Boyer 1971, 67)

In fact, the novel probably had the effect of *increasing* that anxiety among its readers. In the end, *In His Steps* offers a divine legitimation of the capitalist class differences of the late nineteenth century; this story about "a class distinct" both reflects and reinforces the social hierarchy.

Analysis: Class Domination

Not only does the novel contribute to the reproduction of a class hierarchy; we can also see how it contributes to class *domination*. Domination, as I have defined it, takes place when classes are set in a relationship that makes it easier for one class to serve its own interests than it is for the other. There was clearly a relationship of domination between the wealthier or professional classes and the working class in the late nineteenth century. As we see in the novel, for instance, most of the characters at the church are members of Maxwell's class, and as such have a greater access to capital, privilege, and authority, as well as a greater ability to alter the social arrangements in which they are situated when compared with members of the working class. Edward Norman, Alexander Powers, and Milton Wright have within their power the ability to change the conditions in which they work: Norman completely changes the paper (despite his employees' resistance), Powers has the ability to set up a break room and subject his employees to Maxwell's preaching during lunch, and Wright has the ability to change his company's policies. The laborers who work with them obviously do not have this power, and consequently are subject to a relationship of domination.

In addition, however, and considerably more problematic, is the fact that the habitus of the laborers is counted against them—having a working habitus is tantamount to being stupid (as Powers implies when he speaks "simply" to his workers) or, worse, being demonic. Their access to a position of privilege is prohibited not necessarily because of any *real* lack of merit, but in part simply due to their alternative habitus. Since the requirement that one acclimate to a number of arbitrary social codes is in part what might define domination, and since discrimination on the basis of habitus is, in fact, arbitrary, then this furthers the evidence that the laborers are in a relationship of domination. Since Sheldon's novel reinforces the social hierarchy by recommending on the one hand the extension of unfair privileges to members of the professional class (such as when Norman gives Fred a job simply because he shares the same sympathies or the same habitus) and on the other hand demonizing the working class, this novel can be said to contribute to the reproduction of domination.

What is additionally intriguing about Sheldon's novel is the extent to which it is an exercise in misdirection: the novel seems designed to direct the reader's attention away from the causes of poverty and homelessness of the type seen in the Rectangle (although "designed" here should be subordinated to the "seems" that comes before it—I am sure that no such thing was consciously intended by Sheldon). The actual cause of the tramp's joblessness is very clearly stated in the first chapter of the novel—he lost his job *not* because he was lazy or unproductive (that is, there was no question of his merit), but instead because of the fact that the company he worked for bought machines that made his position redundant:

> I lost my job ten months ago. I am a printer by trade. The new linotype machines are beautiful specimens of invention, but I know six men who have killed themselves inside of the year just on account of those machines. Of course I don't blame the newspapers for getting those machines. Meanwhile, what can a man do? I know I never learned but one trade and that's all I can do. I've tramped all over the country trying to find something. There are a good many others like me.
>
> (Sheldon 1899, 10)

The tramp's situation is entirely plausible: these sorts of innovations were widespread during the late nineteenth century, and resulted in a great deal of joblessness for those displaced and low wages for everyone else. "[T]he machine eats work" (Scott 1985, 154).

The problem, of course, was that businesses in competition with one another were in the pursuit of maximum profit. Profits could be raised and prices could be lowered if laborers could be replaced by machines that would perform the same labor more cheaply. However, once one company makes these sorts of changes, others are necessarily quick to follow. This is the nature of market competition: if one company introduces machines and consequently lowers the price of the products they manufacture, they are likely to draw consumers away from other companies. Competing companies are likely to go out of business unless they introduce the same labor-saving devices. Once this cycle starts, a relatively inescapable downward spiral results, where all companies are making the same innovations and laying off laborers.

In addition, once the job market is flooded with laid-off workers, wages go down for workers in general. If there are more jobs than workers, workers can afford to be choosy and negotiate higher salaries; if there are more workers than jobs, workers cannot afford to be choosy and must take whatever they can get. Businesses therefore adjust to the "labor market" and lower the wages offered.

The effects of the combination of the pursuit of profit and market competition are well documented; indeed, it was during the second half of the nineteenth century—at the height of industrialization, but before the rise of substantial laws protecting laborers—that we saw the appearance of extremely exploitative and unsafe labor practices, as well as the wide use of child labor. Karl Marx documented the use of child labor (sometimes starting at even five or six years old), where the children would work fourteen or sixteen hours a day, in working conditions that were literally deadly (often because of poisons or toxins the children were working with; Marx 1990). This sort of exploitative domination resulted directly from the form of market capitalism regnant at the time (these effects of market competition—in particular how they lead to the "squeezing" of labor—are explained with precision by various writers: Marx 1990; Fishman 2006; Reich 2008; Shell 2010).

So the effects of market capitalism appear in the novel: the tramp is left homeless after he is laid off because his business replaced him with a machine. The presence of the tramp's experience in the novel proves that Sheldon had some idea of the negative consequences of capitalism. However, while the novel criticizes profiteering as selfish, never is the capitalist system subjected to substantial criticism. In fact, the one character in the novel who criticizes "the whole of our system" is immediately dismissed by the other characters (see Boyer 1971, 65). The actual *cause* of the tramp's suffering is noted but set aside, and the novel goes on to chastise Christians for not helping people in the tramp's position. This is, of course, the classic problem of recommending a Band-Aid to cover up a symptom rather than getting at the heart of the problem. The sorts of exploitation of children Marx documented and criticized were not corrected until systematic labor laws were put in place to protect children from those kinds of exploitation. Rather than propose substantial changes to the system, Sheldon redirects attention away from the root disease and instead proposes placing a Band-Aid where symptoms appear. In addition, Sheldon replaces a possible critique of the causes of poverty at the time with a critique of the "Satan of rum." As one commentator puts it:

> The pejoratives that Sheldon attached to the slum dwellers pack a powerful, inadvertent message. Why fight for social and economic justice, for a living wage or an eight-hour day or unemployment insurance? These people are incorrigible. Their sins drive them into poverty. And, despite all the big-hearted missionary efforts, they refuse to repent, reform, and rise.
>
> (Morone 2003, 245)

Since they are responsible for their own poverty—rather than a capitalist system that replaces people with machines—why bother doing anything systematic to help? The novel leaves the reader with the impression that it may not be worth the bother.

Why this act of misdirection? Why might Sheldon focus on license and saloons rather than the stated causes of the tramp's misfortune? We cannot, of course, know what might have motivated Sheldon. Perhaps it was ignorance, or perhaps he simply believed that alcohol is literally demonic. Either way, we can see that this act of misdirection is one that could, in some instances, serve the interests of his class. The way that the hierarchy between laborers and Maxwell's "professional" class was set up tended to make it easier for members of the professional class to serve their own interests. First, members of wealthier or professional classes profited from the replacement of laborers, insofar as they owned stock for which the value increased as laborers were displaced. Second, the members of the professional class were not subject to the same sort of displacement. Third, members of the professional class simply experienced a great deal of social privileges that resulted from class distinction and the coordinated collusion; were class distinctions obliterated they would lose those privileges (such as the privilege—seen in the novel—to hire people who shared their own habitus). The interests of the professional class Sheldon apparently identifies with would be better served were the system of collusion and domination to remain in place; the maintenance of the status quo was better for the professional class than the working class. For Sheldon to challenge the system that produces these privileges for the professional class would be for him to risk working against his own class's interests. We cannot know why Sheldon drew attention away from the cause of the tramp's poverty, but we can know that avoiding those systemic causes could have reinforced the class domination from which Sheldon's class benefitted.

Analysis: Authority and Projection

The members of the pact in Sheldon's novel are absolutely certain that Jesus would use his abilities to oppose "license" and "saloonism." We can, however, ask the question: is it possible that they are projecting their values onto the figure of Jesus?

What do we know about Jesus and alcohol? There is not much information to be had in the Bible. It appears that just about everyone in the Christian scriptures drinks alcohol (with a few exceptions, like Samson or John the Baptist). In a few places the Christian scriptures prohibit drunkenness. However, Jesus never appears to have prohibited the use of alcohol. In fact, there are stories where he is said to drink alcohol (including the "Last Supper"), and in the gospel of Luke he admits to drinking, and that he has even been accused of being a drunkard (although here he is referring to himself in the third person as the "Son of Man"): "For John the Baptist has come eating no bread and drinking no wine, and you say 'He has a demon'; the Son of Man has come eating and drinking, and you say, 'Look, a glutton and a drunkard, a friend of tax collectors and sinners!'" (Luke 7:33–4). It is unclear whether he sees the accusation of "drunkard" as fair (he doubtlessly assumes that the parallel charge that John is demonic is false), but either way he claims to be a drinker. Apart from this there is little of note about Jesus and alcohol, apart from a rather significant story in the gospel of John. According to John, Jesus' first miracle was to turn water into wine at a wedding. Here is the story:

> On the third day there was a wedding in Cana of Galilee, and the mother of Jesus was there. Jesus and his disciples had also been invited to the wedding. When the wine gave out, the mother of Jesus said to him, "They have no wine." And Jesus said to her, "Woman, what concern is that to you and to me? My hour has not yet come." His mother said to the servants, "Do whatever he tells you." Now standing there were six stone water-jars for the Jewish rites of purification, each holding twenty or thirty gallons. Jesus said to them, "Fill the jars with water." And they filled them up to the brim. He said to them, "Now draw some out, and take it to the chief steward." So they took it. When the steward tasted the water that had become wine, and did not know where it came from (though the servants who had drawn the water knew), the steward called the bridegroom and said to him, "Everyone serves the good wine first, and then the inferior wine after the guests have become drunk. But you have kept the good wine until now." Jesus did this, the first of his signs, in Cana of Galilee, and revealed his glory; and his disciples believed in him.
>
> (John 2:1–11)

What is particularly telling is that this event is remarkable to the steward *not* because it is miraculous (the steward is not aware that this was a miracle), but because the wedding party seems to have saved the best wine for last. This is remarkable because what normally happens is that expensive wine is produced until people are drunk, at which point the cheap stuff is brought out—since at this point the guests can no longer tell the difference. What this implies is that Jesus has converted water into wine *after* everyone is drunk—otherwise the steward's amazement does not make any sense.

Of course, we do not know if this story ever took place; and, in fact, if we're assuming a hermeneutic of suspicion, we need to be sceptical as a matter of course. Perhaps this story never happened and was instead invented by the author of this gospel. However, Sheldon's form of Christianity probably saw these biblical miracles as literally having taken place. If that is the case, this leaves us with a key question: when Sheldon insists (through the voice of Maxwell) that Jesus would definitely have been opposed to license, is he *projecting* his values onto his favorite authoritative figure (based on what he could know about this figure given his knowledge of the Bible)? The charge that projection is taking place is not only possible, but plausible. It is also worth noting that, insofar as Sheldon's version of Jesus is tied up with capitalist class distinctions that simply did not exist in the first century when Jesus lived, those elements of Sheldon's Jesus are beyond doubt projected.

It is clear why Sheldon might have used the figure of Jesus: Jesus carried a broad authority in Sheldon's social context, an authority that Sheldon by himself could not possibly have held. If Sheldon could successfully project his values onto Jesus, he might more easily legitimate his favored social agenda.

Conclusion

If we apply a hermeneutic of suspicion to Sheldon's novel, focusing on the questions "who is speaking?," "to whom?," "in what context?," and "if persuasive, who stands to gain and who stands to lose?," we get a very interesting set of answers. Sheldon is speaking primarily to a professional Christian audience, in late nineteenth-century America. The context of the novel and its reception is a nation sharply divided into the working class and wealthier classes. If Sheldon was persuasive—and there is evidence he was: the book was an instant bestseller (Boyer 1971, 61)—what might the effects have been? Obviously, one social agenda Sheldon hoped to advance was the prohibition of the sale of alcohol. And, in fact, Sheldon was one of many Christian propagandists writing and working in the late nineteenth century and early twentieth century whose propaganda was, in fact, persuasive; their efforts resulted in precisely what they desired: prohibition. That is, works like Sheldon's were so broadly persuasive that the United States passed an amendment to their constitution (about twenty years after Sheldon's novel appeared) forbidding the sale of alcohol. Obviously, Sheldon and *In His Steps* were not solely responsible for prohibition, but his work was one of many in support of the agenda that eventually won.

Who stood to gain and who stood to lose? Obviously, those people who sold and consumed alcohol stood to lose. In addition, as I have demonstrated, working class people stood to lose from Sheldon's novel—to the extent that it was persuasive—insofar as it taught wealthy people that the working class was not only different because of dress and habit (i.e., habitus), but perhaps also demonic. Despite Sheldon's apparent hope that class lines would be crossed (that is, he seemed to want Christians to convert working class people to Christianity), his implicit demonization of the working class as a whole would probably have had the effect of sharpening class divisions. Given the way that class habitus works, and given the way that the differences in habitus were reinforced in the novel as divine on the one side and demonic on the other, those members of Maxwell's class would be less likely to extend privileges to those outside their class and more likely to discriminate. To the extent that it was persuasive in the context in which it originally appeared, this novel worked to reflect and reinforce the domination of wealthy classes over and against the working class.

This chapter, then, shows how one could apply the theory of religion proposed in this book to Sheldon's novel, and that doing so sheds light on "what's going on" with Sheldon's form of late nineteenth-century Christianity. Sheldon's *In His Steps* is a great artifact for demonstrating the usefulness of critical terms such as habitus, domination, legitimation, authority, and projection.

Afterword

This book has not offered a comprehensive explanation of religion or how religious traditions work. Instead, it is an introduction to how religious traditions can be used to create, maintain, and contest social order. My purpose has been to introduce readers to what I find to be the most useful concepts for thinking critically about religions:

- the hermeneutics of suspicion and social functionalism,
- classification and essentialism,
- group boundaries, social hierarchy, and social positions,
- assigned behaviors, social roles, moral norms, and behavioral codes,
- socialization and social reproduction,
- naturalization and mystification,
- internalized domination,
- habitus, normalization, privilege, and discrimination,
- legitimation and manufacturing consent,
- cultural toolbox and cultural tools,
- authority and projection,
- return-to-origins narratives and false universalism, and
- authenticity claims.

These concepts permit us to answer these sorts of critical questions:

- In general, *how are religious traditions used to create, shape, or modify societies or social groups?*
- How do cultural tools function to reflect and reinforce:
  - group boundaries?
  - social hierarchies?
  - social roles, moral norms, etc.?

- For any given text or interpretation of a religious text, who is trying to convince whom of what? What would be the social implications or social consequences if the text or interpretation were received as persuasive?
- How does a shared habitus sustain social classes, social relations, social boundaries, "normal" practices, etc.? How can a shared habitus be connected to one's religious tradition?

My interest in these issues is the same as Bruce Lincoln's when he claims the following:

> even the most pacific and seemingly benevolent of these rituals still serve to produce subjects who will thereafter accept the propositions, statuses, and modes of being that society desires for and demands of them: persons whom it can use for its own purposes, as productive workers, for example, docile spouses, nurturant mothers, or anaesthetized lovers (in the last case, I think particularly of the many initiatory rituals that feature clitoridectomy). In truth, persuasion can be more insidious than coercion, for while the latter generally provokes some measure of resentment and resistance, skillful persuasion can avoid sowing these seeds of future struggle, insofar as it leads its subjects to desire . . . for themselves precisely what society desires of them.
>
> (Lincoln 1991b, 112)

Here Lincoln is talking about rituals that reinforce the subordination of women, but what he is describing could extend to all elements of cultural toolboxes. If we are attentive to how domination is reinforced, we can more easily resist its pull.

In Mark Twain's *Huckleberry Finn*, which is set in the United States prior to its Civil War, a young boy named Huck Finn runs away from his foster mother's home along with a slave named Jim. Because of his nineteenth-century, conservative Christian upbringing, Huck experiences a great deal of guilt because he feels that by helping Jim escape he has basically stolen Jim from his foster mother, and as such he has committed a sin that will doom him to hell. Helping Jim escape was a "low-down thing" (Twain 1885, 270). Huck thinks to himself,

> The more I studied about this, the more my conscience went to grinding me, and the more wicked and low-down and ornery I got to feeling. And at last, when it hit me all of the sudden that here was the plain hand of Providence [i.e., God] slapping me in the face and letting me know my wickedness was being watched all the time from up there in heaven, whilst I was stealing a poor old woman's nigger that hadn't ever done me no harm, and now was showing me there's

> One [i.e., God] that's always on the lookout, and ain't agoing to allow no such miserable things to go only just fur and no further, I most dropped in my tracks I was so scared.
>
> (270)

He admits that people who steal go "to everlasting fire" (270), and he decides to repent and make right what he has done. So he sits down and writes out a letter to his foster mother, telling her what happened and where she can find Jim. However, although he felt "clean of sin" upon having written the letter, he soon begins reflecting on Jim's interests, rather than his own. He thinks about what Jim had done for him, and about the fact that he was Jim's only friend left in the world. In the middle of these thoughts,

> I happened to look around, and see that paper.
>
> It was a close place. I took it up, and held it in my hand. I was a trembling, because I'd got to decide, forever, between two things, and I knowed it. I studied for a minute, sort of holding my breath, and then says to myself:
>
> "All right, then, I'll *go* to hell"—and tore it up.
>
> (271–2; emphasis original)

Like Huck Finn, we are all surrounded by social orders that serve the interests of some at the expense of others, and we have been subjected to legitimations that make those exploitative power relations seem natural, right, and fair—and we have often been told that to violate the social codes we've inherited will result in cosmic consequences. However, like Huck Finn, some of us have the ability to compare what seems natural or divine with how human interests are served by the social orders that are regularly legitimated by appeals to nature and divinity.

If we pay more attention to all the things that are naturalized for us or that we take for granted, it will be easier for us to identify and reconsider disproportionate social structures. Like Huck Finn, some of us may choose to "go to hell" if the alternative means participating in the reproduction of exploitative social relations.

References

Abbott, Lyman. 1899. *Christianity and Social Problems*. Boston, MA: Houghton, Mifflin and Company.

Abdel Haleem, Muhammad A.S., trans. 2004. *The Qur'an*. Oxford, UK: Oxford University Press.

Althusser, Louis. 2001. *Lenin and Philosophy and Other Essays*. Ben Brewster, trans. New York, NY: Monthly Review Press.

Althusser, Louis. 2008. *On Ideology*. London, UK: Verso.

Ariely, Dan. 2010. *Predictably Irrational: The Hidden Forces that Shape Our Decisions, Revised and Expanded Edition*. New York, NY: Harper Perennial.

Arnal, William. 2005. *The Symbolic Jesus: Historical Scholarship, Judaism and the Construction of Contemporary Identity*. London, UK: Equinox Publishing.

Avalos, Hector. 2007. *The End of Biblical Studies*. Amherst, NY: Prometheus Books.

Avalos, Hector. 2009. "Is Biblical Illiteracy a Bad Thing? Reflections on Bibliolatry in the Modern Academy." *Council of Societies for the Study of Religion Bulletin* 38/2: 47–52.

Bartkowski, John P. 2001. *Remaking the Godly Marriage: Gender Negotiation in Evangelical Families*. New Brunswick, NJ: Rutgers University Press.

Bayart, Jean-François. 2005. *The Illusion of Cultural Identity*. Steven Rendall, Janet Rottman, Cynthia Schoch, and Jonathan Derrick, trans. Chicago, IL: University of Chicago Press.

Berger, Peter. 1967. *The Sacred Canopy: Elements of a Sociological Theory of Religion*. New York, NY: Doubleday.

Berger, Peter and Thomas Luckmann. 1967. *The Social Construction of Reality: A Treatise in the Sociology of Knowledge*. New York, NY: Doubleday.

Botham, Fay. 2009. *Almighty God Created the Races: Christianity, Interracial Marriage, and American Law*. Chapel Hill, NC: University of North Carolina Press.

Bottici, Chiara. 2007. *A Philosophy of Political Myth*. Cambridge, UK: Cambridge University Press.

Bourdieu, Pierre. 1984. *Distinction: A Social Critique of the Judgment of Taste*. Richard Nice, trans. Cambridge, MA: Harvard University Press.

Bourdieu, Pierre. 1990. *The Logic of Practice*. Stanford, CA: Stanford University Press.

Bourdieu, Pierre. 1998. *Practical Reason: On the Theory of Action*. Stanford, CA: Stanford University Press.

Bourdieu, Pierre. 1999. *Language and Symbolic Power*. Cambridge, MA: Harvard University Press.

Boyer, Paul S. 1971. "*In His Steps*: A Reappraisal." *American Quarterly* 23/1: 60–78.

Candland, Douglas Keith. 1993. *Feral Children and Clever Animals: Reflections on Human Nature*. Oxford, UK: Oxford University Press.

Cavanaugh, William T. 2009. *The Myth of Religious Violence: Secular Ideology and the Roots of Modern Conflict*. Oxford, UK: Oxford University Press.

Cook, Michael. 2000. *The Koran: A Very Short Introduction*. Oxford, UK: Oxford University Press.

Dennett, Daniel C. 2007. *Breaking the Spell: Religion as a Natural Phenomenon*. New York, NY: Penguin.

Douglas, Mary. 1986. *How Institutions Think*. Syracuse, NY: Syracuse University Press.

Durkheim, Émile. 1982. *The Rules of Sociological Method*. W. D. Halls, trans. New York, NY: Free Press.

Durkheim, Émile. 2001. *The Elementary Forms of Religious Life*. Carol Cosman, trans. Oxford, UK: Oxford University Press.

Ehrman, Bart D. 1999. *After the New Testament: A Reader in Early Christianity*. Oxford, UK: Oxford University Press.

Epley, Nicholas, Benjamin A. Converse, Alexa Delbosc, George A. Monteleone and John T. Cacioppo. 2009. "Believers' Estimates of God's Beliefs are More Egocentric than Estimates of Other People's Beliefs." *Proceedings of the National Academy of Sciences of the United States of America* 105/51: 21, 533–38.

Evans-Pritchard, E.E. 1965. *Theories of Primitive Religion*. Oxford, UK: Oxford University Press.

Evans-Pritchard, E.E. 1976. *Witchcraft, Oracles, and Magic among the Azande*. Oxford, UK: Oxford University Press.

Fausto-Sterling, Anne. 1993. "The Five Sexes." *The Sciences* March/April: 20–5.

Fausto-Sterling, Anne. 2000. *Sexing the Body: Gender Politics and the Construction of Sexuality*. New York, NY: Basic Books.

Fey, Tina. 2011. *Bossypants*. New York, NY: Little, Brown and Company.

Fishman, Charles. 2006. *The Wal-Mart Effect: How the World's Most Powerful Company Really Works—And How It's Transforming the American Economy*. New York, NY: Penguin.

Fitzgerald, Timothy. 2007. *Discourse on Civility and Barbarity: A Critical History of Religion and Related Categories*. Oxford, UK: Oxford University Press.

Frontline. 2003. "A Class Divided: Introduction." *Frontline*. 1 January. Available at http://www.pbs.org/wgbh/frontline/article/introduction-2/.

Gandhi, Mohandas K. 1993. *An Autobiography: The Story of My Experiments with Truth*. Boston, MA: Beacon Press.

Giddens, Anthony. 1984. *The Constitution of Society*. Berkeley, CA: University of California Press.

Gluckman, Max. 1965. *Politics, Law, and Ritual in Tribal Society*. Chicago, IL: Aldine.

Goodall, Dominic, ed. 1996. *Hindu Scriptures*. Berkeley, CA: University of California Press.

Gould, Stephen Jay. 1981. *The Mismeasure of Man*. New York, NY: W.W. Norton & Company.

Graham, Marty. 2013. "Yoga Not Teaching Religion In Encinitas Schools, California. Judge Rules, Appeal Expected." Huffington Post, 1 July. Available at www.huffingtonpost.com/2013/07/01/yoga-school-religion-_n_3530347.html.

Grant, Robert M. 1997. *Irenaeus of Lyons*. London, UK: Routledge.

Guthrie, Stewart Elliott. 1993. *Faces in the Clouds: A New Theory of Religion*. Oxford, UK: Oxford University Press.

Hacking, Ian. 2002. *Historical Ontology*. Cambridge, MA: Harvard University Press.

Hagerty, Barbara Bradley. 2010. "Is the Bible More Violent than the Quran?" *National Public Radio*, 21 March. Available at www.npr.org/templates/story/story.php?storyId=124494788&ps=cprs.

Hammer, Olav, ed. 2009. *Alternative Christs*. Cambridge, UK: Cambridge University Press.

Hammer, Olav and James R. Lewis, eds. 2007. *The Invention of Sacred Tradition*. Cambridge, UK: Cambridge University Press.

Huffstutter, Patricia J. 2009. "Missouri's Yoga Enthusiasts Go to the Mat Over Sales Tax." *Los Angeles Times*, 18 December. Available at articles.latimes.com/print/2009/dec/18/nation/la-na-yoga-tax18-2009dec18.

Hughes, Aaron W. 2007. *Situating Islam: The Past and Future of an Academic Discipline*. London, UK: Equinox.

Ingersoll, Julie. 2003. *Evangelical Christian Women: War Stories in the Gender Battles*. New York, NY: New York University Press.

Jaffee, Martin S. 1999. "Fessing Up in Theory: On Professing and Confessing in the Religious Studies Classroom." In *The Insider-Outsider Problem in the Study of Religion*, ed. by Russell T. McCutcheon. New York, NY: Cassell.

Jha, Dwijendra. N. 2009. *Rethinking Hindu Identity*. London, UK: Equinox Publishing.

Jordan-Young, Rebecca M. 2010. *Brain Storm: The Flaws in the Science of Sex Differences*. Cambridge, MA: Harvard University Press.

Kertzer, David. 1988. *Ritual, Politics, and Power*. New Haven, CT: Yale University Press.

Lillback, Peter A. 2006. *George Washington's Sacred Fire*. King of Prussia, PA: Providence Forum Press.

Lincoln, Bruce. 1981. *Emerging from the Chrysalis: Studies in Rituals of Women's Initiation*. Cambridge, MA: Harvard University Press.

Lincoln, Bruce. 1989. *Discourse and the Construction of Society: Comparative Studies of Myth, Ritual, and Classification*. Chicago, IL: Chicago University Press.

Lincoln, Bruce. 1991a. *Death, War, and Sacrifice: Studies in Ideology and Practice*. Chicago, IL: University of Chicago Press.

Lincoln, Bruce. 1991b. *Emerging from the Chrysalis: Studies in Rituals of Women's Initiation*. Chicago, IL: University of Chicago Press.

Lincoln, Bruce. 1994. *Authority: Construction and Corrosion*. Chicago, IL: University of Chicago Press.

Lincoln, Bruce. 1996. "Theses on Method." *Method and Theory in the Study of Religion* 8: 225–27.

Lincoln, Bruce. 2006. "How to Read a Religious Text." *History of Religions* 46/2: 127–39.

Lincoln, Bruce. 2007. *Religion, Empire, and Torture: The Case of Achaemenian Persia, with a Postscript on Abu Ghraib*. Chicago, IL: University of Chicago Press.

Locke, John. 2003. "A Letter Concerning Toleration." In *Two Treatises of Government and A Letter Concerning Toleration*, ed. by Ian Shapiro. New Haven, CT: Yale University Press.

Lopez, Donald S. (ed.). 2004. *Buddhist Scriptures*. New York, NY: Penguin.

Lorber, Judith. 1994. *Paradoxes of Gender*. New Haven, CT: Yale University Press.

Lui, Meizhu, ed. 2006. *The Color of Wealth: The Story Behind the U.S. Racial Wealth Divide*. New York, NY: New Press.

Luther, Martin. 1991. *On Secular Authority*. In *Luther and Calvin on Secular Authority*, ed. by Harro Höpfl. Cambridge, UK: Cambridge University Press.

Martin, Craig. 2010. *Masking Hegemony: A Genealogy of Liberalism, Religion, and the Private Sphere*. Sheffield, UK: Equinox Publishing.

Martin, Craig. 2014. *Capitalizing Religion: Ideology and the Opiate of the Bourgeoisie*. London, UK: Bloomsbury.

Marx, Karl. 1990. *Capital, Volume 1*. Trans. by Ben Fowkes. New York, NY: Penguin.

Marx, Karl and Friedrich Engels. 1998. *The Communist Manifesto*. London, UK: Verso.

McCutcheon, Russell. 2001. *Critics not Caretakers: Redescribing the Public Study of Religion*. Albany, NY: State University of New York Press.

Miller, Barbara Stoler, trans. 1986. *The Bhagavad Gita: Krishna's Council in Time of War*. New York, NY: Bantam.

Misra, Amalendu 2004. *Identity and Religion: Foundations of Anti-Islamism in India*. New Delhi, India: Sage Publications.

Morone, James A. 2003. *Hellfire Nation: The Politics of Sin in American History*. New Haven, CT: Yale University Press.

Murphy, Tim. 2007. *Representing Religion: Essays in History, Theory, and Crisis*. London, UK: Equinox Publishing.

Nanda, Serena. 2000. *Gender Diversity: Crosscultural Variations*. Long Grove, IL: Waveland Press.

Needham, Rodney. 1979. *Symbolic Classification*. Santa Monica, CA: Goodyear Publishing Company.

Nongbri, Brent. 2013. *Before Religion: A History of a Modern Concept*. New Haven, CT: Yale University Press.

Nye, Malory. 2008. *Religion: The Basics, Second Edition*. London, UK: Routledge.

Ontario Consultants on Religious Tolerance. 2007. "Which, if any, of the world's 10,000 religions is the true one?" 7 September. Available at http://www.religioustolerance.org/reltrue.htm.

Otto, Rudolf. 1958. *The Idea of the Holy*. Oxford, UK: Oxford University Press.

Owen, Suzanne. 2008. *The Appropriation of Native American Religion*. London, UK: Continuum.

Pagels, Elaine. 1979. *The Gnostic Gospels*. New York, NY: Random House.

Pelikan, Jaroslav. 1985. *Jesus through the Centuries: His Place in the History of Culture*. New Haven, CT: Yale University Press.

Prothero, Stephen. 2003. *American Jesus: How the Son of God became a National Icon*. New York, NY: Farrar, Straus, and Giroux.

Putnam, Hilary. 2004. *Ethics without Ontology*. Cambridge, MA: Harvard University Press.

Reich, Robert. 2008. *Supercapitalism: The Transformation of Business, Democracy, and Everyday Life*. New York, NY: Random House.

Rothstein, Mikael. 2007. "Scientology, Scripture, and Tradition," in *The Invention of Sacred Tradition*. James R. Lewis and Olav Hammer, eds. Cambridge, UK: Cambridge University Press.

Rousseau, Jean-Jacques. 1983. *The Essential Rousseau*. Lowell Bair, trans. New York, NY: Meridian.

Sahlins, Marshall. 1987. *Islands of History*. Chicago, IL: University of Chicago Press.

Schiappa, Edward. 2003. *Defining Reality: Definitions and the Politics of Meaning*. Carbondale, IL: Southern Illinois University Press.

Schweitzer, Albert. 1910. *The Quest of the Historical Jesus*. London, UK: A. & C. Black.

Scott, James C. 1985. *Weapons of the Weak: Everyday Forms of Peasant Resistance*. New Haven, CT: Yale University Press.

Sheldon, Charles M. 1899. *In His Steps*. Chicago, IL: Advance Publishing Co.

Shell, Ellen Ruppel. 2010. *Cheap: The High Cost of Discount Culture*. New York, NY: Penguin.

Smith, Brian K. 1989. *Reflections on Resemblance, Ritual, and Religion*. New York, NY: Oxford University Press.

Smith, Jonathan Z. 2004. *Relating Religion: Essays in the Study of Religion*. Chicago, IL: University of Chicago Press.

Sullivan, Winnifred Fallers. 2005. *The Impossibility of Religious Freedom*. Princeton, NJ: Princeton University Press.

Swartz, David. 1997. *Culture and Power: The Sociology of Pierre Bourdieu*. Chicago, IL: University of Chicago Press.

Tajfel, Henri. 1981. *Human Groups and Social Categories: Studies in Social Psychology*. Cambridge, UK: Cambridge University Press.

Tolle, Eckhart. 1999. *The Power of Now: A Guide to Spiritual Enlightenment.* Novato, CA: New World Library.

Twain, Mark. 1885. *Adventures of Huckleberry Finn (Tom Sawyer's Comrade).* New York, NY: Charles L. Webster and Company. Available at http://openlibrary.org/books/OL7244099M/ Adventures_of_Huckleberry_Finn.

Twain, Mark. 1981. *Pudd'nhead Wilson.* New York, NY: Bantam.

Wade, Lisa. 2010. "Why Is Kim Kardashian Famous?" *Sociological Images*, 21 December. Available at https://thesocietypages.org/socimages/2010/12/21/why-is-kim-kardashian-famous/.

Watson, Burton, trans. 2002. *The Essential Lotus: Selections from the Lotus Sutra.* New York, NY: Columbia University Press.

Welch, Gina. 2010. *In the Land of Believers: An Outsider's Extraordinary Journey into the Heart of the Evangelical Church.* New York, NY: Metropolitan Books.

Index